STRAIGHT TALK

STRAIGHT TALK

*Overcoming Emotional Battles with the
Power of God's Word*

JOYCE
MEYER

New York   Boston   Nashville

Unless otherwise indicated, all Scripture quotations are taken from *The Amplified Bible* (AMP).
The Amplified Bible, Old Testament, copyright © 1965, 1987 by The Zondervan Corporation.
The Amplified Bible, New Testament, copyright © 1954, 1958, 1987 by The Lockman Founda-
tion. Used by permission.

Scriptures marked KJV are taken from the *King James Version* of the Bible.

Scriptures noted NKJV are taken from the NEW KING JAMES VERSION. Copyright © 1979,
1980, 1982, Thomas Nelson, Inc., Publishers.

Scriptures noted TLB are taken from *The Living Bible*, copyright © 1971. Used by permission of
Tyndale House Publishers, Inc., Wheaton, Illinois 60189. All rights reserved.

Warner Faith

Time Warner Book Group
1271 Avenue of the Americas, New York, NY 10020
Visit our Web site at www.twbookmark.com

Warner Faith® and the Warner Faith Logo are trademarks of Time Warner Book Group Inc.

Printed in the United States of America
First Warner Books Edition: January 2005
10 9 8 7 6

Library of Congress Control Number: 2004106437
ISBN: 0-446-57800-2

CONTENTS

STRAIGHT TALK ON *Stress*

CONTENTS

INTRODUCTION

———— ❧ ————

Those who believe in Jesus live *in* the world but are not *of* the world (see John 17:14–15). This is good news for us as believers living in today's stress-filled world!

People in the world are under such intense pressure, they are often hurried, rude, short-tempered, and frustrated. They experience financial and marital stress and the stress of raising children in a changing and uncertain world. Because of mental stress on the job and physical stress from overwork and frayed nerves, some people appear to be time bombs on the verge of explosion.

We as believers do not need to succumb to the stress that affects people "of the world"—people who do not know Jesus as Savior and Lord. We do not have to operate in the world's system by thinking, talking, and acting like the people of the world. In fact our attitude and approach should be entirely different from the world's.

We are to be lights in the darkness (see Matthew 5:16 and Ephesians 5:8). It is hard for us to be lights, though, if we are as stressed as the people in the world! God has provided ways for us to live without being affected by that type of stress.

I have learned something in my own pursuit of peace: To enjoy peace, I must choose in every situation to obey the Lord rather than living under the pressure of stress.

Jesus is the Prince of Peace! Obedience—following the leading of the Holy Spirit—will always lead us to peace and joy, not to anxiety and frustration. Through God's Word we can learn more about the Prince of Peace and the inheritance made available to us by Him. We can find and maintain peace and avoid or overcome stress.

As you read this book, allow the Holy Spirit to speak to you and lead you into living in the wonderful peace of the Lord.

Part One

IS JESUS EXALTED OR ARE YOU EXHAUSTED?

1

❧

EXCEEDING REASONABLE LIMITS

Do you not know that your body is the temple (the very sanctuary) of the Holy Spirit Who lives within you, Whom you have received [as a Gift] from God? You are not your own, You were bought with a price [purchased with a preciousness and paid for, made His own]. So then, honor God and bring glory to Him in your body.

1 Corinthians 6:19–20

The word *stress* was originally an engineering term used to refer to the amount of force a beam or other physical support could bear without collapsing under the strain.

In our time, the word has been expanded to refer not only to physical pressure but also to mental and emotional tension.

As human beings, you and I are built to handle a normal amount of stress. God has created us to withstand a certain amount of pressure and tension. The problem comes when we push ourselves beyond our limitations, beyond what we were intended to bear without permanent damage.

For example, a chair is built to be sat upon. It is designed and constructed to bear a certain amount of weight. If it is used properly, it will seemingly last forever. But if it is overloaded beyond its capacity, it will begin to weaken or even break down completely under the strain.

In the same way, you and I were designed and created to bear a certain amount of physical, mental, and emotional strain day after day. The problem arises when we allow ourselves to come under more weight than we are capable of supporting.

Everyone is under stress. Stress is a normal part of everyday life. As long as we keep that stress within reasonable limits, there is no problem. But when we allow it to exceed its reasonable limits, trouble begins.

A few years ago, I went to see a doctor because I was constantly sick. I had one of those diseases you hear about where no one can determine what is wrong. But the doctor told me the symptoms were the result of being under stress!

When he said that, I was aggravated. I did not believe my problem was stress! I used to handle situations by throwing stressful, emotional fits, but had now grown into a fairly calm person. So being told I was under stress upset me. I thought, "You, doctor, are giving me stress!"

I went to several different doctors who told me the same thing. One told me I was too intense. It *really* aggravated me to be told I was sick because I was too intense! I thought I had successfully redirected my intense nature in a positive way by working intensely for the Lord.

After a while I realized what the doctors were telling me was true. I *was* under stress. I was working too hard and not sleeping right or eating properly. I was pushing myself harder and harder—all in the name of doing the work of Jesus! I was doing the work *I* had determined He wanted me to do without actually seeking Him to find out which work *He* wanted me to do, *when* He wanted me to do it, and *how much* of it He wanted me to do.

In my particular case, I was under stress because I was doing an excessive amount of all kinds of "good works"—church work and other activities related to spiritual things. I was going to Bible studies and prayer meetings. I was counseling people. I was running from one seminar to the next, preaching sometimes twenty or twenty-five times a month.

Besides the physical strain I was placing on my body, I was fighting the mental pressure of learning to run a new ministry with all the challenges involved. I was also dealing with the emotional tension that goes along with having a family and a ministry.

As a result, I was constantly having headaches, backaches, stomachaches, neck aches, and all the other symptoms of stress. Yet I

would not recognize or admit I was under stress so I could deal with it.

You may be pushing yourself beyond your physical limits as I was. If we abuse ourselves in the name of doing Jesus' work by pushing our bodies beyond God's intentions, we will suffer results similar to the ones we would if we were exhausting our bodies in the pursuit of wealth, fame, success, or any other goal.

As we saw before, everybody has some stress. None of us can get through the day without experiencing stress of one kind or another. In handling or overcoming stress, it is important to recognize it for what it is, learn how to control it, and make it work for us rather than against us.

Thermal Stress

I learned some interesting things about stress from my doctors. There are many kinds of stress. For example, the body experiences thermal stress when it goes from one temperature to another.

One doctor explained: "If it is 90 degrees outside and you leave your air-conditioned house, run out through the heat to the curb, jump into your air-conditioned car and wait for it to cool off, your body is experiencing drastic change. Downtown you get out of your cool car and run through the heat again on your way into an air-conditioned building. From the air-conditioned building, you hurry back out into the heat to the parking lot, then jump back into your car and start up the air conditioner. You travel home in relative comfort, then rush from the car through the heat into an air-conditioned house. All that change in temperature puts pressure on your body. It is called thermal stress."

Just as thermal stress places a strain on the physical body, so mental stress places strain on the mind and nerves.

Mental Stress

Mental stress comes from trying to figure everything out, from worrying, from thinking about the same thing over and over without making any progress toward a solution, and from allowing the mind to run on and on by dwelling on little deceptive thoughts inspired by the devil. It can also result from concentrating intently on something for a long period of time.

For example, our son David works for my husband, Dave, and me in our ministry. In the past he worked on computers and designed flyers; his job was primarily mental. One time he commented that when he got home in the evening after a long day's work, he felt as though there was a film over his eyes and a fog over his brain. For a while he felt as if he couldn't think right.

Was his body telling him he was working too hard? Not necessarily. It simply meant his body was sending him the message, "I am moving into overload now; let me rest."

When our bodies are giving us the message to rest, instead we often push ourselves into greater overload. Many times if we would just sit down, get quiet, and do something peaceful for even fifteen minutes, we would feel refreshed. Our bodies have an amazing ability to rebuild and renew themselves and return to normal pretty quickly.

But if we refuse to give our bodies the rest they are calling for, we are asking for trouble. Pushing our bodies into overload and continuing to push and push as if we are Superman (or SuperChristian) will cause something to give, physically, sooner or later.

If I start to sit down in a chair and hear the legs crack, I had better take my weight off the chair fast so I won't end up on the floor! However, many people end up in a state of exhausted collapse because they do not heed the telltale warning signs in their bodies just as severe as the legs cracking on that chair!

I hear young people say things like, "Oh, I can eat anything I want, go without much sleep for days, and it doesn't bother me a bit."

If you are a young person repeatedly pushing your body beyond its physical limits, you may continue on this way for quite a while and feel great. But you may, and probably will, severely damage yourself. All of a sudden, one day your body will say, "I can't do this anymore," and something in your body or mind will break down or become ill.

Pushing your body to the point of damage by not supplying it with the rest and food God created it to have is disobedience. Your body can become severely damaged as a result of this disobedience.

Of course, God is the Healer and He is merciful, but after years of disobeying Him, you may find it more difficult to receive your healing. Believe God for a lifetime of divine health while you're healthy, and add obedience to God's laws of health to your believing. The Bible teaches us to eat properly, get good rest, and not be lazy—to get physical exercise.

Physical Stress

Physical stress occurs simply because our bodies get tired. That is normal. We are supposed to get tired. It feels good to be able to crawl into bed and get a good night's sleep after a good day's work.

However, it does not feel good to keep going and going no matter how tired we are, then fall into bed, restlessly lying there with our mind working overtime. We are adding mental or emotional stress to the physical stress.

I used to come home from long ministry trips every weekend worn out. I didn't sleep very much while gone because we worked hard and lived in changing conditions. Each night we were in a different hotel and a different bed. I prayed for people until late at night, then got up early the next morning to start ministering again.

When I went on those weekend trips, my body was under a lot of strain because I was not able to treat it properly while we were gone. But I made the mistake of getting up on Monday morning and heading right back to the office as if I had been off all weekend.

I don't do that anymore. Now I take time off to be with the Lord. I sit in His presence and spend time with Him getting myself built back up again. Then after being renewed, I am able to do what I am supposed to be doing—what He wants me to do.

Medical Stress

Sometimes if I exhaust myself physically and get a virus or a cold, I slow down or take some time off to rest. But the minute I start feeling a little better, I go back to work full force. Then I get tired or have a relapse and wonder why! I call this "medical stress."

Dave tries to tell me, "Take it easy for a while. Your body is still under strain because you haven't been feeling well. You may need to go to bed a little early for a week or two or get a little extra rest in the evening."

But like so many people, because I have things to do, I just keep pushing myself even though it is causing me physical damage.

Of course, when sickness tries to come on Dave or me, we immediately pray for healing. But if you become sick as a result of running your body down by pushing it beyond the limits God set for you to operate in good health, you need rest as well as prayer to restore your health. The boundaries He has set for us are for our own good. If we disobey by going outside of those boundaries, we open ourselves up to suffer the consequences. The body will not operate properly if it is repeatedly pushed beyond its capabilities. As previously stated, God is very merciful, but repeated disobedience can also cause us to "reap what we have sown" (see Galatians 6:8).

Prudence

I, Wisdom [from God], make prudence my dwelling, and I find out knowledge and discretion.

Proverbs 8:12

A word you don't hear very much teaching about is one the book of Proverbs discusses: *prudence* (or being *prudent*). *Prudence* means "careful management: economy."[1] In the Scriptures *prudence* or *prudent* means being good stewards or managers of the gifts God has given us to use. Those gifts include time, energy, strength, health, and material possessions. They include our bodies as well as our minds and spirits.

Just as each one of us has been given a different set of gifts, each of us has been given a different ability to manage those gifts. Some of us are better able to manage ourselves than are others.

Each of us needs to know how much we are able to handle. We need to be able to recognize when we are reaching "full capacity" or "overload." Instead of pushing ourselves on over into overload to please others, satisfy our own desires, or reach our personal goals, we need to listen to the Lord and obey what He is telling us to do. We must follow wisdom to enjoy blessed lives.

Nobody can remove all the stressors—the things causing or increasing stress—from our lives. For that reason, each of us must be prudent to identify and recognize the stressors that affect us most and learn how to respond to them with the right action. We must recognize our limits and learn to say, "No!" to ourselves and other people.

Stressors

Anything can become a stressor.

For example, going to the grocery store and becoming upset by high prices may be a stressor for you. Then the process of paying for your groceries may become a stressor. The checker in your lane runs out of change in the register and has to shut down. You switch into a new lane and learn you have selected five items that don't have prices on them. The checker has to call for a price check on each one while you wait, and the line behind you grows.

Another stressor could be your car conking out and stopping in the middle of traffic.

If the stressors are not managed properly, one by one they can mount up to bring us to the breaking point. Because we may not be able to eliminate or reduce many of the stressors in our lives, we must concentrate on reducing their effects on us. We must learn to obey Romans 12:16 and adapt: " . . . readily adjust yourself to [people, things]." When we can't control all of our circumstances, we can adapt or adjust our attitude so we don't let our circumstances pressure us.

Fight or Flight

The human body is constructed so that any time it senses fear or danger, it reacts defensively.

For example, if you are driving down the street and see that another vehicle looks as though it is about to collide with yours, without any conscious thought on your part your body will go into action. It will automatically take defensive measures, such as secreting adrenaline, in preparation to meet that crisis situation or to avoid it.

This reaction is what professionals refer to as "fight or flight." Your body is preparing you to stand and face the situation—to fight—or to escape from the danger.

In either case your body is reacting inwardly in ways of which you may not be fully aware. Those reactions, obviously, are causing stress on your system.

Imagination Is As Powerful As Reality

For as he thinks in his heart, so is he.

Proverbs 23:7

Something very interesting about this fight-or-flight phenomenon is that you do not have to be in an actual threatening situation for your body to react. Just thinking or dreaming about, imagining, or even remembering such a situation can cause your body to produce the same physical, mental, and emotional responses.

Have you ever been lying in bed late at night and heard some little noise that caused your mind to start playing games with you? You are lying there in safety and security, yet you begin to perspire, your mouth becomes dry, your heart starts pounding, and so forth.

Isn't it amazing that just the mere *thought* of danger can produce exactly the same reaction as real danger? We can see why the Bible warns us of the tremendous importance and impact of our thoughts and emotions on our everyday lives!

Another example is the response to hearing a vague rumor of some possible layoffs at work. When people hear that type of rumor, they usually start worrying. Some people worry to the point of having stomach trouble. The rumor has had the same effect on them as would the actual fact, yet the rumor is nothing but imagination.

The power of the mind, of thought, of imagination and emotion is immense and every bit as real as the power of the physical realm. We should make every effort not to worry, become fearful, or mentally relive situations that have been emotionally upsetting to us.

The Results of Stress

Every frightening or stressful situation brought on by our mind or emotions has the same effect on our bodies as a real crisis situation.

I've read several descriptions of what happens to the body when it reacts to a stressful situation. The stressor, whatever it may be, causes an impulse to be sent to the brain. The brain combines and integrates emotions with reasoning. In this process, the person reacting to the stressor analyzes the situation. If he perceives it as threatening, his body continues the fight-or-flight response.

The nervous system responds in three ways: It directly stimulates certain organs—the heart, muscles, and respiratory system—with electrical impulses to cause a quick increase in heart rate, blood pressure, muscle tension, and respiration. It signals the adrenal medulla, a part of the adrenal gland, to release the hormones adrenaline and noradrenaline, which alert and prepare the body to take action. This reaction begins a half minute after the first, but lasts ten times as long.

The nervous system also stimulates the hypothalamus in the brain to release a chemical that stimulates the pituitary gland. The pituitary gland releases a hormone causing the adrenal glands to continue releasing adrenaline and noradrenaline and to begin releasing cortisol and corticosterone, which affect metabolism, including the increase of glucose production. This third prolonged reaction helps maintain the energy needed to respond in a threatening situation. Nearly every system of the body is involved, some more intently than others, in the response to the stressor.

Every time we become excited, stimulated, or upset, even though we may not realize it, our entire system is gearing up for either fight or flight to defend itself from the perceived threatening or dangerous situation.[2]

Then, when we calm back down, our body comes out of that emergency state and begins functioning normally, the way it is supposed to function most of the time.

The next time we face a stressful situation or become upset, the whole process starts over. Then when we calm down, the body settles back into functioning normally again.

And so it goes, up and down according to our changing mental and emotional state. But the effects of that excessive stressing and unstressing can have long-lasting and far-reaching consequences.

Tied Up in Knots?

A rubber band has an amazing ability to be stretched to its maximum length then return to its precise original form. But how many times can it do that without becoming weakened or even breaking?

When I am working in my office and break a rubber band, I tie the ends back together because I need to use it to put around something. Sometimes in our daily lives, we stretch ourselves beyond what is reasonable and bearable until we snap like that rubber band. Then we try to "tie the ends back together" and go on with the same behavior that causes us to stretch and stretch and break again.

When a rubber band I have tied breaks again, it usually breaks in a different spot, so I tie the ends together in another knot. When we keep stretching and breaking and "tying the ends together," we feel as though we are tied up in knots inside and out!

We might like for the solution to be to get rid of the causes of the problems tying us up in knots, but the source of stress is not really difficulties, circumstances, and situations. The major source of stress results from approaching problems with the world's perspective rather than with our perspective as believers in Jesus Christ, the Prince of Peace.

Jesus left us with His peace.

> Peace I leave with you; My [own] peace I now give and bequeath to you. Not as the world gives do I give to you. Do not let your hearts be troubled, neither let them be afraid. [Stop allowing yourselves to be agitated and disturbed; and do not permit yourselves to be fearful and intimidated and cowardly and unsettled.] (John 14:27)

Jesus never said we wouldn't have to deal with anything disturbing or disappointing. John 16:33 says, "In the world you have tribulation and trials and distress and frustration." But He did say He would deliver us out of all our afflictions (see Psalm 34:19)! John 16:33 begins, "In Me you may have [perfect] peace and confidence."

It ends with, "But be of good cheer [take courage; be confident, certain, undaunted]! For I have overcome the world. [I have deprived it of power to harm you and have conquered it for you.]"

Even though we will have disturbing things to deal with, we can have Jesus' peace because He has "overcome the world" and "deprived" the world of its "power to harm" us. He left us with the power to "stop allowing" ourselves "to be agitated and disturbed"! Peace is available, but we must choose it!

The Power of the Lord

Jesus sent the twelve disciples and seventy others out two by two into every place He was about to go. Before they left, He told them, "Go your way; behold, I send you out like lambs into the midst of wolves" (Luke 10:3). But He had equipped them for the opposition they would encounter. After they returned and reported, "Even the demons are subject to us in Your name!" (v. 17), He said, "Behold! I have given you authority and power to trample upon serpents and scorpions, and [physical and mental strength and ability] over all the power that the enemy [possesses]; and nothing shall in any way harm you" (Luke 10:19).

What He was saying to them is also for us today: "What you are about to do will not be easy. There will be problems to face. But you do not need to be agitated and disturbed! I have given you the authority, power, strength, and ability you need to overcome the power of the enemy, and nothing will defeat you—if you handle things the right way."

2

❧

The Key to Relieving Stress

*Now we serve not under [obedience to] the old code of written regula-
tions, but [under obedience to the promptings] of the Spirit in newness
[of life].*

Romans 7:6

*If you will listen diligently to the voice of the Lord your God, being
watchful to do all His commandments which I command you this day,
the Lord your God will set you high above all the nations of the
earth . . . And the Lord shall make you the head, and not the tail; and
you shall be above only, and you shall not be beneath.*

Deuteronomy 28:1,13

When I began to prepare this message on stress, I asked the Lord
to show me how He wanted me to present the material. I could have
approached the subject many different ways. The answer He gave
me, I believe, is a message, a word, from the heart of the Father for
the body of Christ for this hour, this season.

That word is *obedience*.

The Lord said to me, "If people will obey Me and do what I tell
them to do they will not be under stress."

We may have stress, but we will be on *top* of it, not *under* it.
There is a big difference between being *under* stress and being *on top*
of a situation!

Jesus came to destroy the works of the devil (see 1 John 3:8).

Jesus was given all "authority . . . power . . . in heaven and on earth" (Matthew 28:18) and has made that authority and power over the power of the enemy available to us (as we saw in Luke 10:19).

Ephesians 6:12 tells us "we are not wrestling with flesh and blood" but against "the spirit forces of wickedness in the heavenly (supernatural) sphere." Verse eleven instructs us how "successfully to stand up against [all] the strategies and the deceits of the devil." Jesus has given us power to stop the devil's attacks on us.

However, nobody can stop from happening every situation that carries the potential to cause our hearts to "be troubled." All of us have things come our way we don't like. But, with the power of God, we can go through those situations stress free. We can be on top— "the head, and not the tail," "above only" and "not be beneath"—in every situation coming our way.

Even though, like the people in the world, we will sometimes experience stressful times, if we are obedient to God's Word, and to His promptings, we can be on top of stress and not under it. We will live *in* the world without being *of* the world.

The Major Importance of Minor Obedience

But thanks be to God, Who in Christ always leads us in triumph.

2 Corinthians 2:14

Do you believe God is leading you into a place of victory and triumph, not into a place of defeat? Your answer as a child of God and believer in Jesus Christ would be yes! It makes sense, then, that if we believers would listen to everything the Lord tells us and obey Him, we would not get into that state of defeat, would we?

However, when many Christians hear the word *obedience*, they immediately think the Lord will ask them to give away a huge sum of money, move to Africa to go on the mission field or do something else really big they don't want to do. They don't realize that obeying the Lord usually involves some minor thing that will make a major difference. Obeying Him in the little things makes a major difference in keeping stress out of our life.

Simply obeying the promptings of the Holy Spirit will often relieve stress quickly, while ignoring the promptings of the Holy Spirit will more than likely cause stress and cause it to increase equally quickly!

The Promptings of the Spirit

But now we are discharged from the Law and have terminated all intercourse with it, having died to what once restrained and held us captive. So now we serve not under [obedience to] the old code of written regulations, but [under obedience to the promptings] of the Spirit in newness [of life].

Romans 7:6

According to this passage, we are no longer under the restraints of the law but now serve the Lord under obedience to the promptings of the Holy Spirit. A prompting is a "knowing" down on the inside of you telling you what to do. First Kings 19:11–12 describes the "still, small voice" the Lord used with Elijah:

And behold, the Lord passed by, and a great and strong wind rent the mountains and broke in pieces the rocks before the Lord, but the Lord was not in the wind; and after the wind an earthquake, but the Lord was not in the earthquake; And after the earthquake a fire, but the Lord was not in the fire; and after the fire [a sound of gentle stillness and] a still, small voice.

A prompting from the Lord is not like hitting someone over the head with a hammer to prompt them to do something! The Lord did not use the great and strong wind, the earthquake, or the fire as a prompting, but instead came as "a sound of gentle stillness" and "a still, small voice."

The prompting of "a still, small voice" is not necessarily a voice; it can be God's wisdom giving you direction in that moment. First Corinthians 1:30 tells us, "But it is from Him that you have your life in Christ Jesus, Whom God made our Wisdom from God." If we are born again, Jesus is living inside us. If He is inside us, we have God's wisdom in us to draw on at any moment! But unless we *listen* to wisdom, it won't do us any good.

Since a prompting is very gentle, it is easy to question whether it is from God, and it is also easy to completely ignore it. One time when I was shopping at the mall, after I had been there for three or four hours, I heard a prompting from the Holy Spirit which said, "You need to go home now." I had been able to purchase only half of the eight or so items on my shopping list, so I ignored the prompting.

The remaining items on my list were not immediate needs. Even though the prompting of the Spirit within me told me to stop what I was doing and go home, like many determined, goal-oriented people, I was not going to leave until I purchased every item on my list.

I had come for eight items, and I was leaving with eight items! I didn't care if I had to be dragged bodily out of the mall, I was going to leave with what I had come to buy!

I had reached the point of being so tired and upset I wasn't thinking clearly beyond, "I just want to finish and get out of here!" Simply being civil any time anyone asked me anything was becoming extremely difficult. I can't remember how many times I've done that to myself—pushing beyond the prompting of the Holy Spirit. And because of the state I've brought on myself, I even start an argument with Dave. A telltale sign of being on overload is if we are no longer displaying the fruit of the spirit—love, joy, peace, patience, kindness, goodness, faithfulness, gentleness, and self-control—Galatians 5:22–23 tells us about.

I could have simply obeyed the prompting of the Holy Spirit—that "still, small voice"—and by going home, relieved the stress from the situation. Instead, I moved ahead in my own fleshly determination to achieve my goal and brought stress on myself and everyone around me!

God's Anointing Is on Obedience

God's grace and power are available for us to use. But God enables us, gives us an anointing of the Holy Spirit, to do what *He* tells us to do. Sometimes after He has prompted us to go in another direction, we still keep pressing on with our original plan, while actually asking Him to help us do what He said not to do! "God, help me! I'm so close to finishing, Lord. Just help me do a little more and I'll be done!" If we are doing something He has not approved, He is under no obligation to give us the energy to do it.

We are functioning in our own strength rather than under the control of the Holy Spirit, because we are doing something God has told us not to do! Then we get so frustrated, stressed, or burned out, we lose our self-control, as I did at the mall, simply by ignoring the prompting of the Spirit.

I believe a major reason many people are stressed and burned out is that they are going their own way instead of God's way. They end up in stressful situations when they go in a different direction from the one God prompted. Then they burn out in the midst of the disobedience and, struggling to finish what they started outside of God's direction, beg God to anoint them.

God is merciful, and He helps us in the midst of our mistakes. But He is not going to give us strength and energy to disobey Him continually. We can avoid many stressful situations and living "tied up in knots" simply by obeying the Holy Spirit's promptings moment by moment.

God Blesses Obedience

Sometimes God does give direction requiring major change. He does tell some people to go on the mission field in Africa or to give away large sums of money. But God created the body of Christ with different abilities, strengths, and desires to reach people in many different ways (see 1 Corinthians 12). Jesus came that we might "have and enjoy life, and have it in abundance (to the full, till it overflows)" (John 10:10).

God loves you and wants to bless you abundantly (see Ephesians 3:17–20 and 1 John 4:16, 19). Once you have an understanding of how great His love is, you will no longer be afraid He will ask you to do something that would be bad for you. As we have seen, obedience to the promptings of the Holy Spirit will always lead us to peace and joy—victory, not defeat.

When you stop to really consider it, do you think God would ask us to obey Him in something as big as going to the mission field when He knows we have a hard time obeying Him in something as small as going home from the mall when He tells us? He works with us on our level. As we grow in obedience to minor things, He leads us into major things.

Special Obedience

God places specific requirements on each of us that may not make sense to anybody else. He knows what each of us needs to fulfill the plan He has for us.

Jesus was obedient to the requirements of God's plan that would enable Him to bring salvation to mankind.

> Although He was a Son, He learned [active, special] obedience through what He suffered And, [His completed experience] making Him perfectly [equipped], He became the Author and Source of eternal salvation to all those who give heed and obey Him. (Hebrews 5:8–9)

A young man who works for our ministry told me of a specific requirement God gave him. Paul and his wife, Roxane, are a tremendous blessing to us both through the work they do in our ministry and also to us and our children, personally.

Paul is one of the calmest and most easygoing people you would ever want to meet. Nothing ruffles or bothers him. But Paul told me he wasn't always that way. When he gave his life to the Lord, he was just the opposite. He couldn't sit still. He couldn't stay home even for five minutes.

Paul's family told Roxane that as a child, Paul was almost hyperactive. They were amazed at his transformation after he gave his life to the Lord. The transformation resulted from Paul obeying one specific thing the Lord asked him to do.

The Lord required that Paul stay home with his family for one full year. One of the reasons for the requirement was that Paul didn't know how to be still. Asking a young man in his twenties to stay home night after night with Mom and Dad seemed almost unreasonable, but Paul knew God was leading him. Paul's obedience helped prepare him for his current ministry.

Acknowledge the Lord

*Lean on, trust in, and be confident in the Lord with all your heart
and mind and do not rely on your own insight or understanding. In
all your ways know, recognize, and acknowledge Him, and He will
direct and make straight and plain your paths.*

Proverbs 3:5–6

One of the most important things we can learn in this day and hour
is how to be still.

Although some of the time we move too slowly and most of the
time we move too fast, the major problem is that we move in the
flesh. We jump up and do things without acknowledging the Lord.

Be Still and Know God

*Let be and be still, and know (recognize and understand) that I am
God. I will be exalted among the nations! I will be exalted in the
earth!*

Psalm 46:10

One of the main reasons so many of us are burned out and stressed
out is that we don't know how to be still—to "know" God and "acknowledge" Him. When we spend time with Him we learn to hear
His voice. When we acknowledge Him, He directs our paths. If we
don't spend time being still, getting to know Him, and hearing His
voice, we will operate from our own strength in the flesh. As we saw
before, we can burn out because God is not obligated to anoint us in
doing something He didn't direct.

We need to learn to be quiet inside and stay in that peaceful state
so that we are always ready to hear the Lord's voice.

Many people today run from one thing to the next. Because their
minds don't know how to be still, they don't know how to be still. At
one time I didn't know how to stay home for an evening, and I was
a full-grown adult!

I felt I had to find something to do every evening. I had to be involved and on the go, being a part of whatever was going on. I

thought I couldn't afford to miss anything that happened because I didn't want anything to go on I didn't know about. I couldn't just sit and be still, look at a tree in the backyard, or drink a cup of coffee. I had to be up doing something. I was not a human being—I was a human doing.

Our young friend Paul was like that. At the age of twenty-two he had the call of the Lord on him but didn't know what it was. Paul was so used to doing, the Lord required Paul to do only one thing—stay home with his family for a year.

Even though the requirement was simple, obeying would be hard. Paul was used to running around with his friends every evening. Paul knew every night his flesh would start screaming, "I want to go out with my friends!" For Paul to obey God's requirement took special obedience.

One of the reasons the Lord told Paul to stay home for a year was to establish good family relationships. So for the next year Paul was there in the family barbecuing for them, watching good movies with them—spending time with his mom, dad, brothers, and sisters. But he was still so full of his old lifestyle, he found it hard to be still. In the evening he roamed all over the house.

"I would rotate around the house at night. My mother said she saw me in the kitchen at least six or seven times a night. I just couldn't be still; I had to be up doing something."

The difference in him between then and now is amazing. It's hard to believe he was ever that way. The Lord wanted to keep Paul still for a year so He could do the work needed in Paul. I believe if Paul had not obeyed God for that year, he would not be in the position he is in now, experiencing the blessings, including the peace and joy, that result from doing God's will.

Prompt, Exact Obedience

One of the areas in which I have had to learn obedience to the Lord is in talking—or more precisely, when to *stop* talking.

If you are a big talker like me, you understand why I say there is anointed-by-the-Holy-Spirit talk, then there is vain, useless, idle talk, the kind the apostle Paul warns about in his letter to young Timothy.

"But avoid all empty (vain, useless, idle) talk, for it will lead people into more and more ungodliness" (2 Timothy 2:16).

There have been times when we have had guests in our home and I have finished saying what the Lord wanted me to say, but then continued talking. We can usually pinpoint the moment when what we are doing switches from being anointed by God to being *us* continuing on in the flesh—in our own strength. After that point I was rambling, really saying nothing, or repeating the same things over and over.

Sometimes when people left our house to go home, I was exhausted. If I had quit talking two hours earlier when the Lord told me, I wouldn't have been worn out from all my empty, vain, useless, idle talking!

Another time I asked the altar workers to assemble in order to give them a word of instruction about a few changes in the way we were handling the prayer lines. I talked to them for about an hour and shared with them what I had planned to say. That was fine. But then I thought of a little something about obedience and shared that, then shared about something else.

I was just about to really get on a roll, when all of a sudden Dave stood up and said, "Well, it's time to go home." He saved me from going on and on with vain, useless, idle talk. And because I had continued beyond God's prompting, I was starting to feel rattled.

The special requirement the Lord had for me was to learn to say what He wanted me to say, then stop.

> For God sets Himself against the proud (the insolent, the overbearing, the disdainful, the presumptuous, the boastful)—[and He opposes, frustrates, and defeats them], but gives grace (favor, blessing) to the humble. (1 Peter 5:5)

When we feel frustrated, we usually want to blame the devil. But the frustration we feel when we push beyond the point God tells us happens because we are continuing on in our own strength—He has quit helping us! If God's approval is on what we are doing—whether it is shopping, doing dishes, or talking—He is energizing us because He is doing it through us.

Have you ever been talking with someone about a tender subject when the discussion suddenly takes a turn and becomes a little heated? You can tell feelings are starting to get out of control and that little prompting on the inside of you says, "That's enough. Don't say any more." That prompting, though small, is very strong, and you know saying one more thing would not be wise. But after thinking for a minute, you decide to plunge on in with the flesh! You press right on in and make your comment. A few minutes later, you're in an all-out war!

I used to do this when Dave and I started to discuss something, and without stopping to think began tossing slightly heated comments back and forth. Immediately the Holy Spirit would quicken me with that little prompting inside, "Don't say another word."

I would think, *One word? Just one more word won't be that bad. Surely one more word won't get me in much trouble!* After I would plunge on in with the "one more word," I was always reminded of the importance of prompt, exact obedience! I discovered from Dave's reaction I couldn't have picked a worse thing to say if I had tried! I was also reminded of the Lord's special requirement for me to say only what He wants me to say and no more.

When we say something after the "still, small voice" prompts us to stop, and the person we speak to reacts, later we often ponder the whole incident, baffled. We say, "God, I don't understand what happened!" What happened is so simple and can be avoided so easily: God told us to do something and we disobeyed. The minute we disobeyed, His anointing lifted and the frustration began. In the situations above, if we had obeyed the promptings and kept quiet, things probably would have settled back down, even in five minutes. Then the Spirit would have let us know it was all right to continue that conversation.

Sometimes all we need is a little break just to let things said, settle. But because the prompting is so small, it's easy to think, *Oh, it won't make any difference if I just say this*, and press on in the flesh. The prompting is so slight, pushing ahead in spite of it doesn't seem like disobedience, but that's exactly what it is!

We soon discover how much difference disobeying the "still, small voice" made! The minute the Spirit says, "That's enough," we need to stop. If we keep going, we are asking for frustration and defeat.

If He says, "Don't say another word," He means exactly that. Sometimes we have our own version of obedience. We interpret a prompting like that from the Lord to mean, "Don't say another *word*. But if you want to say two or three *sentences* more, that's fine!"

When we realize that continuing on beyond the Lord's prompting even just a little is moving into disobedience, we are able to understand what happened—His anointing lifted; therefore, frustration was able to immediately come in. We are also able to understand why obeying the Lord's promptings in the small things is so important.

Five Minutes of Obedience

Recently when I was studying extremely hard, I was becoming very tired mentally. A little prompting said to me, "Just get up and walk away from it. Take a five-minute vacation."

A few years before, I would have pushed on ahead in order to make sure I covered the amount of material I had set as my goal. But instead, I obeyed the Holy Spirit's prompting. I went downstairs, walked around a bit, talked to my daughter, drank something, stretched a little, and looked out the window for a few minutes. When I felt ready again, I went upstairs and dived back into my studies refreshed!

Just five minutes of obedience relieved the pressure and stress building in me. If I had ignored the prompting and continued studying until I reached my goal, my studying wouldn't have been as fruitful. And I would have probably been exhausted and irritable!

If we keep pushing, the work we do from the point we disobey will not compare in quality to the work we would have produced under the Holy Spirit's anointing.

3

⁂

Set Up for Blessing

Samuel said, Has the Lord as great a delight in burnt offerings and sacrifices as in obeying the voice of the Lord? Behold, to obey is better than sacrifice, and to hearken than the fat of rams.

1 Samuel 15:22

When God prompts us to do little things, He is never trying to take anything away from us. He is always trying to set us up for a blessing.

He prompted me to go home from the shopping mall that time knowing I was heading into overload and about to display anything *but* the fruit of the Spirit! If from the beginning I had slowed down and quieted my mind enough to hear His promptings, He could have shown me which mall stores to look in for the items I needed. I could have finished my shopping trip in thirty minutes and in peace!

Things the Lord asks us to do that look unimportant to us are apparently very important from His point of view! Once we fully understand the importance of hearing and immediately obeying the Lord's promptings, we will want to set as a priority doing what we need to do to stay in a place of peace, ready to hear.

"That It Might Go Well with Them"

Deuteronomy 5:29 states, "Oh, that they had such a [mind and] heart in them always [reverently] to fear Me and keep all My commandments, that it might go well with them and with their children forever!" If we will simply listen to the Lord and do what He says, things will go well for us. To bring the result God intends, we need to add action to the hearing.

Our young friend Paul had to add action to the Lord's instructions for him to stay home for a year in order for the result the Lord wanted, to come to pass. It was hard for Paul to obey the Lord's particular requirement for him, and the process took some time, but the Lord was setting him up for blessings! Because Paul was obedient, the result was total transformation!

Often the Lord wants us to spend a little time with Him so He can refresh us. At night many people sit down in front of the television because they're tired. Then when they sense the Holy Spirit prompting, "Turn it off and come away with me," they don't realize the Lord is trying to set them up for a blessing!

They say, "Lord, you know I work all day. I would like to just relax a little bit in front of the television."

If they are in that state, they are not relaxing! Usually, the longer they sit there, the more tired they become. But by obeying the Lord, even ten minutes in His presence can bring the refreshing they are trying to find by watching television.

I don't mean to imply watching television to unwind is a bad thing. Sometimes I like to make popcorn, get something to drink, and watch a good movie on television with my family just to relax. The point I'm making is how important it is to obey the Lord's promptings.

While I'm sitting there watching the movie, the Holy Spirit may prompt me, "Come upstairs for half an hour." The problem would be if I thought, *But God, I prayed this morning*, and disobeyed the prompting! It may have been one of those times when I thought, *It can't make that much difference if I watch this movie with my family and spend some time with the Lord later*. If I continue watching, usually the movie is one I don't enjoy. Then I go to bed frustrated, thinking, *Oh, I just wasted the whole evening.*

Instead I could have immediately responded to the Lord's prompting by saying to my family, "Excuse me—I'll be back." After spending half an hour with the Lord, I would have come back with His peace all over me and could have easily heard any promptings He was giving me to change the channel to a particular movie we would enjoy much better!

Simply Obeying God

Most people have no idea how simple it is sometimes to relieve stress, and Satan works to keep it that way! He works to complicate people's lives in every imaginable way because he knows the power and joy simplicity brings.

Satan wants to exhaust the energies God has given us by keeping us too busy and stressed out trying to handle all the things complicating our life. He knows that if we learn to simply obey God, we will turn that power and energy against him by hearing and doing the work God directs!

The transformations many people desire in different areas of their life come through forming a pattern of obeying God in the little things. He may ask you to come away and visit with Him for half an hour or an evening instead of watching television, going to a party, or talking on the phone. The more consistent you are in keeping yourself still enough to hear His voice, then obey His promptings, the sooner the needed work will be done in you for the transformation to be complete. God uses our obedience in the little things to transform our life.

No matter what the situation, listen to the Lord and obey. As we saw before, Proverbs 3:6 states, "In all your ways know, recognize, and acknowledge Him, and He will direct and make straight and plain your paths." You may not understand the reasons the Lord asks you to do particular things or see any changes or results immediately, but keep obeying the Lord and things will go well with you and your children.

Obedience Is Better Than Sacrifice

First Samuel 15:22 says, "To obey is better than sacrifice." There are times we must make sacrifices in true obedience to the Lord, but sacrifices we make as a result of moving out in the flesh will lead to stress. We may "work hard for God" according to *our* ideas of what we should do for Him rather than taking time to be still in order to hear *Him* tell us what *He* wants us to do.

When we "work for Him" in the flesh, we sacrifice time the Lord really desires to use in another way, and we may also sacrifice our health, peace, and the quality of our relationships, as we saw before.

If we continue on with what the Holy Spirit prompts us to do after He tells us to stop, we *will* sacrifice, because doing the work without His anointing won't be easy! However, God will never abandon us (see Hebrews 13:5), and He continues to work with us in the midst of our wrong choices.

Even if we make a wrong choice and are functioning in our own strength, we may still accomplish some things for God. According to Romans 8:28, "All things work together for good to them that love God, to them who are the called according to his purpose" (KJV).

We need to remind ourselves we aren't perfect. We won't always make the right choice, do the right thing, or obey God perfectly every time. We all make mistakes and when we do, the only thing we can do is ask God to forgive us and go on.

But by obeying God, we will accomplish *specifically* what He wants done at the time and in the way He wants it done, which promotes peace instead of stress. Through obeying the Lord, we place ourselves in position for Him to be able to bless us in the way He desires and plans.

The Prince of Peace, Jesus, Who lives inside those of us who have received Him, knows and will reveal to us the specific actions we need to take in every situation to lead us into peace. He also knows what we need to do in order to prepare for what He has planned for us.

The particular requirements He places on each of our lives may not make sense to anybody else or even to us at the time. But once we understand how much God loves us and fully comprehend that everything He asks us to do is to take us up into a higher level of blessing, we will want to abandon ourselves to Him in trust. As a priority, we will want to keep ourselves in a place of peace to be able to hear and respond immediately to Him.

He may prompt you to go home from the shopping mall to keep you from becoming exhausted, irritable, and hard to get along with. He may tell you to zip your lip because he knows you are about to say something you will wish you hadn't! He may ask you to obey

Him by stopping what you are doing, to getting up, walking away, and taking a five- or ten-minute vacation to relieve pressure building up and to refresh you. Or He may ask you to come away and be still in His presence for half an hour.

Exalt Jesus

Relieving stress—leading a peaceful, happy life, free from exhaustion and burnout—does not need to be complicated!

It is helpful to have a general understanding of the physical effects of stress and important to have a spiritual understanding of the source of stress and the solution to relieving it through Jesus. But we don't need to learn all the details of the medical causes and cures or go into a deep theological study of stress to be relieved of it!

The Lord told me if we will begin to exalt Jesus, we won't be exhausted. If we will begin to exalt Jesus by giving Him first place in our everyday lives through listening to Him, obeying Him, and doing what He shows us to do, we won't be exhausted.

We may lift up our hands and say, "We exalt You," but we are truly exalting the Lord when we obey Him in everything He asks.

The apostle Paul mentions "the simplicity that is in Christ" (2 Corinthians 11:3 KJV). There is a wonderful simplicity available to us through Jesus. Relieving stress is simple: Obey the promptings of the Holy Spirit. Obey immediately. Do exactly what the Lord says to do, no more and no less.

You can probably think of specific areas in your life in which obedience to small things God is telling you to do would relieve a great deal of stress. I think you will be quite amazed to discover that by beginning to apply this principle of immediately obeying the prompting of the Holy Spirit, a week later you will be able to say you experienced less stress than you did the week before.

When you feel like that rubber band all tied up in knots stretched out to the point of breaking again, take a deep breath and remember: Jesus left us His peace. He gave us the power to be on top of stress and not under it. We can live in the world and not be of it by drawing on the power of the Prince of Peace, listening to His voice and responding with prompt, exact obedience to live peacefully, happily, and free from exhaustion and stress.

SCRIPTURES TO OVERCOME STRESS

In this section, Scriptures are grouped together to use in practical application to everyday life.

To Relieve Stress

Receive Power and Strength from the Lord

When we are tired, the Lord can strengthen and refresh us. He will refresh our body and soul.

Sometimes when I'm ministering to a very long prayer line, I can feel myself just starting to cave in physically and even mentally. I stop for a second and inside I say, "Lord, I need help here—I need You to refresh me." And as the Scripture promises, He increases my strength, causing it to multiply and making it to abound.

If you are sitting at your desk or cleaning your house; if you have worked all day then need to go home and cut the grass or change the oil in the car; the Lord can refresh you. Lean back for a minute and let Him give you that power.

> Have you not known? Have you not heard? The everlasting God, the Lord, the Creator of the ends of the earth, does not faint or grow weary; there is no searching of His under-standing. He gives power to the faint and weary, and to him who has no might He increases strength [causing it to multiply and making it to abound]. (Isaiah 40:28–29)

ord can renew your strength.

n youths shall faint and be weary, and [selected] young
en shall feebly stumble and fall exhausted; But those who
wait for the Lord [who expect, look for, and hope in Him]
shall change and renew their strength and power; they shall
lift their wings and mount up [close to God] as eagles
[mount up to the sun]; they shall run and not be weary, they
shall walk and not faint or become tired. (Isaiah 40:30–31)

Come to Me, All You Who . . . Have Burnout!

The answer to burnout is spending time with God. No matter how
much material you read or how many seminars you attend on stress,
you will only find the relief you want from stress and burnout by
going to God and letting God refresh your soul.

The Lord will give rest to the overburdened. In other words, the
Lord will give rest to the burned-out!

> Come to Me, all you who labor and are heavy-laden and
> overburdened, and I will cause you to rest. [I will ease and
> relieve and refresh your souls.] (Matthew 11:28)

> The Lord is my shepherd; I shall not want. He maketh me to
> lie down in green pastures: he leadeth me beside the still wa-
> ters. He restoreth my soul. (Psalm 23:1–3 KJV)

The Lord's burden is to be light and easy to carry. We take His
yoke upon us by obeying His promptings.

> Take My yoke upon you and learn of Me, for I am gentle
> (meek) and humble (lowly) in heart, and you will find rest
> (relief and ease and refreshment and recreation and blessed
> quiet) for your souls. For My yoke is wholesome (useful,
> good—not harsh, hard, sharp, or pressing, but comfortable,
> gracious, and pleasant), and My burden is light and easy to
> be borne. (Matthew 11:29–30)

Enter into the Lord's rest by believing, trusting, and relying on
Him.

For we who have believed (adhered to and trusted in and relied on God) do enter that rest, in accordance with His dec-
laration that those [who did not believe] should not enter
when He said, As I swore in My wrath, They shall not enter
My rest; and this He said although [His] works had been
completed and prepared [and waiting for all who would be-
lieve] from the foundation of the world. (Hebrews 4:3)

Enjoy Your Life

The thief comes only in order to steal and kill and destroy. I
came that they may have and enjoy life, and have it in abundance (to the full, till it overflows). (John 10:10)

And now I am coming to You; I say these things while I am
still in the world, so that My joy may be made full and complete and perfect in them [that they may experience My delight fulfilled in them, that My enjoyment may be perfected
in their own souls, that they may have My gladness within
them, filling their hearts]. (John 17:13)

To Prevent Stress

Use Wisdom
Your body is the temple of the Holy Spirit.

Do you not know that your body is the temple (the very
sanctuary) of the Holy Spirit Who lives within you, Whom
you have received [as a Gift] from God? You are not your
own, You were bought with a price [purchased with a preciousness and paid for, made His own]. So then, honor God
and bring glory to Him in your body. (1 Corinthians
6:19–20)

The Lord gives power to the faint and weary; but remember, if
you are worn out from continually exceeding your physical limitations you need physical rest. The Lord may mercifully give you supernatural energy in particular instances, but you are in

disobedience when you abuse your body, the temple of the Holy Spirit. As we have seen, the anointing lifts when you operate outside of God's promptings.

If you want God to flow through and work through you, you need to take care of your body so God can use you. If we wear out the body we have, we don't have a spare in a drawer somewhere to pull out!

Take a Sabbath Rest

It is important to take a Sabbath rest because we need certain periods of time to just let go of all the usual things we do and think about. We need to spend time with God to restore our energies and let Him restore our soul.

You may not take your Sabbath on Sunday. It may be Saturday or Friday, or a half day on Tuesday and Thursday. The issue is not what day to set aside but to definitely set aside a certain portion of time in which to just totally and completely rest and relax.

> Six days you shall do your work, but the seventh day you shall rest and keep Sabbath, that your ox and your donkey may rest, and the son of your bondwoman, and the alien, may be refreshed. (Exodus 23:12)

Obey God in Making Commitments

Commit only to those things the Lord tells you to do, and say no to the others. You only have so much energy. If you don't use it doing the things God has told you to do, you will run out and have none left to use for the things you should be doing.

To release God's anointing on your life, find out what He wants you to do, then make your yes be yes and your no be no. In other words, stick to what you know in your heart is right for you.

> Let your Yes be simply Yes, and your No be simply No; anything more than that comes from the evil one. (Matthew 5:37)

Be a God-pleaser—not a man-pleaser.

Now am I trying to win the favor of men, or of God? Do I seek to please men? If I were still seeking popularity with men, I should not be a bond servant of Christ (the Messiah). (Galatians 1:10)

Stay Calm

Blessed (happy, fortunate, to be envied) is the man whom You discipline and instruct, O Lord, and teach out of Your law, That You may give him power to keep himself calm in the days of adversity, until the [inevitable] pit of corruption is dug for the wicked. (Psalm 94:12–13)

Do not fret or have any anxiety about anything, but in every circumstance and in everything, by prayer and petition (definite requests), with thanksgiving, continue to make your wants known to God. And God's peace . . . which transcends all understanding shall garrison and mount guard over your hearts and minds in Christ Jesus. (Philippians 4:6–7)

Casting the whole of your care [all your anxieties, all your worries, all your concerns, once and for all] on Him, for He cares for you affectionately and cares about you watchfully. (1 Peter 5:7)

Promote Peace in the Way You Live

And the servant of the Lord must not be quarrelsome (fighting and contending). Instead, he must be kindly to everyone and mild-tempered [preserving the bond of peace]; he must be a skilled and suitable teacher, patient and forbearing and willing to suffer wrong. He must correct his opponents with courtesy and gentleness, in the hope that God may grant that they will repent and come to know the Truth [that they will perceive and recognize and become accurately acquainted with and acknowledge it]. (2 Timothy 2:24–25)

Live in harmony with one another; do not be haughty (snobbish, high-minded, exclusive), but readily adjust yourself to [people, things] and give yourselves to humble tasks. Never overestimate yourself or be wise in your own conceits. (Romans 12:16)

Fathers, do not provoke or irritate or fret your children [do not be hard on them or harass them], lest they become discouraged and sullen and morose and feel inferior and frustrated. [Do not break their spirit.] (Colossians 3:21)

Trust the Lord

He who dwells in the secret place of the Most High shall remain stable and fixed under the shadow of the Almighty [Whose power no foe can withstand]. I will say of the Lord, He is my Refuge and my Fortress, my God; on Him I lean and rely, and in Him I [confidently] trust! (Psalm 91:1–2)

Trust (lean on, rely on, and be confident) in the Lord and do good; so shall you dwell in the land and feed surely on His faithfulness, and truly you shall be fed. (Psalm 37:3)

Prayer to Overcome Stress

Father,

I set as my priority spending time with You to hear Your voice clearly and to obey You. Help me to keep my priorities in order.

I know that as I place You first by spending time with You, You will cause me to do supernaturally all the things I need to do.

I know that You want me to have peace in every area of my life and have made that peace available to me. I thank You that when I ask for wisdom, You give it to me. I ask that You guide me and give me wisdom so that I know clearly the commitments to make.

I thank You, Lord, that I use my energies in the way You want them used. In Jesus' name I pray, amen.

STRAIGHT TALK ON *Loneliness*

CONTENTS

INTRODUCTION

———— ❧ ————

A major problem facing people today is grief and loneliness. The two often go together because many people grieve over being lonely.

Loneliness has become even more of a major issue than in the past. In my ministry, an increasing number of people request prayer for guidance and help in handling loneliness.

In His Word, God tells us we are not alone. He wants to deliver, comfort, and heal us. But when people encounter painful major losses in their lives, sadly, many never get over them. When tragedy occurs and the hurt seems unbearable, Satan sees it as an opportunity to attempt to bring an individual or a family into permanent bondage.

The death of a loved one, divorce, or the severing of a close relationship can bring grief, and most people go through a grieving process. A key to victory is in understanding the difference between a normal, balanced "grieving process" and a "spirit of grief." One helps the grieving person recover from the loss with the passing of time; the other causes him to grow worse and sink deeper into despair.

I believe one of the reasons why people, especially Christians, become bound by grief and loneliness following a loss is due to a lack of understanding about the grieving process. Sometimes when God heals, the result is instant. But more often, especially when recovering from a loss, the healing is a process through which the Lord walks His children step by step. Obviously, all people do not respond to a loss in the same way or in the same degree, but we all have emotions that can be wounded and bruised and must be healed.

Jesus came to earth to destroy the works of the devil and to give us abundant life (see 1 John 3:8 and John 10:10)! If we will learn how to receive what He has made available to us, we will experience that abundant life free from grief and loneliness.

God delivered me from the bondage of grief and loneliness, and I believe He will use the step-by-step process in this book to help you find release also!

Part One

—————— ❧ ——————

NEVER FORSAKEN

1

You Are Not Alone

And Jesus came and spake unto them, saying . . . lo, I am with you al-
ways, even unto the end of the world.

Matthew 28:18, 20 (KJV)

Because he has set his love upon Me, therefore will I deliver him; I will
set him on high, because he knows and understands My name [has a
personal knowledge of My mercy, love, and kindness—trusts and relies
on Me, knowing I will never forsake him, no, never]. He shall call
upon Me, and I will answer him; I will be with him in trouble, I will
deliver him and honor him. With long life will I satisfy him and show
him My salvation.

Psalm 91:14–16

God wants you to know you are not alone. Satan wants you to believe you are all alone, but you are not. He wants you to believe that
no one understands how you feel, but that is not true.

In addition to God being with you, many believers know how
you feel and understand what you are experiencing mentally and
emotionally. Psalm 34:19 tells us: "Many evils confront the [consis-
tently] righteous, but the Lord delivers him out of them all." There
are many accounts in the Bible of "the afflictions of the righteous"
(KJV) and the Lord's deliverance from them.

God Is a Deliverer

God delivered Paul and Silas from prison (see Acts 16:23–26).

In 1 Samuel 17:37 we read of the Lord delivering David from afflictions: "David said, The Lord Who delivered me out of the paw of the lion and out of the paw of the bear, He will deliver me out of the hand of this Philistine. And Saul said to David, Go, and the Lord be with you!"

When you are making progress, Satan often brings affliction to discourage you and will try to make you feel alone. But what Satan intends for our harm, God will work to our good (see Genesis 50:20). You can do as David did in the Scripture above and encourage yourself by remembering past victories.

Shadrach, Meshach, and Abednego experienced affliction when they remained firm in their commitment to the one true God (see Daniel 3:10–30). When they refused the command of the wicked king Nebuchadnezzar to worship the golden image he had set up, Nebuchadnezzar cast them into the fiery furnace which he heated seven times hotter than usual!

Nebuchadnezzar was "astounded" (v. 24) to see that Shadrach, Meshach, and Abednego met a fourth man in their fiery furnace— One Who was "like the Son of God" (v. 25 KJV). Not only did the three come out of the furnace totally unharmed, they didn't even smell like smoke (v. 27)!

Verse thirty tells us the king promoted Shadrach, Meshach, and Abednego. God will not only bring you out of your afflictions, but He will also bring you up!

Daniel was also afflicted. As punishment for his integrity and commitment to God, Daniel was placed into a lions' den. But Daniel chose to trust in God, and God delivered him by sending an angel to shut the lions' mouths. Daniel came out unharmed (see Daniel 6:3–23)! Keep your trust in God, and you will come out unharmed.

All of these people found that God was faithful. I have also experienced His goodness and faithfulness. I was abused sexually, mentally, and emotionally as a child. I have been sick during my life, including ten years of migraine headaches and an attack of cancer as well as several more minor, but nonetheless painful and distressing ailments. In each case God delivered me and provided answers. But there was a time of waiting on God and being steadfast.

First Peter 5:8–9 states:

> Be well balanced (temperate, sober of mind), be vigilant and cautious at all times; for that enemy of yours, the devil, roams around like a lion roaring [in fierce hunger], seeking someone to seize upon and devour. Withstand him; be firm in faith [against his onset—rooted, established, strong, immovable, and determined], knowing that the same (identical) sufferings are appointed to your brotherhood (the whole body of Christians) throughout the world.

As we have seen, afflictions come upon all of us. We all experience a certain amount of grief and loneliness in this life from time to time, but we are not alone. The Bible tells us to resist the devil: "resist" him "steadfast in the faith" (v. 9 KJV). But we can also draw strength from knowing that others know how we feel.

God Is Working for Our Good

God is good, and He is faithful. Several years ago I encountered a major emotional shock that separated me from many people and things very dear to me. God wanted me to move on, but I was not obeying Him. God was working for my good, even though I could not see the good at the time. When I would not move, God moved me and some of the people in my life. I realize now that it was one of the best things that ever happened to me, but at the time I thought my whole world was falling apart. I wasn't sure I would ever recover.

Death and divorce are not the only devastating losses people face. Losing longtime relationships or a career that has been important to you may be traumatic. Personal injury preventing you from pursuing a hobby or sport that has been a major part of your life can be very hard emotionally. Actually, losing anyone or anything that is important to us is hard.

My complete recovery took almost three years, but I made steady, definite progress throughout that time. Something that finally helped me be healed of the major pain was an understanding of "soul ties."

"Soul Ties"

Spending a great deal of time with any person or thing leads to a bonding relationship with that person or thing.

As humans, we are spirit, we have a soul, and we live in a body. The soul can be thought of as being composed of the mind, the will, and the emotions.

Involvement requires mental time, thought, and plans. Generally, we talk about what we are most involved in with our mind, our will, and our emotions. By giving it a little thought, we can see how involved our "souls" are in the people and things into which we invest most of our time and energy.

If my arm were tied to my side and kept there, immobile, for years, it would have a devastating effect. If it was suddenly untied, I would find it not only withered and weakened, but also disabled. It would be impossible for me to use that arm properly until it had gained back its strength and mobility. I would have to learn new ways to function and to develop the muscles that had atrophied from disuse.

The same thing holds true with our souls. When we have been involved with a person, place, or thing for a long period of time, we have developed "soul ties." When that person or place or thing is taken from us, we react as if we are still involved with it. Like an arm that was tied to our side, even though it is later set free, it still feels as if it is bound. It does not function properly until some time has passed and some effort has been made to restore it.

Even when we voluntarily walk away from someone or something, our soul may still want to remain where we were. Feelings are very strong, and can cause us much pain and anguish. We must realize we can use our will to decide to do or not to do something. A solid, willful decision will override raging, surging emotions.

There are right and wrong "soul ties." Right ones will balance out in time; wrong ones must be dealt with.

No matter what kind of situation you are dealing with right now, if not handled properly it can cripple you. However, God knows how to handle it!

If you have been injured in an accident, you may have to learn to walk all over again.

If you have lost your spouse to death or divorce, you may have to learn to function as an individual. You may have to learn to do things you have forgotten how to do or have never done before. You may have to get a job or learn to cook and care for children or make decisions you are not used to making in matters you know nothing about.

If you have lost a job, you may have to learn how to market yourself all over again or even relocate to a new and strange environment.

While you are doing these new things, you may still hurt, but you can take satisfaction in knowing you are moving forward. Each day you are making progress. God promises to be with you in trouble. While you are waiting for Him to deliver you, you can be comforted by knowing He is with you and working on your behalf even though you cannot always see what He is doing in the natural world. Matthew 28:20 says, "Lo, I am with you always, even unto the end of the world" (KJV).

2

❦

LONELINESS CAN BE CURED

For I will turn their mourning into joy and will comfort them and make them rejoice after their sorrow.

Jeremiah 31:13

Loneliness is not a sin. Therefore, if you are lonely, don't add feelings of guilt to your list of wounds.

Loneliness can be cured, no matter what the cause. Some of those who suffer most from loneliness, in itself a form of grief, are the shy or extremely timid; those who feel misunderstood; those in leadership; the divorced and unmarried; the widowed; the elderly; those who feel rejected; those who feel "odd" or different from other people; the abused; those unable to maintain healthy relationships, especially with the opposite sex; those who must relocate or change employment—and the list goes on and on.

There are many causes of loneliness, but many people don't realize they don't need to live with it. They can confront it and deal with it.

The word comes from the root word *lone*, which *Webster* defines as "without companionship: isolated . . . located or standing by itself."[1] The adjective forms are *lonely*, meaning "solitary . . . desolate . . . dejected by being alone,"[2] and *lonesome*, meaning "dejected, due to a lack of companionship . . . deserted."[3]

Loneliness often manifests as an inner ache, a vacuum or a craving for affection. Its side effects include feelings of emptiness, uselessness, or purposelessness. A more serious side effect of loneliness is often depression, which, in some cases, can eventually lead to suicide.

It is sad to say, but numerous people commit suicide either because they don't know how to handle loneliness or because they don't want to properly face and deal with it in a realistic manner. Even Christians are falling prey to this formidable enemy.

Alone Doesn't Mean Lonely

The dictionary defines the word *alone* as "solitary . . . with nothing further added . . . apart from all others."[4] According to *Webster*, words like *lonely* and *lonesome* convey a sense of isolation felt as a result of a lack of companionship.

Are you alone (independent, solitary, on your own)? Or are you lonely or lonesome (desolate, deserted, dejected due to a lack of companionship)? There is a difference.

It is very important to realize that just because you are alone does not mean you must be lonely or lonesome.

Even being in companionship with other people does not guarantee the absence of loneliness.

The conditions that create loneliness are sometimes passing situations. A person who leaves his companions behind and moves to a new home in a new town may experience a temporary feeling of loneliness, but he will eventually make new friends.

But many situations that create a sense of loneliness are much more permanent, and these are the issues that can be dealt with.

While it may not always be possible to keep from being alone, there are always answers to loneliness!

Loneliness Caused by Crisis or Trauma

Many times loneliness results from trauma or crisis resulting from the death of a loved one (a spouse, child, parent, close friend, or relative), a divorce, or separation.

When something happens to make us realize things are never

going to be the way they once were, it often creates crisis or trauma in our lives, which can lead to a sense of loneliness and despair.

By its very nature, a crisis situation requires us to go one way or the other, to become better or worse, to overcome or to go under.

We have all seen movies that depict a seriously ill or injured person whose doctor calls in the family and says, "I have done all I can do. The patient has reached a crisis point. What happens now is out of my hands." What the doctor is saying is that within a very short time the person is either going to start getting well or he is going to die.

Crisis always provokes change, and change of this type is hard for everyone involved.

The Process of Grief Versus the Spirit of Grief

The word *grief* refers to "deep mental anguish, as over a loss: sorrow."[5] To *grieve* is "to feel grief"[6]—that is, to experience mental anguish, to be sorrowful, to mourn, to be distressed.

The grieving process is necessary and healthy—mentally, emotionally, and even physically. A person who refuses to grieve is often not facing reality, which ultimately has a devastating effect on his entire being.

A *spirit* of grief is another matter entirely. If not resisted, it will take over and destroy the life of the one who has suffered a loss. If not confronted and controlled, it will rob health, strength, and vitality—and even life itself. Let me give you an example.

A friend of mine lost her son to a lengthy battle with leukemia. When the boy died, it was naturally very hard on everyone in the family. They were definitely going through the process of grief, and rightfully so.

However, this friend related to me an incident that exposes the spirit of grief. She said that she was doing laundry one day and began to think about her son, when suddenly she felt something wrap itself around her. It felt gloomy and sad, and she could feel herself almost wanting to "sink" into it.

God gave her discernment that it was a spirit of grief trying to oppress her. She grabbed one of her son's shirts, wrapped it around herself and told the devil that she was using it as a "garment of praise" (Isaiah 61:3). Then she began to dance and shout praises to the Lord. As she did so, she felt the oppression leave.

This woman could have opened the door for major long-term problems had she not aggressively confronted and dealt with that oppressive spirit of grief.

Mourning Turned into Joy

Blessed are they that mourn: for they shall be comforted.

Matthew 5:4 (KJV)

The Bible makes several references to those who are mourning. In Jeremiah 31:13, the Lord says through the prophet,

Then will the maidens rejoice in the dance, and the young men and old together. For I will turn their mourning into joy and will comfort them and make them rejoice after their sorrow.

From this verse we see that it is God's will to comfort those who mourn; therefore, we can determine that comfort should come after mourning. If comfort never comes, then something is wrong.

In Isaiah 61:1–3 we read these words of assurance:

The Spirit of the Lord God is upon me, because the Lord has anointed and qualified me to preach the Gospel of good tidings to the meek, the poor, and afflicted; He has sent me to bind up and heal the brokenhearted, to proclaim liberty to the [physical and spiritual] captives and the opening of the prison and of the eyes to those who are bound. To proclaim the acceptable year of the Lord [the year of His favor] and the day of vengeance of our God, to comfort all who mourn, To grant [consolation and joy] to those who mourn in Zion—to give them an ornament (a garland or diadem) of beauty instead of ashes, the oil of joy instead of mourning, the garment [expressive] of praise instead of a heavy, burdened, and failing spirit.

It is obvious from the principle we see set forth in these Scriptures that God is for complete restoration. He is especially interested in those who are hurting and seeks to restore their joy.

You may be grieving over a loss, but you do not have to stay in that condition the rest of your life. God has promised to turn your mourning into joy. You should hold on to that promise while you are working through the grieving process. Doing so will give you hope for the future.

The Hope Set Before Us

Hope deferred makes the heart sick, but when the desire is fulfilled, it is a tree of life.

Proverbs 13:12

While grieving over a loss is often necessary and even healthy, care must be taken not to fall into despair and hopelessness, which is a heavy burden to bear.

Instead of giving in to hopelessness, heed the words of David in Psalm 27:13–14:

[What, what would have become of me] had I not believed that I would see the Lord's goodness in the land of the living! Wait and hope for and expect the Lord; be brave and of good courage and let your heart be stout and enduring. Yes, wait for and hope for and expect the Lord.

No matter what happens in the earth, there is always hope in God.

In Hebrews 6:17–18 the Bible states that God has assured us of His will to bless us by backing His promise with an oath,

. . . so that, by two unchangeable things [His promise and His oath] in which it is impossible for God ever to prove false or deceive us, we who have fled [to Him] for refuge might have mighty indwelling strength and strong encouragement to grasp and hold fast the hope appointed for us and set before [us].

In verse 19 it goes on to say:

[Now] we have this [hope] as a sure and steadfast anchor of the soul [it cannot slip and it cannot break down under whoever steps out upon it—a hope] that reaches farther and enters into [the very certainty of the Presence] within the veil.

A ship's anchor keeps it from floating away in a storm. Hope does the same thing for our souls. Hope is like an anchor that keeps us on course when we are being tossed to and fro, this way and that, by the storms of life.

You may not understand much when you are hurting and the pain of loss is ripping through your soul, but know and hold on to this one truth: God loves you, and He has a future for you. Hope in Him and trust Him to turn your mourning into joy and to give you beauty for ashes, even as you go through the various stages of grief.

3

❧

THE SEVEN STAGES OF GRIEF

Lean on, trust in, and be confident in the Lord with all your heart and mind and do not rely on your own insight or understanding. In all your ways know, recognize, and acknowledge Him, and He will direct and make straight and plain your paths.

Proverbs 3:5–6

After experiencing a tragedy or loss, almost all of us go through some sort of grieving process. Generally, there are seven basic steps or aspects of this process. Let's look at them individually to try to gain a better understanding of what is happening to us in this process and what we can do to gain the most benefit from it.

Stage 1: Shock and Denial

These are usually the first things encountered when tragedy or loss occurs. God uses them as protection against complete devastation.

Shock
A shock is something that jars the mind or emotions with a violent, unexpected blow.

Shock is actually a built-in protection. It gives us time to become gradually adjusted to the change that has taken place. It prevents us from having to face reality all at once.

Before we can press forward, we must have a new mind-set. Shock provides us time to develop a new way of thinking about our lives and our future.

To illustrate, consider an automobile's shock absorbers. They are designed to cushion the vehicle from unexpected bumps in the road. Without them it would fall apart from the violence of the blows it encounters during its travels.

Often we are the same way. We are traveling on the road of life, and most of us are not expecting bumps and potholes. Therefore we are not ready for them when they suddenly show up. Our Holy Ghost–installed "shock absorbers" cushion the blow until we can readjust and adapt our thinking to accommodate the sudden change in the ride.

The stage of shock can last from a few minutes up to several weeks. But if it goes beyond that, something is wrong.

Healthy shock is like a temporary anesthetic; however, we cannot stay permanently under anesthesia. We must move on. Shock is a temporary escape from reality, but if it is not temporary, it can lead to very serious problems.

I recall being with my aunt when my uncle died. He had been sick for quite some time, and even though it was probably inevitable that he would die, my aunt kept saying over and over, "I just can't believe it; I cannot believe he is gone." She was in the initial stage of shock that often comes with a tragic loss.

When going through shock, it is best not to linger in inactivity too long. A woman on my staff experienced a sudden, devastating crisis. I remember her saying, "God told me to keep moving, so I'm going to come to work."

She shared that she was not sure what the quality of her work would be, but she knew it would be disastrous for her if she gave in to the apathy that was seeking to take over and drag her down. In one day, she had lost what seemed to her to be everything of importance to her life. Her general feeling was, "What's the use? Why try to do anything?" She knew that if she was going to survive, she had to counter those feelings with positive action.

When you are going through shock due to a tragic loss, as a believer you must recognize the division between soul and spirit. Even in a time of tragedy or loss you must discern the difference between your human emotions and the true leading of the Holy Spirit.

Denial

Denial is the refusal to face reality, which can often cause emotional and mental illness in varying degrees.

God has equipped us with His Spirit to empower us to face reality, to take His hand, to walk through the dark valleys, and to overcome all the obstacles that life brings.

With God's Spirit to dwell within us and to watch over us, we can say with King David, "Yes, though I walk through the [deep, sunless] valley of the shadow of death, I will fear or dread no evil, for You are with me; Your rod [to protect] and Your staff [to guide], they comfort me" (Psalm 23:4).

Even when death brings a shadow over our lives, we can live with hope.

In speaking of hope, think again of Shadrach, Meshach and Abednego in the fiery furnace (see Daniel 3:8–27). Even though they had to experience being cast into an oven that had been heated seven times hotter than ever before, the Lord was with them in that blazing inferno.

We can look at scriptural accounts such as the one above to encourage us whenever we find ourselves in a tough place. Just as God was with the Hebrew children in that fiery furnace, so that they came out of it loosed and with no permanent damage done to them, so He will be with us in whatever situation we may have to face in life.

It is God's will for us to face reality, to go through and come out victorious in every way. Facing reality is hard, but running away from reality is even harder.

Stage 2: Anger

The second stage is marked by anger: anger at God, anger at the devil, anger at self, and anger at the person who caused the pain or loss, even if that person died.

Anger at God

We believe that God is inherently good, and that He is also in control of our lives. Therefore, when tragedy strikes or loss occurs, we don't understand why God does not prevent such things from happening to us and hurting us so badly.

Faced with tragic loss, often we become angry and ask, "If God is good and all-powerful, why does He allow bad things to happen to good people?" This question becomes a major issue when it is we, God's own children, who are the ones suffering.

At such times, reasoning wants to scream out, "This make no sense at all!" Over and over the question "Why, God, why?" torments those who are grieving over a loss in their life, just as it also tortures the lonely and the dejected.

In 1 Corinthians 13:12 the apostle Paul indicates there will always be some unanswered questions to deal with in this life:

> For now we are looking in a mirror that gives only a dim (blurred) reflection [of reality as in a riddle or enigma], but then [when perfection comes] we shall see in reality and face to face! Now I know in part (imperfectly), but then I shall know and understand fully and clearly, even in the same manner as I have been fully and clearly known and understood [by God].

Excessive reasoning, trying to figure out things for which we will not be able to find an answer, torments and brings much confusion, but Proverbs 3:5–6 tells us that trust in the Lord brings assurance and direction:

> Lean on, trust in, and be confident in the Lord with all your heart and mind and do not rely on your own insight or understanding. In all your ways know, recognize, and acknowledge Him, and He will direct and make straight and plain your paths.

When we face a time of crisis in life, we need direction. These Scriptures tell us that trusting God is the way to find that direction.

Trust requires allowing some unanswered questions to be in your life!

This truth is hard for us to deal with because human nature wants to understand everything. In Romans 8:6 we are told that "the mind of the flesh . . . is sense and reason without the Holy Spirit."

We want things to make sense, but the Holy Spirit can cause us to have peace in our heart about something that makes no sense at all to our natural mind.

No matter how badly you may be hurting from a loss or tragedy, the Holy Spirit can give you a deep peace that somehow everything will be all right.

Being angry at God is useless because He is the only One Who can help. Only He can bring the lasting comfort and healing that is needed. I encourage you to continue to believe that God is good and to know that whatever has happened does not change that fact. Even when you do not understand your circumstances, continue to believe and say that God is good—because He is!

In Psalm 34:8 the psalmist encourages us, "O taste and see that the Lord [our God] is good! Blessed (happy, fortunate, to be envied) is the man who trusts and takes refuge in Him."

Then in Psalm 86:5 he says of God, "For You, O Lord, are good, and ready to forgive [our trespasses, sending them away, letting them go completely and forever]; and You are abundant in mercy and loving-kindness to all those who call upon You."

Finally, in Psalm 136:1 we are told, "O give thanks to the Lord, for He is good; for His mercy and loving-kindness endure forever."

God is good, but the devil wants us to believe that we cannot trust God and that He does not care for us or love us. If you are having doubts about God's love for you and His faithful care over you, please consider the words of the apostle Paul on this subject as recorded in Romans 8:35–39:

> Who shall ever separate us from Christ's love? Shall suffering and affliction and tribulation? Or calamity and distress? Or persecution or hunger or destitution or peril or sword? Even as it is written, For Thy sake we are put to death all the day long; we are regarded and counted as sheep for the slaughter. Yet amid all these things we are more than conquerors and gain a surpassing victory through Him Who loved us. For I am persuaded beyond doubt (am sure) that neither death nor life, nor angels nor principalities, nor things impending and threatening nor things to come, nor powers, Nor height nor depth, nor anything else in all creation will be able to separate us from the love of God which is in Christ Jesus our Lord.

Don't be mad at God. Receive the ministry of the Holy Spirit. Listen to the words of Jesus in this passage:

> Do not let your hearts be troubled (distressed, agitated). You believe in and adhere to and trust in and rely on God; believe in and adhere to and trust in and rely also on Me . . . And I will ask the Father, and He will give you another Comforter (Counselor, Helper, Intercessor, Advocate, Strengthener, and Standby), that He may remain with you forever . . . I will not leave you as orphans [comfortless, desolate, bereaved, forlorn, helpless]; I will come [back] to you. (John 14:1, 16, 18)

Take comfort in those words and resist the devil who will try to convince you to take out your anger and frustration on God.

Anger at the Devil

The Bible says we should hate evil (see Amos 5:15), and since the devil is the source of all evil, then being angry at him can be healthy—if that anger is expressed in a biblical manner.

In Ephesians 6:12 we are told, "We wrestle not against flesh and blood, but against principalities, against powers, against the rulers of the darkness of this world, against spiritual wickedness in high places" (KJV). *The Amplified Bible* translation says that we war against "the world rulers of this present darkness, against the spirit forces of wickedness."

Our war is definitely not against God or against people, but against the enemy of our souls. How can anger at the devil be effectively expressed? Let me give you an example from my own personal life.

For many years I was mad at Satan because of the fifteen years of child abuse I had endured, but I was venting my anger in the wrong way. I became hard-hearted and harsh in dealing with others. I have since learned that we defeat and overcome evil with good (see Romans 12:21).

I was angry at the devil because he had stolen my childhood from me, but my acting like him—like the devil—was not repaying him for my loss. Now I am preaching the Gospel, helping people who are hurting, seeing countless lives restored and, in so doing, I am overcoming the evil Satan did to me by my being good to others through bringing the good news of God to them.

This is the way to get back at the devil!

When you have been hurt, the quicker you get involved in helping someone else the better off you are going to be. Reaching out to other hurting people helps you forget about your own pain.

The only way to repay the devil for hurt and devastation in your own personal life is to aggressively and vehemently do the works of Jesus.

Anger at Self

When tragedy strikes, the question often arises, "Could I have done anything to prevent this from happening?"

A woman I spoke with mentioned that after her husband had died of a sudden heart attack, she kept remembering he had been saying he felt bad. She was blaming herself for not insisting that he see a doctor.

After a tragedy, especially the loss of a loved one, people think of things they wish they had said or done and things they wish they had not said and done.

We can all find plenty to regret in our lives, but regret only produces more agony on top of what we are already experiencing.

Often Satan will take advantage of that situation by placing blame upon us. His tactic is to throw us into a lifetime of guilt, condemnation, and self-hatred.

In Philippians 3:13–14 the apostle Paul stated, "One thing I do [it is my one aspiration]: forgetting what lies behind and straining forward to what lies ahead, I press on toward the goal."

I like the word *straining*. It tells me that, faced with such situations, I may have to "press on" at times, and that there will be opposition from the enemy to overcome.

Endings always bring new beginnings.

Satan strives to keep us out of the new place that God has prepared for us. He wants to trap us in the past and cause us to live in permanent misery. Self-anger and self-blame will do nothing but accomplish the devil's purpose in our lives.

I encourage you to stop tormenting yourself with regret. Satan will always try to attack you when you are in your most weakened state. Guilt, regret, and remorse are his favorite weapons. Meditate on the encouraging things, not the discouraging things.

Remember: Don't be angry at God, and don't be angry at yourself. Be angry at the devil, and express that anger in a proper way by overcoming evil with good.

Anger at Others

It is normal to experience anger at anyone who has caused us pain or hurt, even if that person died.

My aunt told me that after my uncle died, she would sometimes beat his pillow at night and yell, "Why did you leave me?" Obviously, her intellect knew that he did not purposely leave her, but her emotions were speaking.

We should learn that emotions have a voice, and when they are wounded, they may react like a wounded animal. Wounded animals can be quite dangerous, and so can wounded emotions if they are followed.

When suffering from a loss, it is important not to let hurt emotions turn into resentment or bitterness. When divorce is the cause of the loss, it is quite tempting to hate the one who caused the separation or even to try to take revenge by hurting back.

Do not waste your life being bitter. Instead, trust God to take whatever has happened and allow it to make you better. The same thing that is hurting you is also hurting multitudes of others. Ask God to take your "ashes" and give you "beauty" for them. Ask Him to allow you to ultimately help others who are working through their grief and loneliness.

Even when a loved one dies, there may be a period of time when you feel angry at that person for leaving you. You may have thoughts such as, "You could have lived if you had just tried harder," or, "How could you leave me to raise the children and face all these heavy responsibilities alone?"

Even though this type of thinking may seem ridiculous to a more stable person in ordinary times, when sudden tragedy strikes and grief sets in, often there is a tendency to blame someone else for the pain that is being felt. Thoughts and feelings can be quite erratic, jumping from anger at God, to anger at self, to anger at the devil, and then to anger at the person responsible for the loss. This cycle may be repeated many times and even become quite confusing.

Whenever we are hurt, the natural human way to respond is to become angry and to try to defend ourselves against the unbearable pain we are experiencing.

That's why it is so important to understand the grieving process and to be aware of some of the emotions that accompany it. Often in the past we have been taught to place little or no value on our feelings—to disregard them as unimportant.

Just after experiencing a major loss in your life is not the time to deny your feelings or deal with other issues that are anxiety producing or emotionally upsetting. Instead, you must comfort your emotions and deal with them.

The answer is not to try to stifle emotions but to recognize them for what they are and to express them in the proper manner.

Stage 3: Uncontrolled Emotions

People experiencing tragedy often go through various stages of emotions, including sobbing and hysteria. These may come and go when least expected. One minute the person feels that he is going to be all right, then an hour later he finds sadness overwhelming him.

Even those who are normally quite unemotional may experience a great deal of emotion at times of loss. A man who never cries may find himself sobbing uncontrollably at various intervals.

In general, people are afraid of emotions, and an uncontrolled display of emotion may even be fearful.

If you are going through a difficult emotional time right now, I urge you to "fear not" because what you are experiencing at the moment will pass. Good understanding and a lot of help from the Holy Spirit will bring you through the worst of times.

Some people refuse to weep or show any kind of outward emotion, which is not healthy. Pent-up emotions are powerful and need to be released. If you do not release your emotions in times of deep stress, such as the loss of a loved one, those emotions will eat away at you on the inside and may possibly destroy your mental, emotional, and even your physical health.

Since God has given us tear glands and an ability to cry, that must mean there will be times in life when we need to weep.

The Bible makes several references to tears. For example, in

Psalm 56:8 the psalmist refers to a bottle in which God keeps his tears. In Revelation 21:4, which speaks of the new heaven and the new earth that will one day be brought forth for God's people, we read:

> God will wipe away every tear from their eyes; and death shall be no more, neither shall there be anguish (sorrow and mourning) nor grief nor pain any more, for the old conditions and the former order of things have passed away.

There is healthy weeping and unhealthy weeping. Proper release of wounded emotions is healthy, but beware of self-pity. If left unconfronted, it becomes a monster that will turn you in on yourself in a very unwholesome way.

Compassion is a gift God has placed within each of us to turn outward toward someone else who is hurting. Compassion turned onto ourselves as pity has a crippling effect.

Self-pity is also addictive. You may think it is a way of ministering to yourself, but actually it is Satan's way of preventing you from moving beyond the tragedy.

You must also beware of using tears to control others. When you are hurting, you need for others to show you love and kindness.

From time to time all of us, no matter how strong and independent we may be, need help from others for a while. But we must remember that although there are times when we need special attention, other people cannot solve our problems. When we look to others, expecting them to make our pain go away, we are making a mistake.

First of all, people cannot give us everything we need. Second, expecting others to meet our personal needs for us places too much pressure on them. It often has a negative effect on our relationships, especially if that dependent behavior is continued for an extended period of time.

It would be quite understandable for a woman who loses her husband to turn to her children to fill the void in her life. This is good to do if, and only if, the woman is truly desiring to "give" herself to her children more now that she has the time and ability to do so. But if the woman's intent is to force the children to assume responsibility for her, they will resent it.

Basically, each person has his own life to live, and no matter how much love there may be between two individuals, no one wants to be controlled or manipulated for selfish reasons.

If you are experiencing pain or hurt right now, I encourage you to trust God and let Him make the adjustments in your relationships that He sees fit to make. He knows you have different needs now. He knows that void in your life that needs to be filled. When it occurs, God will fill that void in our lives if we wait on Him and refuse to try to use our emotions to control other people.

People don't usually do that intentionally. We may simply be hurting and searching for anything that might alleviate the pain. But God's way is not to relieve one person's burden by adding that burden to another person.

Tragedy leaves us in a weakened state, and Satan will always try to take advantage of us in our weakest moments. The devil is not shy about attacking when we are already down. He sees those lonely, painful times as golden opportunities to bring us into permanent bondage and misery.

Balance will close the door in Satan's face.

Over the years I have come to realize we must learn to work through many things privately. That does not mean we don't need people, because we do. Other people are definitely used by God to bring comfort to us when we are hurting. However, if our need for people gets out of balance, it can block God from working in our life.

My emotions suffered terribly for a number of years as a result of childhood abuse. During part of that time I expected my husband to meet my emotional needs and to fill the void in my life that had resulted from having the wrong kind of relationship with my father. Certainly the Lord used my husband to help bring emotional wholeness to my life, but I learned that I had to work through most of my problems with God alone.

One of the benefits of having no one to turn to but God is that we get our roots firmly established "in Him." He is the Rock, the solid foundation that never moves. No matter what else around us is shaking, He is always the same.

If you are grieving and lonely due to a tragedy in your life, turn that situation into an opportunity to move into a deeper personal relationship with the Father, Son, and Holy Spirit.

Remember: Satan wants to use such times to destroy you, but

what he means for your harm, God will work for your good, as you trust Him to do so (see Genesis 50:20 and Romans 8:28).

Stage 4: Depression

If you are feeling depressed, don't feel bad about yourself. Everyone has experienced depression at some time or another in his life.

When sadness floods the soul, a feeling of depression is quite common, even among those who know and love the Lord. In the Psalms, King David, who was said to be a man after God's own heart, talked about feeling depressed. If such a man of God as King David had to deal with depression, so must each of us.

Temporary periodic depression is just another of the human emotions which everyone experiences during the normal grieving process. But, like the other emotions that come with grieving, depression left unchecked can become a major problem.

The word *depression* refers to a state of being under, or an area sunk below normal levels.[7] The simple way to think of it is like this: Jesus is our glory and the lifter of our heads (see Psalm 3:3). But while Jesus lifts us up and puts us over, Satan comes to drag us down and to bury us under wounds, hurts, and problems.

Depression steals a person's energy. He becomes apathetic and lethargic, desiring to do nothing. If the depressed state continues and becomes strong enough, every movement can become an effort. Depressed people often sleep much more than is really needed—just to avoid life.

Depression can actually become a way of running and hiding in some instances. It can be used to avoid having to deal with life and its problems. *Facing issues is always much more difficult than running from them.*

In my own case I ran from the problems in my life caused by abuse until I was thirty-two years old. When I was filled with the Holy Spirit, one of the first things He started doing in my life was leading me into truth, just as Jesus promised He would do (see John 16:13). Jesus also said that it is the truth that will make us free (see John 8:32), but the truth must be faced if it is to have any positive effect on our lives.

Let's look at the Scriptures to see how King David responded to the age-old problem of depression. In Psalm 42:5–11 he wrote of his sunken emotional state:

> Why are you cast down, O my inner self? And why should you moan over me and be disquieted within me? Hope in God and wait expectantly for Him, for I shall yet praise Him, my Help and my God. O my God, my life is cast down upon me [and I find the burden more than I can bear]; therefore will I [earnestly] remember You from the land of the Jordan [River] and the [summits of Mount] Hermon, from the little mountain Mizar. [Roaring] deep calls to [roaring] deep at the thunder of Your waterspouts; all Your breakers and Your rolling waves have gone over me. Yet the Lord will command His loving-kindness in the daytime, and in the night His song shall be with me, a prayer to the God of my life. I will say to God my Rock, Why have You forgotten me? Why go I mourning because of the oppression of the enemy? As with a sword [crushing] in my bones, my enemies taunt and reproach me, while they say continually to me, Where is your God? Why are you cast down, O my inner self? And why should you moan over me and be disquieted within me? Hope in God and wait expectantly for Him, for I shall yet praise Him, Who is the help of my countenance, and my God.

I love these Scriptures because they show that King David felt depression attacking and flooding his own soul, and yet he resisted it. In other words, although he experienced depression, he would not give in to it. He talked to himself about his situation, and so we must also talk to ourselves during such times.

David remembered the good things on purpose, so that his soul would not be filled with only negative thoughts and influences.

For our own protection, it is vital that we resist long-standing depression. It is impossible to work through the healthy grieving process without experiencing certain feelings of sadness, loss, and depression. But once again, my desire is to bring a word of caution concerning an out-of-balance situation that has gone beyond the normal and has crossed over the line into the category of the destructive.

Normal emotions and the proper release of them are healthy. But when emotions are allowed to control us, they can become very destructive. Don't repress your emotions, but don't give them full rein in your life.

Any person who refuses to practice self-restraint, allowing his emotions to get out of control, will ultimately live a life of self-destruction.

Emotions are a gift from God. They are vital to human existence. No one would want to live without feelings. But at the same time, we cannot live our lives by or according to our feelings. For one reason, they are too unstable. We can feel a thousand different ways in the course of a month about the same situation.

People experience this lack of stability in their emotions especially during times of crisis and tragedy, which leads us to the next stage of the normal grieving process.

Stage 5: Waves of Overwhelming Emotion

When you are going through the grieving process, there will be times when you feel that you have worked through the emotional trauma of your tragedy or loss.

It is perfectly natural to be anxious for all your painful feelings to subside and finally disappear forever. However, that is not usually the way it works. Generally, those moments of subsiding will invariably be followed by surges of seemingly overwhelming emotion.

A good way to think of this emotional ebb-and-flow is to picture the ocean with its mighty waves which beat against the shore with peaceful, smooth intervals between them.

Initially, there seems to be no break in the waves of despair which flow over you and threaten to drag you down. This is a universal feeling that has been common to all people everywhere throughout history. If you recall Psalm 42:6–7 you will remember how David wrote of his despair, "O my God, my life is cast down upon me [and I find the burden more than I can bear] . . . all Your breakers and Your rolling waves have gone over me."

After some time elapses, however, there begins to be smooth moments between the surging waves. At such moments you may be tempted to think that the pain may never come back again. Then when you least expect it, there it is again in full force. Something may happen that triggers a memory, and suddenly all the old emotions come back with a vengeance.

The anniversary of the death, loss, or separation, and other especially meaningful milestones like holidays and birthdays, are extremely difficult to handle.

I am told that suicide rates rise sharply during holiday seasons. Imagine how hard it is for people to handle the sudden death of a loved one, or any other such tragedy, if they don't know the Lord and His sustaining presence.

Those of us who believe in Jesus Christ receive the comfort of the Holy Spirit, and yet these times are still difficult for us. So we can only imagine what pain must be endured by those who are already empty inside and then suffer the loss of someone or something so meaningful to them.

At such trying times, I am sure it is easy for Satan to convince them there is no point in living, that the pain they are experiencing is just too much to bear.

Sometimes I hear people say ahead of time, "I dread the anniversary of that event; I always get so depressed on that day."

Dread is a forerunner of fear, and it never brings a blessing. When I start dreading something, the Holy Spirit always gently reminds me that I am setting myself up for a miserable time.

When you feel yourself beginning to experience feelings of dread, I recommend that you pray and ask the Lord to strengthen you against those overwhelming emotions.

Sometimes we dread things without even realizing we are doing so. Asking for God's help will bring an awareness of what is happening and better equip us to avoid sinking into confusion, disorientation and fear.

Stage 6: Confusion, Disorientation and Fear

Facing a major change in our lives is one of the most emotionally difficult times that we are called upon to endure. Even if the change was our own choice, it is often hard for us to handle.

If that change comes as a result of tragedy, loss, or crisis, then confusion, disorientation, and fear are normal. Suddenly our plans for the future have collapsed. A vacation, a home purchase, a com-

pany retirement plan that collapses, or other cherished plans are un-
expectedly canceled.

It takes time to get new direction. In such moments, many questions come against our minds all at once, and many of them may be
pressing for immediate answers.

Even well-meaning friends and relatives may seem to be asking
repeatedly, "What are you going to do now? Where will you live? Are
you going back to work soon or will you take some time off?"

All of these are valid questions and must eventually be answered.

If you have experienced a sudden life-changing tragedy or loss,
you know you need to make some serious decisions about the future.
But you may well feel that you are not yet ready to make them!

At such times, your mind is not clear. You may think you have
made a decision, and then, suddenly, you change your mind. Your
emotions start playing tricks on you; they vacillate back and forth,
making decisions even harder than in normal times.

Along with the confusion and disorientation, fear often sets in.
You may begin to ask yourself questions like, "What will I do financially? Who will take care of these things I am not used to handling?"

When faced with such troubling questions, I suggest you meditate on this verse from the book of Hebrews. It always gives me great
comfort and hope, and I believe it will encourage you also:

> He [God] Himself has said, I will not in any way fail you nor
> give you up nor leave you without support. [I will] not, [I
> will] not, [I will] not in any degree leave you helpless nor
> forsake nor let [you] down (relax My hold on you)! [As-
> suredly not!] (Hebrews 13:5)

When we do not know what to do nor what the future holds, it
is comforting to know the One Who does know. In Psalm 139:15–17
the psalmist assures us that our heavenly Father does indeed know
our past, our present, and our future:

> My frame was not hidden from You when I was being formed
> in secret [and] intricately and curiously wrought [as if em-
> broidered with various colors] in the depths of the earth [a
> region of darkness and mystery]. Your eyes saw my un-
> formed substance, and in Your book all the days [of my life]

were written before ever they took shape, when as yet there was none of them. How precious and weighty also are Your thoughts to me, O God! How vast is the sum of them!

God is the Alpha and Omega, the beginning and the end. Since this is the case, He is also everything in between. He knows our situation and will lead us and guide us if we trust Him to do so.

Our heavenly Father usually gives us what we need one day at a time. The grace for each day comes with the day. For this reason, it is difficult to look very far into the future and not feel frightened.

As we look ahead, we often feel we cannot face the difficulties that may come. But we are looking at them without God's grace upon us.

When we arrive at the place, we will find the grace.

For thousands of years, the Twenty-third Psalm has ministered comfort to millions of grieving and lonely people. In times of confusion, disorientation, and fear, use it as an anchor for your soul:

The Lord is my Shepherd [to feed, guide, and shield me], I shall not lack. He makes me lie down in [fresh, tender] green pastures; He leads me beside the still and restful waters. He refreshes and restores my life (my self); He leads me in the paths of righteousness [uprightness and right standing with Him—not for my earning it, but] for His name's sake. Yes, though I walk through the [deep, sunless] valley of the shadow of death, I will fear or dread no evil, for You are with me; Your rod [to protect] and Your staff [to guide], they comfort me. You prepare a table before me in the presence of my enemies. You anoint my head with oil; my [brimming] cup runs over. Surely or only goodness, mercy, and unfailing love shall follow me all the days of my life, and through the length of my days the house of the Lord [and His presence] shall be my dwelling place. (Psalm 23:1–6)

Stage 7: Physical Symptoms

It often occurs that people who are grieving over a death or other traumatic loss begin to experience physical symptoms. It seems almost too much to bear, to feel bad mentally, emotionally, and physically.

Emotional upset places tremendous stress on the physical body. Weaknesses that may have already been there are often stressed beyond their limits. Many times the result is physical pain, sickness, or disease.

Various pains in the head, neck, back, or stomach are not uncommon when under extreme stress. One thing that will relieve stress is physical exercise.

During periods of grief, often the tendency is to just sit and "think" (brood). Although perfectly natural, this tendency must be overcome with forceful, positive action.

If you are going through the grieving process, I recommend that you at least take long walks. If you are up to it, I would suggest even more vigorous physical exercise.

Remember: You are already under strain, so don't overdo it.

But it has been proven that exercise does tend to lessen mental, emotional, and physical stress and to relax tense muscles.

Loss of appetite, of course, is also quite common when grieving, which is understandable. However, it will be detrimental to your health to discontinue eating for very long. If you are unable to eat very much, at least try to eat something of good nutritional quality.

Although it may be difficult, also be sure to get the proper amount of sleep. A tired, weak, undernourished, and overstressed body is an open invitation to sickness and disease. That's why it is important to get as much physical exercise, nourishment, and rest as possible to help the mind and body remain healthy during these stressful times.

I believe it is also important when grieving and lonely to realize that the things you feel and the various stages of grief you are experiencing are all quite normal and must be gone through in order to return to healthy emotional soundness.

As we have noted, repressed feelings and emotions are very hard on the system. If they are not properly expressed, they can do quite a lot of damage.

Remember: When negative emotions are repressed, they will ultimately come out another way.

Often we think we are hiding things within, but they come out in our attitude or conversation, and even in our physical bodies.

In dealing with all these seven stages of the grieving process, the key word is *balance*.

4

RECOVERING FROM TRAGEDY AND LOSS

The Spirit of the Lord [is] upon Me, because He has anointed Me [the Anointed One, the Messiah] to preach the good news (the Gospel) to the poor; He has sent Me to announce release to the captives and recovery of sight to the blind, to send forth as delivered those who are oppressed [who are downtrodden, bruised, crushed, and broken down by calamity].

Luke 4:18

Whatever has happened to cause you to suffer grief and loneliness, you can be sure of one thing: You will be led by the Lord in your recovery. He will definitely let you know when you are becoming excessive or getting out of balance—if you are willing to listen to His Spirit.

It is impossible to know the amount of time it will take to work through the grieving process. That varies with each individual person and situation. But, however long it may be, there will eventually come a time when the Lord will say, "It is time now to get up and go on. You must let go of the past and finish the course I have laid out for your life. I will never leave you nor forsake you, so be bold, be strong, be courageous, and go forward!"

Each Case Is Different

Generally, the first six months of the grieving process will be the most difficult. It could be a little longer or a little shorter depending on the circumstances. There are many factors involved that are unique to each situation:

- *The suddenness of the loss.* If a person is sick for an extended period of time, the family has longer to become mentally and emotionally prepared for the death of their loved one. If the loss is sudden or unexpected, the loss may be more traumatic and thus more difficult to adjust to.
- *The presence or absence of support members.* If a husband or wife dies, for instance, it makes a difference if there are children left to comfort the surviving parent. If a child is lost, other children may help to fill the void left in the home by the child's passing.
- *The quality of the relationship between the bereaved and the lost loved ones.* If the relationship was a strong, loving one, the grieving process will be longer and more difficult than if the relationship had not been as fulfilling.
- *The personality of the survivor.* This is especially true in the death of a spouse. Some people are more dependent than others and it takes a greater effort for them to assume the lead role and proceed with life.
- *The depth of the relationship between the grieving person and the Lord Jesus Christ.* This is a major factor. Tragedy or loss often provokes people to seek a relationship with the Lord, which, of course, brings comfort. But the person who already knows Him "and the power of his resurrection" (Philippians 3:10 KJV) will usually recover much quicker than one who has had no prior personal knowledge of the Lord or who has developed only a surface relationship with Him.

As an illustration of my point about the varying periods of time required for recovery from tragedy or loss, I would like to share with you two actual cases of which I am aware.

The First Case
I know of a strong Christian woman who had been deeply involved with the things of the Lord for many years.

She and her husband had been married for about twenty-five years. Although he was a professing Christian, he was not showing forth the fruits of his relationship with the Lord. He definitely did not treat his wife properly, nor had he done so for many years.

This man's business came before anything else in his life. He was selfish, ego-centered, and even sometimes cruel in his attitude toward his wife and her needs.

As this woman continued in her walk with God, the Lord gave her a special prayer assignment for her husband, warning her that if he did not submit to His (God's) dealings, within six months he would be dead.

The woman prayed, and still the man resisted the dealings of the Lord. Through disobedience, he opened a door for Satan to shorten his life. As a result, the man died of a sudden heart attack.

Although the loss was hard on the wife, it was not nearly as hard as it might have been for someone who had enjoyed a wonderful relationship with her husband. God had warned her, which had prepared her ahead of time.

I noticed that her recovery time was amazingly short. There were issues in her life that had to be dealt with—financial matters and so forth—but overall within a relatively short period of time she was able to adjust and to go on with her life.

The Second Case
This one involved my aunt. She and my uncle had known one another in childhood and were married when she was fifteen and he only a few years older. She had never had another boyfriend, or even dated anyone else.

The two of them were never able to have children, so they were especially close. They worked together in the same bakery for more than thirty years. They did everything together, serving God as partners in the work of the Lord.

They both had experienced a lot of sickness in their lives and had spent a great deal of time caring for each other. Sometimes, the more people have to do for one another, the more they mean to each other.

These two were deeply involved in each other's lives. They fit together like a hand in a glove. They had such fun together: fishing, cooking, going to church, etc.

Even though he had been sick for many years, when my uncle died his loss was extremely difficult for my aunt. At the time she was crippled with arthritis in her knees, but could not have the usually prescribed knee replacement surgery because of a heart condition. Therefore, she was more or less housebound for several years after my uncle's death, which only increased her trauma.

Due to these extenuating circumstances, her recovery took years.

Grieving Is Normal, Living in Grief Is Not

From these two cases, we can readily see how the same type of event can affect different people in different ways. Although it is impossible to make an exact prediction of how long the grieving process will last, progress should be seen regularly throughout it.

This progress may be gradual and difficult to perceive at first, but it *definitely* should be seen.

Like a wound healing, the pain may be felt a long time, but complete recovery requires daily improvement. When a physical wound refuses to heal, it is an indication there is an infection that must be dealt with. I believe the same is true of emotional wounds.

The emotional part of us should heal just like the physical part of us. God gave us emotions just as He gave us physical bodies. He has provided for our emotional restoration in Jesus Christ, just as He has provided for our physical healing in Him. Both of these are our right as believers.

Don't believe the lies of Satan. He will try to tell you that you will never get over the hurt, never be whole again emotionally. While it is true that you may always miss the person or the thing lost, that does not mean you must suffer permanent grief and loneliness.

Given proper time, grief should dissipate, and you should be able to make a transition to a new season of life. If this transition does not occur within a reasonable time frame, it is an indication there is a problem somewhere: an improper mental attitude, refusal to face reality, or perhaps the presence of abnormal and unreasonable fear.

Whatever the root of the problem, God will reveal it to you if you will spend time reading His Word and seeking Him through prayer and meditation.

Just keep in mind that grieving is normal, but living with a spirit of grief is not.

Overcoming Grief and Loneliness

I would like to share with you two vital points to help you overcome grief and loneliness and gain complete emotional recovery:

1. Know that God is with you all the time.

In Matthew 28:20 Jesus said, "I am with you always, even unto the end of the world" (KJV). Then in Hebrews 13:5 we read that God has promised, "I will never leave thee, nor forsake thee" (KJV).

Grief and loneliness often lead to fear, which in turn provokes all kinds of unanswerable questions such as: "What if I get sick and can't work; who is going to provide for me?" "What if I am alone for the rest of my life?" "What if this pain I am feeling never goes away?" "What if a problem arises that I don't know how to handle on my own?"

"What if . . . what if . . . what if . . ." The questions go on and on, endlessly.

You cannot answer all the "what ifs" in life. But as long as you know that Jesus is with you, you can be assured He has all the answers you need.

Consider these Scripture passages and let them bring comfort to you:

A father of the fatherless and a judge and protector of the widows is God in His holy habitation. God places the solitary in families and gives the desolate a home in which to dwell; He leads the prisoners out to prosperity; but the rebellious dwell in a parched land. (Psalm 68:5–6)

Although my father and my mother have forsaken me, yet the Lord will take me up [adopt me as His child]. (Psalm 27:10)

Fear not, for you shall not be ashamed; neither be confounded and depressed, for you shall not be put to shame. For you shall forget the shame of your youth, and you shall not [seriously] remember the reproach of your widowhood any more. For your Maker is your Husband—the Lord of hosts is His name—and the Holy One of Israel is your Redeemer; the god of the whole earth He is called. (Isaiah 54:4–5)

He was despised and rejected and forsaken by men, a Man of sorrows and pains, and acquainted with grief and sickness; and like One from Whom men hide their faces He was despised, and we did not appreciate His worth or have any esteem for Him. Surely He has borne our griefs (sicknesses, weaknesses, and distresses) and carried our sorrows and pains [of punishment], yet we [ignorantly] considered Him stricken, smitten, and afflicted by God [as if with leprosy]. But He was wounded for our transgressions, He was bruised for our guilt and iniquities; the chastisement [needful to obtain] peace and well-being for us was upon Him, and with the stripes [that wounded] Him we are healed and made whole. (Isaiah 53:3–5)

Sickness also brings grief and loneliness. When we are hurting and pain is flooding our body, we want someone to understand how bad we are feeling. Even though our family and friends may do the best they can for us, we can still find ourselves lonely in our suffering.

Extended illness is even worse because after a while we find that others don't want to continually hear how bad we are feeling. Not only does it not edify them, but it does not help our progress to keep talking about how miserable we are.

When you are sick, you will have the same kind of questions you have when you are experiencing a tragedy or loss: "What if I never get well; who will take care of me?" "What if I can never do the things I used to do?" "What if I am never able to go back to work; who will provide for me and my family?" "What if I have to live with this pain for the rest of my life?"

In sickness, you have to apply the same principle we have discussed in our consideration of grief and loneliness. You have to know that God is your Healer and believe that His power is at work in your body to heal and restore you.

Remember that "Death is swallowed up in victory" (1 Corinthians 15:54 KJV) and that God has said, "I am the Lord Who heals you" (Exodus 15:26).

Spend a great deal of time with the Lord and allow His resurrection life that is in you as a believer to minister to your physical needs. As you do so, meditate on these Scripture passages:

The everlasting God, the Lord, the Creator of the ends of the earth, does not faint or grow weary; there is no searching of His understanding. He gives power to the faint and weary, and to him who has no might He increases strength [causing it to multiply and making it to abound]. Even youths shall faint and be weary, and [selected] young men shall feebly stumble and fall exhausted; But those who wait for the Lord [who expect, look for, and hope in Him] shall change and renew their strength and power; they shall lift their wings and mount up [close to God] as eagles [mount up to the sun]; they shall run and not be weary, they shall walk and not faint or become tired. (Isaiah 40:28–31)

Bless (affectionately, gratefully praise) the Lord, O my soul; and all that is [deepest] within me, bless His holy name! Bless (affectionately, gratefully praise) the Lord, O my soul, and forget not [one of] all His benefits—Who forgives [every one of] all your iniquities, Who heals [each one of] all your diseases, Who redeems your life from the pit and corruption, Who beautifies, dignifies, and crowns you with loving-kindness and tender mercy; Who satisfies your mouth [your necessity and desire at your personal age and situation] with good so that your youth, renewed, is like the eagle's [strong, overcoming, soaring]! (Psalm 103:1–5)

Once again, know that you are not alone. The Lord is with you. He understands what you are going through and has promised to be with you in every trial of life. When you feel the loneliest and the most forsaken, open your mouth in faith and say emphatically, "I am *not* alone, for God is with me!"

While you are waiting for your healing to manifest, confess this out loud: "The healing power of God is working in me right now."

Also, read and confess these Scripture verses which assure you of the Lord's presence and power:

But take notice, the hour is coming, and it has arrived, when you will all be dispersed and scattered, every man to his own home, leaving Me alone. Yet *I am not alone, because the Father is with Me.* I have told you these things, so that in Me you may have [perfect] peace and confidence. In the world you have tribulation and trials and distress and frustration; but be of good cheer [take courage; be confident, certain, undaunted]! For I have overcome the world. [I have deprived it of power to harm you and have conquered it for you.] (John 16:32–33)

2. "Press aggressively" into a new life.

Not everything in your life is over; just one part of it has ended. One season has passed; another can now begin—if you are willing to take action.

Don't just passively sit and wait for something to happen or someone to come along. Pray—and then step out in faith.

Earlier I shared with you about my aunt and how difficult it was for her to begin a new life after the death of my uncle. However, as hard as that transition was, she made it. Now she travels with my husband and me and helps in our ministry to others. In our meetings, she sells cassette tapes of our seminars. At home, she cooks for us and, when she can, she babysits our grandchildren.

All of these things are a tremendous benefit to us and to the kingdom of God. She has "pressed aggressively" into a new lifestyle and, in the process, has become a blessing to many.

If you are lonely, don't just sit and wish you would meet others. *Go make new friends!* Find someone else who is lonely too—someone even lonelier than you are—and be a friend to that individual. You will reap what you sow. God will return that friendship to you, multiplied many times over.

Our daughter Sandra went through a lonely time in her young adult years. It seemed that most of her friends had either gone off to college or got married, so she was spending a lot of lonely evenings at home.

Instead of sitting and feeling sorry for herself, she started "pressing aggressively" forward and going places on her own. She would attend church functions alone or go to a singles group at another church by herself. It was not easy for her, but she knew she had to do something besides just sit and wish for companionship.

You may say, "Well, Joyce, I'm not wishing, I'm believing." But I would remind you that the Bible teaches us that faith moves us to take God-inspired action (see James 2:17). I am not suggesting works of the flesh, or just fleshly zeal, but I am saying to be bold and step out as God leads.

Sandra is now married to Steve, a young man she met at a function she attended alone. Her corresponding actions gave her faith a direction and a goal.

In the same way, put hands and feet to your prayers. Let your loneliness give birth to compassion within you for other lonely people and then *decide to do something about it*!

Conclusion

Press aggressively forward into the next season of your life. Things may never be the way they used to be, but don't miss the rest of your life by living in the past.

The time has come to stop thinking and talking about the past. You have a future. The Holy Spirit is standing by ready to help you, comfort you, and assist you in pressing on to fulfill God's marvelous plan for you.

Remember: God is not finished with you!

Endings Always Offer New Beginnings

In John 10:10, Jesus said, "The thief comes only in order to steal and kill and destroy. I came that they may have and enjoy life, and have it in abundance (to the full, till it overflows)."

No matter how good or bad your life before your loss was, you cannot enjoy life in the present and the future while still living in the past.

Whatever you have lost, be determined not to miss what remains.

Remember: God is good.

He loves you very much.
He has a good plan for your life.

Read and meditate on the Scripture passages in the following section, allowing the Lord to speak through them to you in your present situation.

Scriptures to Overcome Loneliness

God Is Always with You

He [God] Himself has said, I will not in any way fail you nor give you up nor leave you without support. [I will] not, [I will] not, [I will] not in any degree leave you helpless nor forsake nor let [you] down (relax My hold on you)! [Assuredly not!] (Hebrews 13:5)

I will never leave thee, nor forsake thee. (Hebrews 13:5 KJV)

Because he has set his love upon Me . . . [I will never forsake him, no never] . . . He shall call upon Me, and I will answer him; I will be with him in trouble, I will deliver him and honor him. (Psalm 91:14–15)

You Cannot Be Separated from God's Love

Who shall ever separate us from Christ's love? . . . For I am persuaded beyond doubt (am sure) that neither death nor life, nor angels nor principalities, nor things impending and threatening nor things to come, nor powers, Nor height nor depth, nor anything else in all creation will be able to separate us from the love of God which is in Christ Jesus our Lord. (Romans 8:35, 38–39)

The Lord Will Take Care of You

The Lord is my Shepherd [to feed, guide, and shield me], I shall not lack. (Psalm 23:1)

A father of the fatherless and a judge and protector of the widows is God in His holy habitation. God places the solitary in families and gives the desolate a home in which to dwell; He leads the prisoners out to prosperity; but the rebellious dwell in a parched land. (Psalm 68:5–6)

Although my father and my mother have forsaken me, yet the Lord will take me up [adopt me as His child]. (Psalm 27:10)

Fear not, for you shall not be ashamed; neither be confounded and depressed, for you shall not be put to shame. For you shall forget the shame of your youth, and you shall not [seriously] remember the reproach of your widowhood any more. For your Maker is your Husband—the Lord of hosts is His name—and the Holy One of Israel is your Redeemer; the God of the whole earth He is called. (Isaiah 54:4–5)

God Will Do a New Thing

Do not [earnestly] remember the former things; neither consider the things of old. Behold, I am doing a new thing! Now it springs forth; do you not perceive and know it and will you not give heed to it? I will even make a way in the wilderness and rivers in the desert. (Isaiah 43:18–19)

Behold, the former things have come to pass, and new things I now declare; before they spring forth I tell you of them. (Isaiah 42:9)

Press On

> I do not consider, brethren, that I have captured and made it my own [yet]; but one thing I do [it is my one aspiration]: forgetting what lies behind and straining forward to what lies ahead, I press on toward the goal to win the [supreme and heavenly] prize to which God in Christ Jesus is calling us upward. (Philippians 3:13–14)

Don't give up, give out, or give in. Instead, press on—aggressively.

God Is Not Finished with You!

> For I know the thoughts and plans that I have for you, says the Lord, thoughts and plans for welfare and peace and not for evil, to give you hope in your final outcome. (Jeremiah 29:11)

Prayer to Overcome Loneliness

Now I want to pray for you and leave you with a final word of encouragement:

Father,

I come to You in Jesus' name, presenting unto You all that He is and asking for Your grace and mercy.

This precious person for whom I am praying is hurting. I ask for the comfort of the Holy Spirit to flow to this individual beginning right now. Your Word says You are the Healer of the brokenhearted. You have promised to bind up our wounds and heal our bruises.

We look to You, Lord, for truly You are our Helper in time of need. You have promised to place the solitary, the lonely, in families. I ask You, Lord, to do according to Your Word and give this child of Yours friends and family who will care for him or her.

Assist this person, Holy Spirit, as he or she takes steps of faith to build a new life. I ask You to prosper this individual mentally, physically, spiritually, financially, and socially. Amen.

Child of God, I believe the anointing of the Holy Spirit is flowing into you right now. I recommend that you remain in His presence for a period of time, allowing Him to minister to you. Let Him take the Word I have shared with you and, as you wait, trust Him to work it in you.

I believe a fresh wind of the Spirit is blowing on you to prepare you for a new season in your life. May the love of God, the grace of our Lord Jesus Christ, and the Communion of the Holy Spirit be with you.

STRAIGHT TALK ON *Fear*

CONTENTS

INTRODUCTION

———— ❧ ————

One of the many benefits available to us in our spiritual inheritance as a believer in Jesus Christ is freedom from fear. But even if we are afraid, we know that we can go ahead and act, because God will be with us to protect us. He will help us, go before to fight the battle for us or deliver us, bringing us through victoriously as we obey Him.

If you feel you have missed out on some things in your life because of fear, you can learn how to handle or overcome fear and begin to experience the abundant life God has planned for you.

Part One

FREEDOM FROM FEAR

1

CONFRONTING FEAR

The Lord your God Who goes with you; He will not fail you or forsake you.

Deuteronomy 31:6

The message of "fear not, for I, the Lord, am with you" is expressed in many different ways throughout the Bible. God does not want us to fear because fear prevents us from receiving and doing all He has planned for us. He loves and wants to bless us and has provided ways for us not to fear.

We can see in the following passage that we who believe in Jesus Christ do not need to fear the things that unbelievers—the people of "the world"—fear. God does not want us to fear those things.

> For the Lord spoke thus to me with His strong hand [upon me], and warned and instructed me not to walk in the way of this people, saying, Do not call conspiracy [or hard, or holy] all that this people will call conspiracy [or hard, or holy]; neither be in fear of what they fear, nor [make others afraid and] in dread. The Lord of hosts—regard Him as holy and honor His holy name [by regarding Him as your only hope of safety], and let Him be your fear and let Him be your dread [lest you offend Him by your fear of man and distrust of Him]. Isaiah 8:11–13

In His Word, God tells us we can live victoriously, strong in Him and in the power of His might. And He has promised never to leave us or forsake us regardless of what happens.

No Fear!

Every one of us has experienced starting to step out in faith and, even at the thought of it, fear rising up in us. We need to realize that the source of fear is Satan. First John 4:18 (KJV) says:

> There is no fear in love; but perfect love casteth out fear: because fear hath torment. He that feareth is not made perfect in love.

Satan sends fear to try to torment us into being so doubtful and miserable, we will be prevented from doing what God wants us to do and receiving all God has for us.

We can live without fear by building our faith on what God has said in His Word. For example:

> For God did not give us a spirit of timidity (of cowardice, of craven and cringing and fawning fear), but [He has given us a spirit] of power and of love and of calm and well-balanced mind and discipline and self-control. (2 Timothy 1:7)

> Be strong, courageous, and firm; fear not nor be in terror before them, for it is the Lord your God Who goes with you; He will not fail you or forsake you. (Deuteronomy 31:6)

Romans 10:17 tells us, "So then faith cometh by hearing, and hearing by the word of God" (KJV). We need to learn and confess aloud Scriptures like the ones above and the ones at the end of this book to drink them in like a glass of water when we are thirsty. When we open our mouth and confess what the Lord says to us and about us, God's Word will give us the power to overcome the fears that torment and prevent.

And this is the confidence (the assurance, the privilege of boldness) which we have in Him: [we are sure] that if we ask anything (make any request) according to His will (in agreement with His own plan), He listens to and hears us. And if (since) we [positively] know that He listens to us in whatever we ask, we also know [with settled and absolute knowledge] that we have [granted us as our present possessions] the requests made of Him. (1 John 5:14–15)

There is power in praying and confessing the Word of God, which is His revealed will. I am convinced that one of the most important things we can do in our prayer time is confess the Word.

When we find ourselves trying to avoid confronting some issue in our life because of fear or dread or wondering or reasoning, what we should do is pray and ask God to do for us what He has promised in His Word—to go before us and pave the way for us. James teaches us that we have not because we ask not (see James 4:2). Jesus tells us to ask, seek, and knock (see Matthew 7:7).

When we are facing a job interview, for example, instead of being afraid that we will make a bad impression and fail to get the position, we need to ask the Lord to be with us, to go before us to prepare the way for us so we can present ourselves in the very best light. Then we can trust that whatever happens, it will turn out for our good in accordance with God's perfect will and plan for us.

Do It Afraid!

Now [in Haran] the Lord said to Abram, Go for yourself [for your own advantage] away from your country, from your relatives and your father's house, to the land that I will show you.

Genesis 12:1

How would you feel if God told you to leave your home, your family, and everything that is familiar and comfortable to you and head out to who knows where? Full of fear?

That is precisely the challenge Abram faced in this passage—and it frightened him. That's why God kept saying to him again and again, "Fear not."

That is the same message He gave to Joshua when He called him to lead the children of Israel to take the land He had promised to give them as their inheritance (see Joshua 1:6–9).

Anyone who is going to do anything for God is going to have to hear the Lord say on a regular basis, "Fear not."

Elisabeth Elliot, whose husband was killed along with four other missionaries in Ecuador, says her life was controlled completely by fear. Every time she started to step out, fear stopped her. A friend told her something that set her free. She said, "Why don't you do it afraid?" Elisabeth Elliot and Rachel Saint, sister of one of the murdered missionaries, went on to evangelize the Indian tribes, including the people who had killed their husband and brother.

Many times we think we should wait to do something until we are not afraid. If we do that, we will probably accomplish very little for God, others, or even for ourselves. Both Abram and Joshua had to step out in faith and obedience to God and do what He had commanded them to do—afraid.

The Lord reminded me of the story about "Why don't you do it afraid?" then began showing me some things about fear.

"Fear Not" Means "Don't Run!"

Fear not; stand still (firm, confident, undismayed) and see the salvation of the Lord which He will work for you today.

Exodus 14:13

What I perceived God was saying to me was that the phrase "Fear not" simply means "Don't run." Then the solution to fear is also simple. When we are faced with fear, rather than bowing our knee to it, we must stand firm against it and do what we fear anyway.

That is precisely what God tells us to do in His Word. Even if our knees are shaking, our mouth is dry, and we feel as though we are about to fall down, we need to keep saying: "Lord, strengthen me. This is what You have told me to do, and with Your help I am going to do it, because it is Your revealed will for me. I am determined that my life is not going to be ruled by fear but by Your Word."

Confront Fear with God's Word

Fear cannot be wished away or hoped away, it must be confronted and dealt with through God's Word.

There are times when people are miraculously delivered from fear through prayer. There is no doubt of that, because we serve a miracle-working God. I have prayed for people to be delivered from fear, and they have come back to me later and said, "After you prayed for me, I never had a problem with fear again." But the majority of the time, we confront and overcome our fears by meditating and speaking God's Word ourselves and resisting fear in the power of the Spirit.

In my own case, I had major problems as a result of the abuse I suffered in my early years. There were many things in my life from which I needed deliverance. But with one minor exception, God delivered me from all of them as a result of my applying His Word. God doesn't always deliver us from things; often He walks us through them.

Fear Is Falsehood

> *The devil . . . was a murderer from the beginning and does not stand in the truth, because there is no truth in him. When he speaks a falsehood, he speaks what is natural to him, for he is a liar [himself] and the father of lies and of all that is false.*
>
> John 8:44

The Bible does not tell us "Tremble not" or "Sweat not" or "Shake not," it says, "Fear not."

There is a difference.

In this context, to fear is to take flight or to run from. Elisabeth Elliot's friend was suggesting that she start doing what she was afraid of instead of running from it.

It is said that the letters in the word *FEAR* actually stand for "False Evidence Appearing Real."

Jesus said the devil is a liar and the father of all lies. The truth is not in him. He tries to use falsehood to deceive God's people into fear so they will not be bold enough to be obedient to the Lord and reap the blessings He has in store for them.

Most of the time the fear of something is worse than the thing itself. Usually, if we will be courageous and determined enough to do whatever it is we fear, we will discover it is not nearly as bad as we thought it would be.

Throughout the Word of God we find the Lord saying to His people again and again, "Fear not." I believe the reason He did that was to encourage them so they would not allow Satan to rob them of their blessing.

In the same way, because He knows we are fearful, the Lord continues to exhort and encourage us to press through what lies before us to do what He is telling us to do. Why? Because He knows that great blessings await us on the other side.

We see an example of this in Abram.

Courage and Obedience Produce Great Rewards

After these things, the word of the Lord came to Abram in a vision, saying, Fear not, Abram, I am your Shield, your abundant compensation, and your reward shall be exceedingly great.

Genesis 15:1

As we saw before, in Genesis 12:1 God gave Abram a tall order. In so many words He said, "Pack up and leave everyone you know and everything you are comfortable with and go to a place I will show you."

If Abram had bowed his knee to fear, the rest of the story would never have come to pass. He would never have experienced God as his Shield, his great compensation, and he would never have received his exceedingly great reward.

In the same way, if Joshua had not overcome his fear and been obedient to God's command to lead His people into the Promised

Land, neither he nor they would ever have enjoyed all that God had planned and prepared for them.

There is power in God's Word to equip us to stop bowing our knee in fear to the devil's desires. We can do what God wants us to do, even if we have to do it afraid.

2

⧜

PRAY ABOUT EVERYTHING AND
FEAR NOTHING!

The earnest (heartfelt, continued) prayer of a righteous man makes
tremendous power available [dynamic in its working].

James 5:16

Some time ago the Lord spoke these words to me: "Pray about everything and fear nothing." He said this to me when I had a vague feeling of fear that a new hairdresser I was going to would not do a good job.

The Holy Spirit spoke to me: "Don't fear it, pray about it. Pray that the Lord will anoint this woman so she is able to do for you what needs to be done."

Then over the next couple of weeks He continued showing me different things about prayer versus fear. Many of them dealt with little areas in which fear would try to creep into my life and cause me problems. He showed me that in every case, no matter how great or important or how small or insignificant, the solution was to pray.

Fear not [there is nothing to fear], for I am with you; do not look around you in terror and be dismayed, for I am your God. I will strengthen and harden you to difficulties, yes, I will help you; yes, I will hold you up and retain you with My [victorious] right hand of rightness and justice . . . For I the

Lord your God hold your right hand; I am the Lord, Who says to you, Fear not; I will help you! (Isaiah 41:10, 13)

In this passage, the Lord tells His people not to look around them in terror or be dismayed, for He is their God.

Sometimes we become afraid just by staring at our circumstances. That is always a mistake. The more we focus our eyes and our mouths on the problem, the more fearful we become. Instead, we are to keep our eyes and our mouths focused on God. He is able to handle anything we may ever have to face in this life.

God has promised to strengthen us, to harden us to difficulties, to hold us up and retain us with His victorious right hand. He also commands us not to be afraid. But remember, He is not commanding us never to feel fear, but rather not to let it control us.

The Lord is saying to you and me personally, "Fear not, I will help you." But we never experience the help of God until we place everything on the line, until we are obedient enough to step out in faith.

Do you know when I experience the anointing of God to preach? When I have walked up on the platform and begun to speak—not before, but *when* I have stepped out.

God is saying to us today, "Stop letting fear rule your life. Begin to do what I am telling you to do, because what I am telling you is for your benefit. I know the blessings that are on the other side, and so does the devil. That's why he is coming against you with fear and why I keep telling you to fear not."

Fear Not, You Are Mine!

Thus says the Lord, He Who created you, O Jacob, and He Who formed you, O Israel: Fear not, for I have redeemed you [ransomed you by paying a price instead of leaving you captives]; I have called you by your name; you are Mine. When you pass through the waters, I will be with you, and through the rivers, they will not overwhelm you. When you walk through the fire, you will not be burned or scorched, nor will the flame kindle upon you.

Isaiah 43:1–2

Here the Lord is telling us not to fear when we go through trials of different kinds. That means we will experience victory in our lives, but only as we go through. If we are going to go through, then we must not run away anymore.

The Lord has promised to be with us and keep us safe when we go through the water, which will not overwhelm us, and through the fire, which will not burn us or scorch us.

Do you remember the story of the three Hebrew children named Shadrach, Meshach, and Abednego? They were thrown into a fiery furnace but came out of it not only unharmed but not even smelling like smoke (see Daniel 3:1–30)!

There are major fears—like being thrown into a trial similar to a fiery furnace—and there are also minor fears—like being afraid our hair won't look right!

We may be afraid of something major like cancer or a heart attack or the death of a loved one, or we may be afraid of something minor such as a picnic being rained out or not being able to find a parking place.

But whatever its magnitude or cause, fear is the same and must be dealt with the same way. As we have seen, it must be confronted through prayer with God's Word. And when we pray, we must believe. Fear is our enemy and we should treat it as such.

Faith: the Antidote for Fear

If any of you is deficient in wisdom, let him ask of the giving God [Who gives] to everyone liberally and ungrudgingly, without reproaching or faultfinding, and it will be given him. Only it must be in faith that he asks with no wavering (no hesitating, no doubting). For the one who wavers (hesitates, doubts) is like the billowing surge out at sea that is blown hither and thither and tossed by the wind. For truly, let not such a person imagine that he will receive anything [he asks for] from the Lord.

James 1:5–7

Faith is the only antidote for fear.

If you or I drank some kind of poison, we would have to swallow an antidote or the poison would cause serious damage or even death. The same is true of the deadly toxin of fear. There must be an antidote for it, and the only antidote for fear is faith.

When fear comes knocking at our door, we must answer it with faith, because nothing else is effective against it. And prayer is the major vehicle that carries faith.

Faith must be carried to the problem and released in some way. It is possible to pray without faith (we do it all the time), but it is impossible to have real faith and not pray.

James tells us that when we find ourselves in need of something, we should pray and ask God for it in *simple, believing* prayer. Those two words are very important. The way we do that is by simply praying and having faith, believing that what we ask for from God we will receive in accordance with His divine will and plan.

So the key to overcoming fear is simple, faith-filled, *continual* prayer.

Pray at All Times!

Pray at all times (on every occasion, in every season) in the Spirit, with all [manner of] prayer and entreaty. To that end keep alert and watch with strong purpose and perseverance, interceding in behalf of all the saints (God's consecrated people).

Ephesians 6:18

In Ephesians 6:10–17 the apostle Paul talks about the armor of God and how we are to use it and the weapon of the Word to engage in spiritual warfare. After each piece has been listed, in verse eighteen Paul sums up his message by saying, "Pray at all times."

How often are we to pray?

At all times.

How are we to pray?

In the Spirit, with all different kinds of prayer.

In the next chapter we will examine the different types of prayer, but right now let's consider praying "at all times."

What does that mean? Does it mean that when we are out doing the grocery shopping and God puts it on our heart to pray we are to drop to our knees right there in the middle of the supermarket aisle?

I often kneel by my bed and pray. There are other times when I feel led by God to lie down, face to the floor, before Him and pray. We have to be careful not to confuse physical posture with prayer. We can also pray silently in the supermarket as we are walking down the aisles.

In the different seasons of life we are able to pray in different ways. A young mother with three or four little children, for example, is going to have to structure her prayer life differently from that of a grandmother whose family is all grown up and out of the house.

If we become too "religious" about prayer, thinking we must do it one way or the other because that is how someone else does it, we will bring condemnation on ourselves. The important thing about prayer is not the posture or the time or place but learning to pray in faith—at all times, unceasingly. Anytime the desire or need arises . . . *pray!*

Pray Without Ceasing

Be unceasing in prayer [praying perseveringly].

1 Thessalonians 5:17

The *King James Version* of this verse says, "Pray without ceasing."

I used to read those words and wonder, "Lord, how can I ever get to the place that I am able to pray without ceasing?" To me the phrase "without ceasing" meant nonstop, without ever quitting.

I couldn't see how that was possible.

Now I have a better understanding of what Paul was saying. He meant that prayer should be like breathing, something we do continually but often unconsciously, without even being totally aware of it.

You and I live by breathing. Our physical bodies require it. In the same way, our spiritual bodies are designed to be nurtured and sustained by prayer.

The problem is that because of religious thinking we have gotten the mistaken idea that if we don't keep up a certain schedule of prayer we are missing the mark. We have become too clock oriented concerning prayer.

The Lord gave me this example to illustrate the way we are to pray. Just as we breathe all day long but never spend time counting our breaths, so we are to pray all day long without keeping track of our prayers.

I have never carried a clock around with me to remind me to breathe every so many seconds. I have never come home from work at night and written down in a manual how many times I breathed that day. I just breathe when I need to, continually and continuously, without giving it a great deal of thought.

That's the way we are to be about our prayers.

I don't know how many times I pray a day; I pray all day long. I start praying when I get up in the morning, and I pray until I go to sleep at night. I enjoy special set-apart times for prayer as well as praying all throughout the day.

Does all this mean I never do anything else? No, there are periods when I have to give myself to other things. But I think as we consider the different type of prayers, we will see that we can pray at all times in every season, on every occasion, in every place, and that God will hear those prayers—which are just as spiritual and powerful as any others we may pray.

Do you know why the devil wants to make us feel so bad about our prayer life? Because he knows if he can make us feel that we are not doing it right, then we will do it out of obligation, but we won't be releasing any faith when we do it; therefore it won't do us any good.

Principles of Prayer

Now Peter and John went up together into the temple at the hour of prayer.

Acts 3:1

Many people feel vaguely guilty about their prayer life. There is no need because each person should have his or her own individual prayer life, and it doesn't have to be just like that of anyone else.

Yes, there are definite principles of prayer that need to be followed. It is good, for example, to discipline ourselves to have a certain time and place for prayer.

Even in the New Testament, as we see here in the book of Acts, the early disciples set aside certain hours of the day when they would go to a designated place to pray. That is good self-discipline, and there is nothing wrong with it. But that should be the start of prayer and not the finish.

The point is that we should discipline ourselves to establish a prayer schedule that is individually suited to us and then stick to it until it becomes such a part of our lifestyle that we do it without even thinking.

There was a time when I had to discipline myself to brush my teeth. But I have done that so long now I don't even think about it anymore, I just do it. I brush my teeth before I go to bed at night, when I get up in the morning, and after every meal. Brushing my teeth is just a normal part of my everyday life.

The same holds true when we start our walk with the Lord. At first we may have to discipline ourselves in some areas because we are so undisciplined in those areas. But after a while they should become such a normal part of our lives that we do them without even thinking.

I believe if we will allow Him to do so, the Holy Spirit will lead us into prayer without ceasing so it becomes like breathing. When that happens we can be continually offering up prayers.

We can get up every day saying, "Good morning, Lord. I love You." We can go to the breakfast table saying, "Father, You are so good to me." We can drive to work saying, "Thank You, God, for all the good things You are going to do for me today."

Throughout the day and evening we can continue to communicate with the Lord, praising and worshiping Him, thanking Him for His presence with us and asking His help in all our problems. Then just before we go to sleep at night, we can offer up a final prayer of gratitude for the blessings of the day and a request for a peaceful and refreshing night's sleep.

Now the devil may try to tell us that is not praying because we are not in the right posture or not praying in formal "church language." That is the time to kick the devil in the teeth! Because prayer is not of the body, or even of the mouth; it is of the spirit, the mind and the heart.

And where there is prayer, there is power!

Prayer Is Power!

The earnest (heartfelt, continued) prayer of a righteous man makes tremendous power available [dynamic in its working].

James 5:16

Simple, believing prayer is powerful! In fact, there is nothing more powerful than heartfelt, continued prayer!

The reason the devil torments us about our prayer life and tries to prevent us from being faithful to it is because he wants us in a weakened condition. He knows it is continual, believing prayer that destroys his works and ushers in the will of God on this earth.

Anytime you and I begin to feel guilty about our prayer life, we begin to lose the ability to release our faith through it.

In order to accomplish what God has called us to do in this life, we need to be assured He does hear our prayers and does respond to them. That is what makes them so powerful and so effective.

That's why we need to stop fearing and start continually praying—in faith—all kinds of prayers!

3

TYPES OF PRAYER

First of all, then, I admonish and urge that petitions, prayers, inter-cessions, and thanksgivings be offered on behalf of all men, For kings and all who are in positions of authority or high responsibility, that [outwardly] we may pass a quiet and undisturbed life [and inwardly] a peaceable one in all godliness and reverence and seriousness in every way. For such [praying] is good and right, and [it is] pleasing and ac-ceptable to God our Savior.

1 Timothy 2:1–3

As we see in this passage, we are to pray all types of prayers for our-selves and for others.

Let's look at some of the different types of prayers we are to pray as we engage in continual, heartfelt prayer.

Prayer of Commitment

Commit your way to the Lord [roll and repose each care of your load on Him]; trust (lean on, rely on, and be confident) also in Him and He will bring it to pass.

Psalm 37:5

First there is the prayer of commitment in which we commit our-selves and our lives to the Lord. We do that when we cast our load of care upon Him as we are told to do in 1 Peter 5:7: "Casting the whole of your care [all your anxieties, all your worries, all your concerns, once and for all] on Him, for He cares for you affectionately and cares about you watchfully."

When we are faced with fears and problems that threaten to overwhelm and destroy us, we need to pray, "Lord, I am not going to carry this load of care around with me and allow it to torment me and prevent me from serving You.

"I am praying right now, Father, that You will strengthen me and enable me to do what You have called me to do even if I have to do it afraid.

"I cast this situation on You, God. Whatever evil, wicked, perverted thing the devil is trying to tell me is going to happen, that is Your problem, and not mine, because I am going to do what You have told me to do and leave the rest to You."

The minute fear arises, if you and I will pray, sooner or later we will see it overcome by the power of God.

The problem is that many times it is not the major fears that cause us the most trouble. Like the little foxes that spoil the vineyards (see Song of Solomon 2:15), often it is all those little pestering fears that assail us day and night that drain the life out of us and steal our joy.

That's why, at the very first sign of fear, no matter how minor it may be, we need to confront it and pray, "Lord, I will not live in fear. Instead, I commit my way unto You and ask You to overcome this thing that is trying to torment and prevent me from living the abundant life You desire for me and fulfilling Your good and perfect will and plan for me."

If we will do that in heartfelt, earnest prayer, the Lord will honor our request and commitment, and will do His part to keep us free.

Prayer of Consecration or Dedication

I appeal to you therefore, brethren, and beg of you in view of [all] the mercies of God, to make a decisive dedication of your bodies [presenting all your members and faculties] as a living sacrifice, holy (devoted, consecrated) and well pleasing to God, which is your reasonable (rational, intelligent) service and spiritual worship.

Romans 12:1

When we give something to God in prayer, that is a prayer of consecration or dedication. We say in essence, "Here, Lord, I give You my money, my time, my mind"—whatever it may be.

The apostle Paul tells us in this passage that we are to give, dedicate, consecrate to the Lord our bodies, all our members and faculties, for His use, which is our reasonable service and worship.

We also pray the prayer of consecration or dedication when we dedicate our children to God, promising to "bring them up in the nurture and admonition of the Lord" (Ephesians 6:4 KJV).

Just as we dedicate and consecrate our lives, our money and possessions, our minds and bodies, ourselves and our children to God, so we also ought to dedicate and consecrate our mouths—which leads us to the next type of prayer.

Prayer of Praise and Worship

Through Him, therefore, let us constantly and at all times offer up to God a sacrifice of praise, which is the fruit of lips that thankfully acknowledge and confess and glorify His name.

Hebrews 13:15

I think we all understand praise and worship.

Praise is really recounting the goodness of God. It is telling the story of all the good things He has done for us.

Worship is simply adoring God. It is acknowledging His "worthship." It is recognizing Him for Who He is and what He is.

That's why the writer of the book of Hebrews tells us we should be praising and worshiping God constantly and at all times.

As we have seen, the prayer of praise and worship should be like breathing, in and out, day and night, moment by moment.

We are to be thankful to God always, continually acknowledging, confessing, and glorifying His name in prayerful praise and worship.

Prayer of Thanksgiving

Thank [God] in everything [no matter what the circumstances may be, be thankful and give thanks], for this is the will of God for you [who are] in Christ Jesus [the Revealer and Mediator of that will].

1 Thessalonians 5:18

Immediately after telling us in 1 Thessalonians 5:17 to pray without ceasing, the apostle Paul directs us to give thanks to God in everything no matter what our circumstances may be, stating that this is the will of God for us.

Just as prayer is to be a lifestyle for us, so thanksgiving is to be a lifestyle for us.

Giving thanks to God should not be something we do once a day as we sit down somewhere and try to think of all the good things He has done for us and merely say, "Thanks, Lord."

That is religion, something we do simply because we think God requires it.

True thanksgiving flows continually out of a heart that is full of gratitude and praise to God for Who He is as much as for what He does. It is not something that is done to meet a requirement, win favor, gain a victory, or qualify for a blessing.

The type of thanksgiving God the Father desires is that which is provoked by the presence of His Holy Spirit within us Who moves upon us to express to the Lord verbally what we are feeling and experiencing spiritually.

True thanksgiving is the kind expressed by the psalmist when he wrote: "O give thanks to the Lord of lords, for His mercy and lovingkindness endure forever" (Psalm 136:3)!

Prayer in the Spirit

But you, beloved, build yourselves up [founded] on your most holy faith [make progress, rise like an edifice higher and higher], praying in the Holy Spirit.

Jude 1:20

We have already seen in Ephesians 6:18 that we are not only to pray at all times with all manner of prayers, but as we are told here by Jude, our prayers are to be "in the Holy Spirit."

It is the Holy Spirit of God within us Who provokes us and leads us to pray. Rather than delaying, we need to learn to yield to the leading of the Spirit as soon as we sense it. That is part of learning to pray all manner of prayers at all times, wherever we may be, and whatever we may be doing.

Our motto should be that of the old spiritual song, "Every time I feel the Spirit moving in my heart, I will pray."

If we know we can pray anytime and anywhere, we won't feel we have to wait until just the right moment or place to pray.

Prayer of Agreement

Again I tell you, if two of you on earth agree (harmonize together, make a symphony together) about whatever [anything and everything] they may ask, it will come to pass and be done for them by My Father in heaven. For wherever two or three are gathered (drawn together as My followers) in (into) My name, there I AM in the midst of them.

Matthew 18:19,20

There is power in agreement.

The Bible tells us that if the Lord is with them one can chase a thousand, and two can put ten thousand to flight (see Deuteronomy 32:30). But that power is available only to those who are in agreement with each other—and with God.

Obviously we cannot argue and fight with one another all the time and then agree in prayer on some need and expect that "prayer of agreement" to be effective. As we are told in 1 Peter 3:7, "In the same way you married men should live considerately with [your wives], with an intelligent recognition [of the marriage relation], honoring the woman as [physically] the weaker, but [realizing that you] are joint heirs of the grace (God's unmerited favor) of life, in order that your prayers may not be hindered and cut off. [Otherwise you cannot pray effectively.]"

In the same way, we cannot gossip and complain about the preacher all week long and then go to him for prayer about some serious personal problem and expect him to pray the prayer of agreement with us.

Why not? Because we are already out of agreement—with each other and with God.

Do you know why God honors the prayer of agreement? Because He knows what a challenge it is to walk and live in agreement. He respects anyone who will do that.

If you and I will come into agreement with each other and with God, then there will be an added force behind our prayers to make them much more powerful and effective.

United or Corporate Prayer

All of these with their minds in full agreement devoted themselves steadfastly to prayer.

Acts 1:14

There is great power in united or corporate prayer, which as we see here in this verse is a form of prayer in agreement.

Throughout the book of Acts we read that the people of God came together "with one accord" (see Acts 2:1, 46; 4:24; 5:12; 15:25 KJV).

Then in Philippians 2:2 we are told by the apostle Paul, "Fill up and complete my joy by living in harmony and being of the same mind and one in purpose, having the same love, being in full accord and of one harmonious mind and intention."

If we will heed these words and come into harmony and agreement with each other and with God, we will experience the same kind of powerful results the first-century disciples enjoyed as recorded in the book of Acts.

Prayer of Intercession

I exhort therefore, that, first of all, supplications, prayers, intercessions, and giving of thanks, be made for all men.

1 Timothy 2:1 (KJV)

To intercede for someone is to "stand in the gap" for him, to plead his case before the throne of God.

In Romans 8:27 we are told by the apostle Paul that the Holy Spirit intercedes for us according to the will of the Lord.

In Hebrews 7:25 we read that Jesus "is always living to make petition to God and intercede with Him and intervene" for us.

Finally, Paul exhorts us here in 1 Timothy 2:1 to offer intercessions "for all men," meaning that we are to pray for all people everywhere.

Intercession is one of the most important ways we carry on the ministry of Jesus Christ which He began in this earth.

Prayer of Silence

The Lord is in His holy temple; let all the earth hush and keep silence before Him.

Habakkuk 2:20

I also call this kind of prayer "waiting on the Lord."

David knew all about waiting on the Lord as we see in Psalm 27:4 in which he wrote: "One thing have I asked of the Lord, that will I seek, inquire for, and [insistently] require: that I may dwell in the house of the Lord [in His presence] all the days of my life, to behold and gaze upon the beauty [the sweet attractiveness and the delightful loveliness] of the Lord and to meditate, consider, and inquire in His temple."

It is very important to learn to wait on the Lord because most people don't understand that waiting is a vital part of prayer.

Prayer is not just doing, it is also an attitude of waiting. Prayer is not talking to God all the time—it is also listening to Him.

Prayer of Petition

Do not fret or have any anxiety about anything, but in every circumstance and in everything, by prayer and petition (definite re-

quests), with thanksgiving, continue to make your wants known to God.

Philippians 4:6

Petition is simply making requests, asking God to meet needs.

I always say that the greatest prayer anyone can pray is what I call the "help me" prayer: "Help me, God, help me, help me! Oh, God, help me!"

I pray that prayer a lot.

Sometimes I get up in the middle of the night to go to the bathroom, and there is not a thing wrong with me, yet I will find myself praying, "Oh God, help me, help me!"

I believe I am led by the Holy Spirit to pray that way.

"Help me, God!" is a powerful prayer. If you and I can do nothing else, we can always pray that way.

Another important prayer of petition is simply: "God I need You."

You and I will see major changes take place in our lives if we will stop trying to do everything ourselves.

Proverbs 3:5–7 tells us: "Lean on, trust in, and be confident in the Lord with all your heart and mind and do not rely on your own insight or understanding. In all your ways know, recognize, and acknowledge Him, and He will direct and make straight and plain your paths. Be not wise in your own eyes; reverently fear and worship the Lord and turn [entirely] away from evil."

Don't wait until after you have already fallen apart and proven you can't handle things on your own before you run to God for help. Know ahead of time that you can't before you even try. Be totally dependent on God.

Learn to pray: "Lord, I can't do this, but You can. Do this through me. I am leaning on, trusting in, and being confident in You with all my heart and mind. Help me, Lord, because I need You."

Just that little prayer of petition is enough to see you through the worst situations of life.

Acknowledging God takes only a few minutes but it can help us to avoid many failures in our everyday life—especially when we realize that without God we can do nothing.

When we have said, "Lord, I am depending on You . . . please help me," we have prayed the prayer of petition—and it is powerful.

Prayers of petition are also requests to have wants, needs, or desires met. We should be comfortable talking to the Lord about anything that concerns us. Remember, He loves us very much and is concerned about anything that concerns us.

Put First Things First!

Now while they were on their way, it occurred that Jesus entered a certain village, and a woman named Martha received and welcomed Him into her house. And she had a sister named Mary, who seated herself at the Lord's feet and was listening to His teaching. But Martha [overly occupied and too busy] was distracted with much serving; and she came up to Him and said, Lord, is it nothing to You that my sister has left me to serve alone? Tell her then to help me [to lend a hand and do her part along with me]! But the Lord replied to her by saying, Martha, Martha, you are anxious and troubled about many things; There is need of only one or but a few things. Mary has chosen the good portion [that which is to her advantage], which shall not be taken away from her.

Luke 10:38–42

By now you may have begun to realize that you may have a better prayer life than you thought. You have seen that although it is good to have a set time and a specific place to pray to the Lord, especially at the beginning of each day, there is great power in being in prayer all the time.

The way to develop a powerful, effective prayer life is by simply spending time in the presence of the Lord. As followers of Christ, that is what our lifestyle should be centered around.

If you and I will just sit in the Lord's presence for a period of time before we start our day, and then remain conscious of His presence throughout the rest of the day, we will see marvelous results in our everyday life.

If you think you don't have time, remember this rule: "The busier I get, the more time I need to spend with God." After all, the more I have to do, the more I need His help.

If, like Martha, you are too busy to spend time with the Lord, then you are just plain too busy. You need to be more like Mary and learn to let some lesser things go for a while so you can sit at the feet of the Lord and learn from Him.

If you will do that, you will receive from Him the very keys to the kingdom!

4

KEYS TO THE KINGDOM

I will give you the keys of the kingdom of heaven.

Matthew 16:19

Now when Jesus went into the region of Caesarea Philippi, He asked His disciples, Who do people say that the Son of Man is? And they answered, Some say John the Baptist; others say Elijah; and others Jeremiah or one of the prophets. He said to them, But who do you [yourselves] say that I am? Simon Peter replied, You are the Christ, the Son of the living God.

Matthew 16:13–16

When Peter made that statement about Jesus being the Christ, the Son of the living God, he was releasing with his mouth the faith that was in his heart.

We must understand that we establish the faith that is in our heart by the words we speak from our mouth, as we read in Romans 10:10: "For with the heart a person believes (adheres to, trusts in, and relies on Christ) and so is justified (declared righteous, acceptable to God), and with the mouth he confesses (declares openly and speaks out freely his faith) and confirms [his] salvation."

That is why prayer is so important. Because we establish the things we believe inwardly when we start talking about them outwardly.

That is also why confessing Scripture in prayer is so important.

When we do that, we are establishing things in the spiritual realm by the words we are speaking in the physical realm. And eventually what is established spiritually will be manifested physically.

You and I should be constantly confessing the Word of God. We should be saying things like:

"Father, I believe in You. I believe You love me so much You sent Your Son Jesus to die for me on the cross.

"I believe you have filled me with Your Holy Spirit. I believe You have a good plan for my life, and You are empowering me to fulfill it.

"I believe Your anointing is upon me so I can lay hands on the sick and they will recover, and cast out devils and they will flee.

"I believe that in accordance with Your Word, everything I put my hand to prospers and succeeds."

On and on we should go, believing in our heart and confessing with our mouth what God has said about us in His Word.

And one thing He has said is that He has not given us a spirit of fear but of power and of love and of a sound mind. Therefore, we should be confessing continually, "I will not fear!"

Faith Shall Prevail

Then Jesus answered him, Blessed (happy, fortunate, and to be envied) are you, Simon Bar-Jonah. For flesh and blood [men] have not revealed this to you, but My Father Who is in heaven. And I tell you, you are Peter [Greek, Petros—a large piece of rock], and on this rock [Greek, petra—a huge rock like Gibraltar] I will build My church, and the gates of Hades (the powers of the infernal region) shall not overpower it [or be strong to its detriment or hold out against it].

Matthew 16:17–18

What rock is Jesus talking about in this passage? He is talking about the rock of faith. He is telling Simon Peter that on the faith he has just displayed He will build His Church, and (as the King James Version puts it) "the gates of hell shall not prevail against it" (v. 18).

That means that the gates of hell shall not prevail against the person who walks in faith.

Fear comes from hell. That's why John tells us that "fear hath torment" (1 John 4:18 KJV). But when fear is confronted by faith, hell cannot prevail against it.

The Keys to the Kingdom

I will give you the keys of the kingdom of heaven; and whatever you bind (declare to be improper and unlawful) on earth must be what is already bound in heaven; and whatever you loose (declare lawful) on earth must be what is already loosed in heaven.

Matthew 16:19

What Jesus was saying here is, "Whatever is taking place in heaven I am giving you the power and authority to bring to pass in the earth."

This is the fulfillment of the prayer to the Father that Jesus had taught the disciples to pray in Matthew 6:10: "Your kingdom come, Your will be done on earth as it is in heaven."

Later on in Matthew 18:18 Jesus gave this same power to bind and loose to all the disciples when He said to them: "Truly I tell you, whatever you forbid and declare to be improper and unlawful on earth must be what is already forbidden in heaven, and whatever you permit and declare proper and lawful on earth must be what is already permitted in heaven."

What Jesus was telling them was that He was conferring upon them the power and authority to use the keys He was giving them to bring to pass on earth the will of God that prevails in heaven.

I believe the keys He gave to Peter and the other disciples—and to us—may be references to the different types of prayer we have been studying.

Earnest Prayer Is Effectual

The effectual fervent prayer of a righteous man availeth much. Elias was a man subject to like passions as we are, and he prayed earnestly that it might not rain: and it rained not on the earth by

the space of three years and six months. And he prayed again, and
the heaven gave rain, and the earth brought forth her fruit.

James 5:16–18 (KJV)

In any organization, who has the power and authority? Isn't it the person who controls the keys? What do keys do? They lock and unlock. That is what binding and loosing mean—locking and unlocking.

When you and I intercede for someone, for example, we unlock a blessing on that person's life. We unlock the door of hell that is holding him or her in bondage.

In the same way, when we offer a prayer of thanksgiving to God, we are unlocking a blessing in our own life.

So you and I have been given the keys to the kingdom of God. With those prayer keys we have the authority and the power to bring to pass the will of God on earth as it is in heaven.

What a privilege!

No wonder the devil wants to deceive us into thinking that our prayer life is ineffectual—so we will give up and quit rather than continuing to use the key ring of prayers to overcome his kingdom of darkness.

Don't let the devil belittle you concerning your prayer life. Begin to acknowledge God, calling upon Him in prayer—all kinds of prayer—trusting that your earnest, heartfelt prayers *are* effectual because your faith is in Him, not in your own ability to live holy or pray eloquently.

Prayer as Requisition

Do not fret or have any anxiety about anything, but in every cir-
cumstance and in everything, by prayer and petition (definite re-
quests), with thanksgiving, continue to make your wants known to
God.

Philippians 4:6

We looked at this passage when we talked about the prayer of petition.

What is a petition? According to this verse it is a definite request. Another word for a definite request is a *requisition*.

What is a requisition? It is a demand or request made on something to which a person is legally entitled but not yet in possession of, as in the military when an officer requisitions equipment or supplies for his men. As a duly commissioned agent of the United States Army, he is entitled to that material, but in order to receive it he has to submit a definite request for it.

The Lord has shown me that when we pray, what we are doing is requisitioning from Him what He has already set aside to provide for us when the need arises.

Let me give you an example from everyday life. You and I may have money in a bank. But in order for us to benefit from that money we must requisition it by writing a check, which is a request to the bank to issue to us or to the person we designate a certain sum of money for a certain purpose.

The same thing happens when managers come to my husband, who is the financial officer of our ministry, asking for money for their departments. Before he will release any funds to them, although that is what the money is set aside for, they must submit a written requisition for it stating the amount requested and the purpose for which it will be used.

That is what prayer is—a heavenly requisition we submit to God for what we need to carry on our daily life and ministry.

Ask in Jesus' Name

So for the present you are also in sorrow (in distress and depressed); but I will see you again and [then] your hearts will rejoice, and no one can take from you your joy (gladness, delight). And when that time comes, you will ask nothing of Me [you will need to ask Me no questions]. I assure you, most solemnly I tell you, that My Father will grant you whatever you ask in My Name [as presenting all that I AM].

John 16:22–23

The Bible teaches that God knows everything about us (see Psalm 139:1–6). He knows what we have need of before we ask Him (see Matthew 6:8, 32). Yet He has commanded that we ask (see Matthew 7:7).

You and I do not receive the things we need by wishing. To go around saying, "I wish I had more money" or "I wish I could get rid of this headache" or "I wish I could live without fear," is not a heavenly requisition.

According to what we read in James 1:5–8 we have to ask for what we need in faith, believing that we receive what we ask for, what we have requisitioned from God's storehouse of blessings.

Here in this passage from John 16, spoken by Jesus to His disciples just before He went to the cross, He makes it clear that when we pray we must not only believe but we must also ask in His name.

Now that does not mean just tacking the phrase "in Jesus' name" on the end of everything we say. If we are not careful we can become so religious that every sentence that comes out of our mouth ends with "hallelujah," "praise God," or "in Jesus' name." When that happens, those words soon lose their meaning.

That is not what Jesus was talking about. He was talking about using the authority of His name, as He has commanded us to do, in order to bring about the will of God on earth as it is in heaven. He was talking about submitting a requisition to God the Father over the signature of His Son for what we need to usher in His kingdom.

In our ministry, our employees earn vacation time. It is legally theirs. But even though it rightfully belongs to them, they cannot receive a day of that vacation time unless they submit a requisition for it.

You and I have an inheritance laid up for us in heaven, bought and paid for by the shed blood of Jesus Christ (see Ephesians 1:11, 12). It is legally and rightfully ours. But the problem is we have not been submitting enough requisitions.

If an employee of our ministry submits a requisition to Dave, our finance manager, and that person does not receive the authorization to take that earned vacation, he soon comes to Dave and asks, "Did you lose my requisition? When am I going to get what is rightfully mine?"

When you and I submit a requisition to God in the name of Jesus, and we do not receive what we have asked for in faith, then we have every right to go to the Lord and ask Him, "Father, You haven't forgotten about my requisition, have You?" That is not impudence, it is faith. It actually honors the Lord because it shows Him that we expect Him to keep His Word because He is faithful.

Use the Name of Jesus!

Up to this time you have not asked a [single] thing in My Name [as presenting all that I AM]; but now ask and keep on asking and you will receive, so that your joy (gladness, delight) may be full and complete.

John 16:24

Jesus commanded us to ask in His name that we might receive so that our joy might be full.

I am convinced one of the main reasons for the lack of joy in the life of believers today is a lack of prayer. And one reason for the lack of prayer is the fact that God's people are trying to do in the flesh what they should be praying about and asking God to do through them and for them.

Jesus told His disciples that after He was resurrected from the dead, things would be different. He told them they would have a new power and authority they had not enjoyed before His death and resurrection.

"When that time comes," He told them, "you won't have to ask Me anything, but you can go straight to the Father, and He will grant you whatever you ask—in My name."

What does it mean to ask in Jesus' name?

According to verse twenty-four, to pray in the name of Jesus is to present to the Father all that Jesus is.

One of the main reasons we are so weak in prayer power is that we go to God trying to present to Him what we are. The problem with that is that if we have failed Him in any way, we think we have nothing to present to Him that will influence Him to act on our behalf.

The Bible says that in the sight of God all our righteousness is as filthy rags (see Isaiah 64:6 KJV). So there is nothing you and I can present to God except the blood of Jesus.

That's why I am so excited about my book titled *The Word, The Name, The Blood* (see the book list in the back). In it I discuss this very issue.

As you and I come before the throne of God's grace covered with the blood of Jesus asking in faith according to His Word and in the name of His Son Jesus Christ, we can know we have the petitions that we ask of Him. Not because we are perfect or worthy in ourselves or because God owes us anything, but because He loves us and wants to give us what we need to do the job He has called us to do.

There is power in the name of Jesus. At the very mention of it, every knee has to bow in heaven, on earth, and beneath the earth (see Philippians 2:10). By the power of that name you and I are to lay hands on the sick and they will recover, cast out demons and they will flee, and do the same works Jesus did and even greater works than these for the glory of God (see Mark 16:17–18; John 14:12).

Jesus has purchased a glorious inheritance for us by the shedding of His blood. We are now joint-heirs with Him (see Romans 8:17 KJV). Everything He has earned by his sacrifice is in the heavenlies stored up for us. We have the keys to that storehouse, and the keys are prayer.

We do not have to live in fear and lack. Let's start using those keys and opening those doors so that heavenly blessings may be showered down upon us for the glory of God, so that His divine will may be done on earth as it is in heaven, and so that our joy may be made complete.

Conclusion

Fear is not from God. Fear is from Satan.

The only acceptable attitude (and confession) that a Christian can have toward fear is this: "It is not from God, and I will not put up with it or let it control my life! *I will confront fear,* for it is a spirit sent out from hell to torment me."

I often say that fear is the spirit Satan uses to try to keep God's people from coming under the leadership of the true Master, Jesus Christ.

I believe God works gently with us in areas to bring us out of bondage and into liberty. The Bible is full of instructions to "Fear not." As mentioned before, events in my own life have led me to understand that "Fear not" means "Do not run."

I encourage you to press on, and if need be, "do it afraid." Don't run from fear; instead confront it in prayer and faith.

Remember, God wants to deliver you from *all* your fear:

F   –   False
E   –   Evidence
A   –   Appearing
R   –   Real

Part Two

———— ✿ ————

SCRIPTURES TO OVERCOME FEAR

Fear not; stand still (firm, confident, undismayed) and see the salvation of the Lord which He will work for you today. (Exodus 14:13)

Behold, the Lord your God has set the land before you; go up and possess it, as the Lord, the God of your fathers, has said to you. Fear not, neither be dismayed. (Deuteronomy 1:21)

Be strong, courageous, and firm; fear not nor be in terror before them, for it is the Lord your God Who goes with you; He will not fail you or forsake you. (Deuteronomy 31:6)

Have not I commanded you? Be strong, vigorous, and very courageous. Be not afraid, neither be dismayed, for the Lord your God is with you wherever you go. (Joshua 1:9)

Fear not [there is nothing to fear], for I am with you; do not look around you in terror and be dismayed, for I am your God. I will strengthen and harden you to difficulties, yes, I will help you; yes, I will hold you up and retain you with My [victorious] right hand of rightness and justice . . . For I the Lord your God hold your right hand; I am the Lord, Who says to you, Fear not; I will help you! (Isaiah 41:10, 13)

Thus says the Lord, He Who created you, O Jacob, and He Who formed You, O Israel: Fear not, for I have redeemed you [ransomed you by paying a price instead of leaving you captives]; I have called you by your name; you are Mine. When you pass through the waters, I will be with you, and through the rivers, they will not overwhelm you. When you walk through the fire, you will not be burned or scorched, nor will the flame kindle upon you. (Isaiah 43:1–2)

For [the Spirit which] you have now received [is] not a spirit of slavery to put you once more in bondage to fear, but you have received the Spirit of adoption [the Spirit producing sonship] in [the bliss of] which we cry, Abba (Father)! Father! (Romans 8:15)

And do not [for a moment] be frightened or intimidated in anything by your opponents and adversaries, for such [constancy and fearlessness] will be a clear sign (proof and seal) to them of [their impending] destruction, but [a sure token and evidence] of your deliverance and salvation, and that from God. (Philippians 1:28)

Do not fret or have any anxiety about anything, but in every circumstance and in everything, by prayer and petition (definite requests), with thanksgiving, continue to make your wants known to God. And God's peace [shall be yours, that tranquil state of a soul assured of its salvation through Christ, and so fearing nothing from God and being content with its earthly lot of whatever sort that is, that peace] which transcends all understanding shall garrison and mount guard over your hearts and minds in Christ Jesus. (Philippians 4:6–7)

For God did not give us a spirit of timidity (of cowardice, of craven and cringing and fawning fear), but [He has given us a spirit] of power and of love and of calm and well-balanced mind and discipline and self-control. (2 Timothy 1:7)

Let your character or moral disposition be free from love of money [including greed, avarice, lust, and craving for earthly possessions] and be satisfied with your present [circumstances and with what you have]; for He [God] Himself has said, I will not in any way fail you nor give you up nor leave you without support. [I will] not, [I will] not, [I will] not in any degree leave you helpless nor forsake nor let [you] down (relax My hold on you)! [Assuredly not!] So we take comfort and are encouraged and confidently and boldly say, The Lord is my Helper; I will not be seized with alarm [I will not fear or dread or be terrified]. What can man do to me? (Hebrews 13:5–6)

There is no fear in love [dread does not exist], but full-grown (complete, perfect) love turns fear out of doors and expels every trace of terror! For fear brings with it the thought of punishment, and [so] he who is afraid has not reached the full maturity of love [is not yet grown into love's complete perfection]. (1 John 4:18)

Prayer to Overcome Fear

Oh, God, deliver me from fear. Help me to be courageous and to have holy boldness.

Help me to "fear not" but to go in and possess all You desire for me to have.

Help me know how much You love me, because perfect love (Your love for me) will cast out all fear. In Jesus' name, amen.

STRAIGHT TALK ON *Depression*

CONTENTS

INTRODUCTION

Many people have bouts with depression. There are many underlying causes for depression and a variety of treatments offered to deal with it. Some are effective, but many are not. Some help temporarily, but can never permanently remove the torment of depression. The good news is that Jesus can heal depression and deliver us from it in the same way He can any other sickness or problem.

As I was preparing to speak on depression one time, I saw very clearly that God has given us His joy to fight depression. It was so clear that it seemed as though I was looking at a movie screen.

If you are a believer in Jesus Christ, the joy of the Lord is inside you. Many believers know this but don't have the slightest idea how to tap into it or release it. We need to experience what is ours as a result of our faith in Jesus Christ. *It is God's will for us to experience joy!*

Many people, including Spirit-filled Christians, not only have had bouts with depression, but major problems with it. I had problems with depression myself a long time ago. But, thank God, I learned I didn't have to allow the negative feeling of depression to rule me. I learned how to release the joy of the Lord in my life!

The message in this section of the book is very simple, but very powerful. No matter what you have gone through in life or are going through now, if you are a believer in Jesus Christ, you have His joy inside you, and you can learn how to release it to win over depression!*

---

* If you do not have a personal relationship with the Lord Jesus Christ, the Source of this joy, see the prayer at the end of this book to learn how to receive Him into your life.

Part One

———— ❧ ————

RELEASING GOD'S JOY

1

PHASES OF DEPRESSION

*I waited patiently and expectantly for the Lord; and He inclined to me
and heard my cry. He drew me up out of a horrible pit [a pit of tumult
and of destruction], out of the miry clay (froth and slime), and set my
feet upon a rock, steadying my steps and establishing my goings.*

Psalm 40:1–2

*D*epression in *Webster's 1828 Dictionary* is said to be "the act of
pressing down . . . a low state; a sinking of the spirits; dejection; [or]
a state of sadness; want of courage . . . a low state of strength."[1]

Who Suffers from Depression?

People in all walks of life can suffer from depression: professionals—
doctors, lawyers, teachers; blue-collar workers—laborers; house-
wives, teenagers, small children, the elderly, singles, widows and
widowers, and even ministers.

The Bible tells of kings and prophets who became depressed.
King David, Jonah, and Elijah are three good examples (see Psalm
40:1–2; 55:4; Jonah 2:7; 4:1–8; 1 Kings 19:4–8).

I believe the reason so many people suffer from depression is that
everyone on the face of the earth has to deal with disappointment. If
we don't know how to properly deal with it, disappointment can lead

to depression. From what I have observed, disappointment is the first phase of depression.

Dealing with Disappointment

All of us must face and deal with disappointment at different times. No person alive has everything happen in life the way they want in the way they expect.

When things don't prosper or succeed according to our plan, the first thing we feel is disappointment. This is normal. There is nothing wrong with feeling disappointed. But we must know what to do with that feeling, or it will move into something more serious.

In the world we cannot live without disappointment, but in Jesus we can always be given re-appointment!

In Philippians 3:13 we read a statement by the apostle Paul:

But one thing I do [it is my one aspiration]: forgetting what lies behind and straining forward to what lies ahead.

Paul stated that one thing of greatest importance to him was to let go of what lay behind and press toward the things that were ahead! When we get disappointed, then immediately get re-appointed, that's exactly what we're doing. We're letting go of the causes for the disappointment and pressing toward what God has for us. We get a new vision, plan, idea, a fresh outlook, a new mind-set, and we change our focus to that. *We decide to go on!*

Isaiah 43:18–19 says it like this:

Do not [earnestly] remember the former things; neither consider the things of old. Behold, I am doing a new thing! Now it springs forth; do you not perceive and know it and will you not give heed to it? I will even make a way in the wilderness and rivers in the desert.

Isaiah 42:9 says:

Behold, the former things have come to pass, and new things I now declare; before they spring forth I tell you of them.

We see from these two Scriptures that God is willing to do a new thing in our lives. He always has something fresh, but we seem to want to hang on to the old. We hang on in our thoughts and in our conversation. It seems that some people want to talk about their disappointments in life rather than their dreams and visions for the future.

God's mercies are new every day. "His [tender] compassions fail not. They are new every morning" (Lamentations 3:22–23). Every day is a brand new start! We can let go of yesterday's disappointments and give God a chance to do something wonderful for us today.

You may be thinking, *Joyce, I've been disappointed so many times, I'm afraid to hope.* That place of hopelessness is exactly where the devil wants you to be! I know about that place because I was there many years ago when Dave and I married. I had been abused, abandoned, and mistreated by so many people that I was afraid to even hope things would ever change.

But, through my study of God's Word, I came to realize that disappointment is a very unhappy place to live. I would rather hope all of my life and receive nothing than live perpetually in a feeling of disappointment.

Hoping doesn't cost anything, and it could pay off generously. Disappointment, however, is very expensive. It costs you your joy and your dreams of tomorrow.

We have a promise from God that those who place their hope in Him will never be disappointed or put to shame (see Romans 5:5). I don't believe this means we will never experience disappointment. As I have already shared, no person can live in the world without being disappointed. I believe that verse means we won't have to *live* in disappointment. Keeping our hope in Jesus will eventually produce positive results.

Dashed Expectations

Dashed expectations lead to disappointment. We have many expectations in different areas every day. For example you may lie down expecting to get a good night's sleep, when in the middle of the night, the phone rings with a wrong number. Then after waking up, you can't go back to sleep for some reason. You toss and turn the rest of the night and get up feeling worn out the next morning.

We may expect the day to be sunny, but instead it rains. We may expect to get a raise at work and we don't.

We have expectations concerning other people. We don't expect good friends to gossip about us, but we find sometimes that they do. We expect our friends to understand us and meet our needs when we go to them, but they don't always do it. We expect things from ourselves we don't fulfill. Many times I have behaved in ways I, myself, did not expect!

I think we all expect more out of ourselves than we can give and frequently become disappointed with ourselves. We expect things from God that actually are not in His plans for us. Yes, our lives are filled with expectations, and some of them are dashed.

From that point when we are disappointed, it is up to us to decide what we will do—how we will respond. I have found that if I stay disappointed for too long, I will start to feel discouraged. Discouragement is an even deeper problem than disappointment.

Discouragement

Webster's 1828 Dictionary defines *discouraged* in part as, "disheartened, deprived of courage or confidence," and *discouragement* as "the act of deterring or dissuading from an undertaking; the act of depressing confidence; that which depresses confidence and hope."[2] One meaning of *discourage* is "to try to prevent."[3]

Discouragement is the opposite of courage. When we are discouraged we have lost our courage. I believe God gives everyone who believes in Him courage, so naturally Satan tries to take it away. Remaining strong and courageous is one of the top rules for succeeding at anything.

God told Joshua that He would cause Joshua to possess the land, but that he had to remain strong and very courageous (see Joshua 1:6). I believe God was warning Joshua that the enemy would try to discourage him. We need to be educated on Satan's tactics and ready to resist each of them at the onset (see 1 Peter 5:9).

Proverbs 13:12 tells us, "Hope deferred makes the heart sick." When we become discouraged about something, we are also hopeless about it. We cannot be discouraged and hopeful at the same time. As soon as hope comes back in, discouragement has to leave. Sometimes when we are fighting to have a right attitude, we may vacillate between hope and discouragement. The Holy Spirit is leading us to be hopeful, and Satan is attacking us with discouragement.

At this point it is vital for the believer to get the victory in the Spirit realm. If he doesn't, his condition will worsen. Then he will begin moving into depression. A short period of discouragement may not have a devastating effect, but long-term discouragement can.

To get the victory and keep our attitude one of hope, we need to renew our mind to God's promises concerning our situation and stand in faith, believing God will do what His Word says He will do.

Levels of Depression

It is also important for the believer to get the victory early because a person who has become depressed can move into other levels or depths—there is depression, then there are the two deeper levels, despondency and despair. A mildly depressed person will not commit or consider suicide, but a person in despair will.

Mildly depressed people may feel sad and not want to talk or go out. They feel as though they just want to be left alone. Their thoughts are negative, and their attitude is sour.

The mildly depressed person may still have occasional rays of hope. It is that hope that will ultimately help pull the person out of depression.

A despondent person has all the symptoms of a depressed person, but the symptoms are deeper. He is "cast down" (in the terminology of Psalm 37:24; 42:5), dejected in mind, failing in spirit, has lost all courage, and is sinking due to a loss of hope.

A person in despair, once again, has similar symptoms to someone who is depressed, but at a still deeper level than even the despondent individual. W. E. *Vine's Expository Dictionary of New Testament Words* translates the Greek word for *despair* in part as, "to be utterly without a way; to be quite at a loss, without resource."[4]

Despair is distinct from despondency in that despair is marked by total loss of hope, whereas despondency is not. People who are despondent are hopeless, but haven't lost *all* hope. Despondency is followed by the abandonment of effort, or cessation of action; despair is sometimes connected with violent action, even rage.

People who take action to commit suicide, a violent act against oneself, are people who are in deep despair. Satan's tactic is to begin leading someone toward that point with dashed expectations or some other form of disappointment.

To avoid taking the path to despair, it is very important to deal with the first phases of depression at the onset!

2

⁓❧⁓

THE POWER OF REJOICING

About midnight, as Paul and Silas were praying and singing hymns of praise to God . . . Suddenly there was a great earthquake, so that the very foundations of the prison were shaken; and at once all the doors were opened and everyone's shackles were unfastened.

Acts 16:25–26

Throughout the Bible, God instructs His people to be filled with joy and to rejoice. For example, Philippians 4:4 says:

Rejoice in the Lord always [delight, gladden yourselves in Him]; again I say, Rejoice!

Any time the Lord tells us twice to do something—the Philippians were told twice in this verse to rejoice—we need to pay careful attention to what He is saying.

The apostle Paul knew the power of rejoicing. When he and Silas were in the Philippian jail:

. . . about midnight, as Paul and Silas were praying and singing hymns of praise to God . . . Suddenly there was a great earthquake, so that the very foundations of the prison were shaken; and at once all the doors were opened and everyone's shackles were unfastened. (Acts 16:25–26)

The same power that opened the doors and broke the shackles of Paul and Silas and the others imprisoned with them is available to people who are imprisoned and shackled today with depression.

Many times people see or hear the word *rejoice* and think, *That sounds nice, but how do I do that*? They would like to rejoice but don't know how!

Paul and Silas, who had been beaten, thrown into prison, and had their feet put in stocks, rejoiced by simply singing praises to God. We don't often realize the "rejoicing" that can release so much power can be just as simple as smiling and laughing, having a good time and enjoying ourselves. And doing that in itself often makes the problem go away!

One time I was preparing to speak on depression when the Lord showed me something so clearly it was as if I were watching it on a movie screen. He said, "People come for all kinds of counseling because they're depressed. People take all kinds of medication because they're depressed. When people start getting depressed, if they would just smile, it would start to go away. Most people really truly do not understand that is how they're going to change their circumstances."

Change is often the result of a simple adjustment in how we respond in a given situation. The Lord was saying, "If they would just smile or sing a song to me, it would go away. If they would just laugh a little, depression couldn't stay on them. If they would immediately react this way just as soon as they start getting depressed, depression would leave."

The Scriptures clearly teach this, even though we might not have looked at the teaching on rejoicing in quite this way before!

Joy is simply a fruit of the Spirit.

> But the fruit of the [Holy] Spirit [the work which His presence within accomplishes] is love, joy (gladness), peace, patience (an even temper, forbearance), kindness, goodness (benevolence), faithfulness, Gentleness (meekness, humility), self-control (self-restraint, continence). Against such things there is no law [that can bring a charge]. (Galatians 5:22–23)

If you have a personal relationship with the Lord—if you are saved—the Holy Spirit dwells within you (see John 14:16–17; 1

Corinthians 12:3). If joy is a fruit of the Spirit, and the Spirit is in you, joy is in you. You're not trying to get joy or manufacture it—it is already there, just as are the ability to love and the other fruit of the Spirit, because the Spirit is there.

It is very important to understand that we as believers are not to try to *get* joy—we *have* joy. Joy is in our spirit. What we need to do is learn how to release it.

A Calm Delight

But none of these things move me; neither do I esteem my life dear to myself, if only I may finish my course with joy and the ministry which I have obtained from [which was entrusted to me by] the Lord Jesus, faithfully to attest to the good news (Gospel) of God's grace (His unmerited favor, spiritual blessing, and mercy).

Acts 20:24

According to *Strong's* concordance, the root of the Greek word translated *joy* in this verse means "cheerfulness, i.e. calm delight."[1] Meanings of one Hebrew word for *joy* are "to rejoice; make glad; be joined."[2] Another Hebrew word translated *joy* can mean "to spin around."[3]

One of the meanings of *joy* in Nehemiah 8:10—"for the joy of the Lord is your strength and stronghold"—is "be joined." You can see that in order for the joy of the Lord to be your strength, you must be joined with God. Being joined with God causes joy in your life!

We can show forth the joy of the Lord in a way another of the meanings indicates by spinning around—in other words, with physical exuberance at times. But that doesn't mean we need to go around jumping up and down and twirling around in circles twenty-four hours a day!

Sometimes when people hear a message they recognize as truth, they want so much to apply it, they move into works—they try to make it happen in their own strength without allowing God to bring it to pass in their life as a result of prayer and God's power and timing. By saying sometimes we express God's joy by physical exuberance, I don't want to push anyone into doing this in the flesh.

When we don't feel joyful, we need to take some action to release joy before we start slipping into depression. Sometimes we must start in the flesh to rejoice whether we feel like it or not. It is like priming a pump by repeatedly moving the handle up and down until the pump kicks in and the water begins to flow.

I remember my grandparents had an old-time pump. Where they lived, folks didn't have running water in the kitchen back then. I can recall standing at the sink as a small child moving the pump handle up and down and sometimes feeling as though it would never take hold and start to supply water. It actually felt as if it was connected to nothing, and I was just pumping air.

But if I didn't give up, moving the handle up and down would soon become more difficult. That was a sign that water would start flowing shortly.

This is the way it is with joy. We have a well of water on the inside of our spirit. The pump handle to bring it up is physical exuberance—smiling, singing, laughing, and so forth. At first the physical expressions may not seem to be doing any good. And after a while it even gets harder, but if we keep it up, soon we will get a "gusher" of joy.

I don't think *joyful* means I am supposed to go around laughing hilariously all the time, spinning around, and jumping up and down with a plastic, frozen smile on my face. We need to use wisdom. I have had experiences with supposedly joy-filled Christians who actually hurt my feelings because they were insensitive.

I remember sharing something I was going through with a friend of mine. It was something that was really hurting me emotionally. Her response was a big smile and a loud, "Well, praise the Lord anyway!" I felt as if she had slapped me in the face.

If she had comforted me properly by showing understanding and concern, her ministry to me could have released real joy in my life. But her fleshly and phony reaction hurt me and made my situation worse.

When I first went to her, I was just sad. By the time she was finished with me, however, I was really depressed!

We always need to use wisdom. There may be times when we feel like spinning around in joy before the Lord. Maybe something really exciting has happened and we feel we can hardly contain it. But if we were in a restaurant or the grocery store, considering the feelings and reactions of those around us would be wise. We don't want to hurt our witness as Christians by doing things that make others think of us as emotional fanatics.

I've had occasions in a restaurant when I've told my family, "I feel like getting up on the top of this table and shouting, 'Praise the Lord!'"

There are times when an expression like that starts to come out of your inner man and you should give way to it. But if you're in a restaurant, grocery store, or some other public place, you might need to wait until you get in your car.

Although we can rejoice exuberantly at times, most of the time we rejoice by being glad and calmly happy. And, as the Lord showed me, that means smiling, or even simply living in a state of calm delight.

3

SMILING IS SERIOUS BUSINESS!

Joy cometh in the morning.

Psalm 30:5 (KJV)

I have a tendency to be a very serious, straight-faced individual. But I learned I also need to become very serious about smiling!

I was brought up in a bad situation and had a heaviness on my life. I didn't have a childhood—I was robbed of the joy of my youth. For as long as I can remember, I lived as if I were an adult because everything in my life was serious. I thought if I stayed serious, maybe I could stay alive. With this type of a background, you don't develop a bubbly, giggly kind of personality. I developed a serious attitude about me that can be misunderstood by people at times.

Once I told one of my assistants I needed to talk to her before she went home. She thought I was going to reprimand her for something. All I wanted was to talk to her about making preparations for an up-coming meeting. I had approached her so seriously, she felt she was in serious trouble!

I began seeking the Lord to find out how to be free from having such a seriousness about me. The Lord ministered to me that I need to express more of the joy that's in my heart. He knows it's there, but He wants it outside of us so that everyone can see it and benefit from it.

He ministered this to me while I was taking a shower one morning. I started to talk to Him, as I always do, when He spoke to my heart and said, "I wish you'd smile when you talk to Me."

My face didn't want to smile. At 6:00 A.M. it was stiff with sleep. But I started smiling! I felt kind of stupid smiling in my shower. I thought, *I'm glad no one can see me do this!*

Psalm 30:5 (KJV) tells us, "Joy cometh in the morning." When you open your eyes in the morning, joy is right there with you. You can't always feel joy until you activate it by purposely operating in it. Often the decision comes first, then feelings follow.

When the joy is obvious in your life, it rubs off on people. But when it's only inside you without being evident to others, you can create an atmosphere around you that is so serious, it brings a heaviness.

One night when Dave and I were talking, he said, "I feel there's almost too much seriousness in our home."

I started thinking about that. I asked the Lord, "God, there's nothing that I know of wrong in my life. I'm spending all my time praying, studying, loving You, and taking care of my family. What is this Dave is sensing?"

The Lord ministered to me that we can have a serious commitment in our heart without being so serious on the outside about it that everybody else doesn't know how to react to us.

I began to realize that as a homemaker I could set the climate in our home. Joy is of light, and sorrow is of darkness. The two cannot dwell together. If I wanted my home full of light, I needed to "lighten up." I realized I needed to smile more at the people in my own home—not just give the children orders about their homework and chores, but smile or have a pleasant look on my face while giving those instructions. I needed to take the time to laugh with them and with Dave.

I believe our homes should be happy places. We should operate in the joy of the Lord. If a woman is joyful, her husband will be glad to come home. Everyone wants to go to a happy place. If he has a grouchy boss and complaining coworkers, he doesn't want to come home to more of the same.

Of course, the husband and children should also do their part to make the home a happy place. Joy is infectious. One person gets it, then another, and another, and before you know it, everybody is happy!

Rejoicing Changes Your Circumstances

At times you reach a certain point in your walk with God in different areas and feel you're stuck there. You know there's much more, but you can sense something is blocking more from coming to you.

Dave and I reached that point in the area of prosperity. We had come from the point of having practically nothing to entering into a realm of at least not being concerned about how we were going to pay our bills. God was beginning to bless us. But I knew God had so much more for us.

God wants to bless us so much. He wants us to live in nice homes, drive nice cars, and be able to wear nice clothes. We are His children and He wants to take good care of us. Unbelievers should not have all the nice things while believers live on "barely-get-along" street.

There are certain things we do that bring prosperity because they set Bible principles into operation. When we give because we love the Lord and we want the gospel to go forth, we will receive (see Luke 6:38). When we tithe, God rebukes the devourer for our sake (see Malachi 3:10–11).

Dave and I were experiencing the kind of prosperity that results from giving and tithing, but because I sensed in my spirit it was time to go on into another level, I asked the Lord to show me what was blocking it. One of the things the Lord ministered to me was that joy is part of our receptacle to receive things from Him. Not showing outward joy in our life blocks prosperity from coming to us.

If the joy of the Lord is inside, but you don't smile and show forth the brightness of it, you'll look like a sourpuss. From a natural standpoint, how people see you has a great deal to do with their willingness toward you in many areas. People don't usually want to bless or help someone do something who looks like he might bite their head off because he looks so serious!

Every one of us knows how to smile. It's one of the greatest gifts God has given us. A smile makes people feel good, and people look so beautiful when they smile.

I would never have thought smiling was such a serious matter, but God spent several months trying to get this point across to me. Many times when God tries to tell us something and we don't heed it, we get ourselves in a mess before we realize how serious it is. Expressing joy through the calm delight of smiling will bring good things into your life besides showing forth the light of Jesus to others.

In the Bible the Lord told His people to rejoice when they faced their enemies. He told them to rejoice when they went into battle or when it looked as though they were going to die. He told them to rejoice no matter what—to sing, to praise with a loud voice (see 2 Chronicles 20).

When we are going through difficult times, we are to consider them wholly joyful. *The King James Version* says that we are to "count it *all* joy" (see James 1:1–5).

God spoke to my heart, "Most people really, truly do not understand how expressing joy will change their circumstances." Operating in the joy of the Lord will chase off circumstances that are not godly because they are full of the devil. The devil can't stand God's joy, so if we operate in that joy, the devil and the circumstances will move out of the way.

Releasing the spirit of joy in the morning stops the circumstances Satan is setting up before they ever get started that day.

4

~~~

SING AND SHOUT FOR JOY

Be glad in the Lord and rejoice, you [uncompromisingly] righteous
[you who are upright and in right standing with Him]; shout for joy,
all you upright in heart!

<div align="right">Psalm 32:11</div>

Let the word [spoken by] Christ (the Messiah) have its home [in your
hearts and minds] and dwell in you in [all its] richness, as you teach
and admonish and train one another in all insight and intelligence and
wisdom [in spiritual things, and as you sing] psalms and hymns and
spiritual songs, making melody to God with [His] grace in your
hearts. And whatever you do [no matter what it is] in word or deed, do
everything in the name of the Lord Jesus and in [dependence upon] His
Person, giving praise to God the Father through Him.

<div align="right">Colossians 3:16–17</div>

Sing Unto the Lord

We have already seen the power of joy and rejoicing in winning over depression.

In the above verse the apostle Paul tells us that one of the ways we are to express that joy and rejoicing in accordance with the Word of God is through the singing of psalms, hymns, and spiritual songs.

In Ephesians 5:19–20 Paul goes on to instruct us: "Speak out to one another in psalms and hymns and spiritual songs, offering praise with voices [and instruments] and making melody with all your heart to the Lord, at all times and for everything giving thanks in the name of our Lord Jesus Christ to God the Father." The *King James Version* of Ephesians 5:19 says, "Speaking to yourselves in psalms and hymns and spiritual songs, singing and making melody in your heart to the Lord."

Let's have happy conversation with others and in speaking what the Word says to ourselves.

Sing and Shout Deliverance!

You are a hiding place for me; You, Lord, preserve me from trouble, You surround me with songs and shouts of deliverance.

Psalm 32:7

Be glad in the Lord and rejoice, you [uncompromisingly] righteous [you who are upright and in right standing with Him]; shout for joy, all you upright in heart!

Psalm 32:11

In Psalm 5:11 David says to the Lord: "Let all those who take refuge and put their trust in You rejoice; let them ever sing and shout for joy, because You make a covering over them and defend them; let those also who love Your name be joyful in You and be in high spirits."

A few years ago a laundry product named Shout was advertised on television with the slogan, "Shout out tough stains!" That message prompted me to preach a message entitled, "Shout It Out!" In this message I encouraged believers that when Satan came around harassing and disturbing them, they should shout him out of their lives.

In my own life I used to be a screamer, but never a shouter. There is a difference. Finally the Lord came to me and said, "Joyce, either you will learn to start shouting or else you will end up screaming. Which do you want?"

So now when things start to go wrong in my life, instead of yelling and screaming at the top of my voice, I have learned to shout praise and glory to God. I "shout it out." You should try it—it beats screaming in anger and frustration.

Like David, I surround myself with singing and shouting. I have noticed that when I do that, I begin to feel better, because as David said, the singing and shouting act as a wall surrounding me on all sides.

But singing and shouting can also tear down walls and strong- holds! We read in Joshua 6:20 an account of the Lord directing the people to shout and bring down a wall: "So the people shouted, and the trumpets were blown. When the people heard the sound of the trumpet, they raised a great shout, and [Jericho's] wall fell down in its place, so that the [Israelites] went up into the city, every man straight before him, and they took the city."

Now that does not mean you and I are to go running all over town shouting at the top of our lungs wherever we may be! But at home there is nothing to prevent us from getting up in the morning with a song on our lips and praise in our mouth to the Lord God as a means to dispel depression.

I used to like the atmosphere to be as quiet as possible—espe- cially in the mornings. I wanted to think! Actually, though, instead of thinking productively, I ended up worrying and reasoning exces- sively about things for which I could have never figured out a solu- tion. What I needed to be doing was praying and trusting God about those things.

Within five or ten minutes after getting up in the morning, my husband would start singing or humming. He would have enjoyed listening to music, but I complained if he turned it on, telling him I wanted it quiet.

Since then, I have learned to listen to music as I start my day. During part of my prayer and fellowship time, I often listen to music.

God actually spoke very clearly to me in my heart on several oc- casions and told me that I did not listen to enough music. I had to develop a habit of doing it. At first, I did it in obedience. I was so used to quiet, I wanted it that way even though it wasn't always the best way to get my day started.

I don't mean to say that we don't need quiet because we do. God speaks in the still, quiet times, and they are precious. But I was out of balance. I needed to start my days happy, and the music helped me do that.

Even the great spiritual giant, David, had to battle with depression. We saw that David said to ever "sing and shout for joy." To overcome his downcast feelings and emotions, he used songs and shouts of deliverance. That's why so many of his psalms are songs of praise to God to be sung in the very midst of disturbing and unsettling situations.

When I am feeling down, I often go through the psalms and read them out loud, because I know that the promises in the Word of God will come to pass—as long as we don't just read it and confess it, but also do it, despite how we may feel at the time.

That is what Paul was referring to when he wrote to the Corinthians: "For you are still [unspiritual, having the nature] of the flesh [under the control of ordinary impulses]. For as long as [there are] envying and jealousy and wrangling and factions among you, are you not unspiritual and of the flesh, behaving yourselves after a human standard and like mere (unchanged) men?" (1 Corinthians 3:3).

In other words, these people were not doing what the Word of God told them to do, but were doing what they felt like doing. Paul said that by so doing they were not operating by the Spirit of God, but by their own flesh. In Galatians 6:8 he warned, "He who sows to his own flesh (lower nature, sensuality) will from the flesh reap decay and ruin and destruction, but he who sows to the Spirit will from the Spirit reap eternal life."

That is why we must learn to do as David did and speak to our soul, our inner self; otherwise, it will take control over us and lead us to decay, ruin and destruction.

Wait Expectantly for God

Why are you cast down, O my inner self? And why should you moan over me and be disquieted within me? Hope in God and wait expectantly for Him, for I shall yet praise Him, my Help and my God.

Psalm 42:5

Does your inner man ever feel cast down? Sometimes mine does. So did David's.

When he felt that way, when his soul was moaning and disquieted within him, David put his hope in God and waited expectantly for Him, praising Him as his Help and his God.

This must have been an important issue with David because in verse eleven of that same psalm he repeated almost the same words: "Why are you cast down, O my inner self? And why should you moan over me and be disquieted within me? Hope in God and wait expectantly for Him, for I shall yet praise Him, Who is the help of my countenance, and my God."

David knew that when he got down, his countenance went down with him. That is why he talked to himself, his soul (mind, will, and emotions), and encouraged and strengthened himself in the Lord (see 1 Samuel 30:6).

When we find ourselves in that same depressed state, we should wait expectantly for the Lord, praise Him Who is our Help and our God, and encourage and strengthen ourselves in Him.

We who are righteous—in right standing with God by believing in Jesus Christ—we who take refuge and put our trust in the Lord can sing and shout for joy! The Lord makes a covering over us and defends us. He fights our battles for us when we praise Him (see 2 Chronicles 20:17–22).

5

⁂

RESIST THE DEVIL AT THE ONSET

Withstand him; be firm in faith [against his onset].

1 Peter 5:9

There are many causes of depression—but only one source: Satan. He wants to keep us pressed down and feeling badly about ourselves so we won't receive all that Jesus died to give us. One of his biggest tools to try to make us feel bad about ourselves is condemnation.

Condemnation can certainly be a cause of depression. Satan uses it to steal our joy. He knows the "joy of the Lord" is our "strength" against him (see Nehemiah 8:10). Satan wants us weak and unable to do anything except put up with whatever he decides to throw on us.

People can also be depressed because of something that is wrong physically—sick people are frequently depressed; a chemical imbalance or being excessively tired and worn out can cause depression. If the body is depleted due to stress or lack of rest, the person may be restored simply by using wisdom and getting the needed rest and nutrition. If the depression is a medical depression, one that is caused from a chemical imbalance or other physical problems, obtaining proper physical help is prudent.

In other words, playing music or singing and shouting will not fix people who are in a state of collapse due to overwork, depressed because their body isn't functioning properly with their hormones or body chemicals out of balance. We must pay attention to the physical need also.

Depression can result from physical, mental, emotional, or spiritual causes. King David was depressed because he had unconfessed sin in his life (see Psalm 51). Jonah was depressed because he was running from the call of God and living in disobedience (see Jonah 1–2). Elijah was depressed because he was tired. First Kings 19:5–8 tells us the angel of the Lord fed him two good meals and let him get some sleep.

We cannot always put all the causes of a problem in one box and pull out one right answer. But Jesus always is the right answer, and no matter what cause Satan has used to bring depression, Jesus will lead us to victory when we follow Him. He will show each of us what we need to do in order to live joy-filled lives.

No matter what the cause, as soon as we feel depression coming on, we need to resist it immediately and take whatever action the Lord leads us to take.

Don't Flirt with the Devil

Don't play around with depression. As soon as we start feeling disappointed, we must say to ourselves, "I had better do something about this before it gets worse." If we don't, we will ultimately get discouraged, then depressed. Jesus gave us "the garment of praise for the spirit of heaviness" to put on (see Isaiah 61:3 KJV). If we don't use what He has given us, we will sink lower and lower into the pit of depression and could end up in real trouble.

When we know to do right and we don't do it, we are what I will call "flirting with the devil." In the world a man or woman might flirt with someone at the office, yet never move into a full-blown adulterous affair. But we cannot flirt with the devil like that. Once we open a door, he may get a foothold. Once he gets a foothold, he can obtain a stronghold. He is progressive and aggressive in his action against us, and we must be aggressive against him.

I remember when God revealed to me how wrong self-pity is. He told me that I could not be pitiful and powerful. I had lived in self-pity most of the time. At that time, I made a real commitment not to allow that negative emotion to rule my life any longer. When something didn't go my way, and I felt like feeling sorry for myself, I re-sisted the feeling right away. If I had let it go on, I would have moved deeper and deeper into it.

I recall one time thinking that I wanted to feel that way only for a while and then I would pull myself out of it. I was sitting in my prayer chair drinking my morning coffee. Dave had hurt my feelings so I wanted to feel sorry for myself. I knew I could not stay that way but was not ready to give it up just yet. The Lord showed me that by my not wanting to give up that feeling immediately, it was as if I wanted to have one cup of coffee with Mr. Pity. That may not sound too harmful, but it might be all the time the devil needs to get a stronghold that cannot be easily broken.

God covers us to a greater degree when we're ignorant and really don't know what we're doing. But once we know what is right and we willfully choose to do wrong, it puts us in a different arena. God still loves us and still wants to help us, but we have a greater degree of accountability. Knowledge gives us accountability.

Someone handed the following story to me during a conference where I was teaching on sin and how to handle it. It really brings across the point I am making.

> A young girl was walking along a mountainous path. Making her way up the mountain it became very cold. While on her journey a snake approached her. The snake said, "Please pick me up, I am cold." The girl said, "I can't do that." The snake said, "Oh, please make me warm." She gave in and said, "You can hide inside my coat." The snake coiled itself and became warm. The girl thought everything was okay. Suddenly the snake bit her. She dropped the snake and said, "I trusted you; why did you bite me?" The snake said, "You knew what I was when you picked me up."

If we flirt with the devil, we will always get hurt. Refusing to put on the garment of praise because we don't feel like it or don't want to is dangerous. It opens a door for deeper problems that can cause serious consequences.

Resist Depression Immediately

Be well balanced (temperate, sober of mind), be vigilant and cautious at all times; for that enemy of yours, the devil, roams around like a lion roaring [in fierce hunger], seeking someone to seize upon and devour. Withstand him; be firm in faith [against his onset—rooted, established, strong, immovable, and determined], knowing that the same (identical) sufferings are appointed to your brotherhood (the whole body of Christians) throughout the world.

1 Peter 5:8–9

Resisting Satan at his onset will stop extended bouts of depression.

We resist the devil by submitting ourselves to God and by wielding the sword of the Spirit, which is His Word (see Ephesians 6:17).

When Jesus was tempted three times by Satan in the wilderness, He did not get all wild and emotional. He simply said, "It is written . . . It is written . . . It is written" (see Luke 4:4, 8, 12). That is the way we are to resist Satan when he comes to tempt us into condemnation, depression, or any other wrong thing he is trying to give us.

You and I must realize and remember that depression is not part of our inheritance in Jesus Christ. It is not part of God's will for His children. Anytime we feel anything that is not part of the will of God for us, that is when we need to begin to wield the sharp, two-edged sword of the Word (see Hebrews 4:12).

The Bible has promised that if we will do that, if we will resist Satan firmly at his onset, he will flee from us (see James 4:7; 1 Peter 5:8–9).

The moment we begin to experience any feelings of depression brought on by condemnation or guilt or remorse or regret, we need to stand on the Word of God and refuse to allow those negative feelings to weigh upon us and depress us.

In Isaiah 61:1–3 we see that Jesus was anointed and sent by God to preach the gospel of good tidings to the poor in spirit, to bind up and heal the brokenhearted, to proclaim liberty to the captives, to open the prison doors and the eyes of those who are bound, and to grant consolation and joy to those who mourn—to give them an ornament of beauty instead of ashes, the oil of joy instead of mourning, and a garment of praise instead of a heavy, burdened, and failing spirit.

In Christ There Is No Condemnation

Therefore, [there is] now no condemnation (no adjudging guilty of wrong) for those who are in Christ Jesus, who live [and] walk not after the dictates of the flesh, but after the dictates of the Spirit.

Romans 8:1

According to this Scripture, we who are in Christ Jesus are no longer condemned, no longer judged guilty or wrong. Yet so often we judge and condemn ourselves.

In my own case, until I learned and understood the Word of God, I lived a large part of my life feeling guilty. If someone had asked me what I felt guilty about, I could not have answered. All I knew was that there was a vague feeling of guilt that followed me around all the time. Fortunately, when I came to better understand the Word of the Lord, I was able to overcome that nagging feeling.

But not too long ago I went through a short period in which I felt that old sense of guilt. It took me a couple of days to recognize what was happening, because I had not had a problem like that for a long time.

From that experience, God gave me a real revelation about walking free from guilt and condemnation. He showed me that you and I must not only receive forgiveness from Him, we must also forgive ourselves. We must stop beating ourselves over the head for something He has forgiven and forgotten (see Jeremiah 31:34; Acts 10:15).

That does not mean that we are now perfect or incapable of error. It just means we can go on with our lives without being weighed down with a constant burden of guilt and condemnation for what is in the past.

As long as we are doing the best we can, we truly repent for our sins, and our heart is right before God, we can stay out from under the burden of guilt and condemnation.

God not only looks at what we do, He looks at our heart. He

knows that if our heart is right, our actions will eventually come into line with our heart.

During the period I was going through feelings of guilt and condemnation, everything I did bothered me. I felt guilty and condemned for every little mistake I made. Finally I told my husband, "Dave, I believe I am being attacked by a spirit of condemnation."

That happens from time to time to each of us. We may wake up one day and for no apparent reason suddenly feel that we have done something wrong. If that feeling continues, we may begin to ask ourselves, "What's wrong with me?"

That is when we need to exercise the spiritual authority that has been given to us over the demonic forces in the name and by the blood of Jesus. That is when we need to use the Word of God to overcome the powers that would try to rob us of our peace and joy in the Lord.

God Wants to Help You

Some people born with more of an "up" personality don't have problems with depression. But there are many others, including born-again, Spirit-filled Christians, who suffer from it regularly.

If you are suffering from depression, know that God loves you more than you can imagine and cares about your problem. He doesn't want you to have to suffer with it anymore. But if you do become depressed again, which you may, you don't need to become guilty or feel condemned over it.

I apply in my life the principles in this book on a regular basis. If I didn't, I could end up depressed four to five days a week.

I believe it is nearly impossible to get depressed if the mind is kept under strict control. That is why we are told in Isaiah 26:3 that God will guard and keep us in perfect and constant peace—if we will keep our mind stayed on Him.

If we are in perfect and constant peace, then we will not be depressed. Ninety-nine-and-nine-tenths percent of our problems begin in our mind.

> You will guard him and keep him in perfect and constant
> peace whose mind [both its inclination and its character] is

stayed on You, because he commits himself to You, leans on You, and hopes confidently in You. So trust in the Lord (commit yourself to Him, lean on Him, hope confidently in Him) forever; for the Lord God is an everlasting Rock [the Rock of Ages]. (Isaiah 26:3–4)

6

REJECTION, FAILURE AND
UNFAIR COMPARISONS

Although my father and my mother have forsaken me, yet the Lord will take me up [adopt me as His child].

Psalm 27:10

Rejection causes depression. To be rejected means to be thrown away as having no value or as being unwanted. We were created for acceptance, not rejection. The emotional pain of rejection is one of the deepest kinds known. Especially if the rejection comes from someone we love or expect to love us, like parents or a spouse.

I once knew a woman who was deeply depressed most of the time even though she was a Christian and had a lovely family. Her depression seemed to stem from the fact that she was adopted. She said she had a deep feeling that something was wrong with her and because of that she was unwanted. She expressed it as a big hole in her heart that nothing seemed to fill up.

She desperately needed to *receive* the love of God. I emphasize "receive" because many people mentally assent that God loves them, even saying it, but it is not a reality in their life.

Psalm 27:10 says, "Although my father and my mother have forsaken me, yet the Lord will take me up [adopt me as His child]."

God had accepted her and loved her very much, but she was ruining her life trying to get something she would never have—the love of her natural parents.

This longing made her feel depressed. Satan had taken advantage of her emotions through this open door early in her life. Depression had become a habitual pattern. She was so accustomed to feeling that way, just floating along in those same old negative feelings was easy.

When we are saved by Jesus from our sins, our emotions are not saved. We may still "feel" many negative things. But at that moment or time of salvation—the time when we accept Jesus Christ as our Lord and Savior and believe in Him—we do receive the fruit of the Holy Spirit.

One of the fruits is the fruit of self-control (see Galatians 5:23). It is this fruit that will save us from all these negative emotions. We learn what God's Word says about emotions, then we begin with the help of the Holy Spirit to control the negative ones and not give them expression through our bodies which now belong to Jesus Christ.

This young woman, although a Christian, was living in the carnal realm. She was following ordinary impulses. She needed to begin getting her worth and value out of the fact that Jesus loved her enough to die for her and stop feeling that she was unloved and valueless because her parents did not keep her. She eventually got the victory, but it was a long, hard battle.

If you have been depressed it might be due to a root of rejection in your life. Overcoming rejection is certainly not easy, but we can overcome it through the love of Jesus Christ.

In Ephesians 3:18–19 Paul prayed for the church that they would know "the breadth and length and height and depth" of the love God had for them and that they would experience it for themselves. He said this experience far surpasses mere knowledge.

Watch for all the ways that God shows His love for you, and it will overcome the rejection you may have experienced from other people.

While I was working on this chapter of the book I received a phone call letting me know that a certain very well-known pastor had called. He has many wonderful meetings in his church, but had never wanted to make his building available for other ministries to use. This pastor had absolutely never allowed ministries like mine to use his church auditorium to hold a conference, but he called stating that God had placed on his heart to let us use it!

We had outgrown the church we had been using previously and were at the point of needing to quit using that building because we couldn't fit in it. The only option we saw was to rent a civic center which can sometimes be very costly and usually involves a lot of red tape.

So often we just let things that happen like that go by without realizing they are from God Who is showing His love for us. Every time God gives us favor, He is showing us that He loves us. There are many, many ways He shows His love for us all the time; we simply need to begin watching for them. Having a deep revelation concerning God's love for us will keep us from depression.

When people reject us, Jesus takes it personally.

Luke 10:16 states: "He who hears and heeds you [disciples] hears and heeds Me; and he who slights and rejects you slights and rejects Me; and he who slights and rejects Me slights and rejects Him Who sent Me."

Think about it—even if someone slights us, Jesus takes it personally. It is an evil thing for one person to reject another. James 2:8–9 teaches us that love is the new law and that "if you show servile regard (prejudice, favoritism) for people, you commit sin and are rebuked and convicted by the Law as violators and offenders." We are breaking that law of love.

Although rejection is an evil thing, we don't have to allow the evil to control our emotions and depress us. Romans 12:21 states, "Do not let yourself be overcome by evil, but overcome (master) evil with good."

Putting a smile on our face and being joyful on purpose is a good thing, and it will overcome the evil of rejection and the result of depression.

Failure

We are programmed by society to believe that winning is everything and that success means living without failure. I personally believe that failure is part of true success.

What I mean is this: Everyone on their way up has a few things to learn. One of those things is humility. People are not just automatically humble; we all deal with a generous portion of pride. A few rounds of failure works humility into our character very quickly!

Peter was a powerful apostle. We might say he was a success and made it to the top—he obeyed the Lord and allowed Him to accomplish great things for the kingdom of God through him. But Peter failed miserably when he denied three times that he even knew Jesus.

Paul also was a mighty man of God, yet he stated that he had weaknesses. David was a tremendous king and psalmist and prophet, but he failed in that he committed adultery with Bathsheba and arranged to have her husband Uriah killed.

I have a very successful ministry now, but I sure made a lot of mistakes and failed at various times on my way to the position I now have. I thought I was hearing from God at times, then discovered I wasn't. I stepped out in things that were not God's will for me and had to back down, sometimes very embarrassed. I failed to always treat people with the love and mercy that Jesus would have.

My failures disappointed me and sometimes discouraged and even depressed me. As a matter of fact that was my normal response until I realized that God was using my weaknesses, turning them to the good to develop my character and make me a better person.

No person has truly failed until they stop trying. I keep the outlook that Satan may knock me down, but he is not going to knock me out. Failing at something is quite different from being a failure. We must learn to separate our *who* and our *do*. I may do something that I fail at, but *I* am not a failure. I am a child of God who is still being changed into His image, from glory to glory (see 2 Corinthians 3:18).

It is really not failure that causes depression; it is our attitude toward it. If we believe God is greater than our failures, then they have no power over us! Our weaknesses are an opportunity for Him to show His strength.

Romans 5:20 says, "Where sin abounded, grace did much more abound" (KJV). How can anyone fail with a system like that set in motion on their behalf?

Don't be depressed over weaknesses and failures. Rejoice in knowing that because of Jesus, you don't have to stay that way. People without the Lord in their lives only have depression to go to when they fail, but we can go to Jesus. That should make us happy, not sad!

Remember that you are no surprise to God. He knew what He was getting when He chose you, the same as He knew what He was getting when He chose me. Ephesians 1:4 says, "He chose us [actually picked us out for Himself as His own] in Christ before the foundation of the world." He already knew every weakness, every flaw, every time we would ever fail, and He still said, "I want you." Ephesians 1:5 states that He foreordained us to be adopted as His own children.

I think I'll be happy—God is my daddy! With God on our side things are bound to work out all right in the end. So let's rejoice now and not waste all that time being sad.

Unfair Comparisons

Comparing our lives with other people's lives frequently causes depression. We can look at other people and wonder why we don't look like they look, know what they know, own what they own or do what they do. But it's interesting to note that Satan never points out what they don't have, only what they do have that we don't have.

Others may have some things we don't, but we also have some things they don't have. We must believe that God equipped each of us with just what we need to fulfill His call on our lives. If I don't have it, I must not need it, or it just isn't time yet for me to have it.

I spent many unhappy, depressed days comparing myself with other people. Why couldn't I cast my care like Dave? Why couldn't I be sweet, merciful, and submissive like my pastor's wife? Why couldn't I sew like my neighbor? Why can't I have a faster working metabolism so I can eat more and not gain weight? Why? Why? Why?

God never answered me except with the same answer he gave Peter when he compared himself with John. In John 21:18–22 Jesus had told Peter that Peter was going to enter a time of suffering. He was speaking of the kind of death Peter would die and thereby glorify God.

Peter's initial response was to ask what was going to happen to John. Jesus promptly said, "If I want him to stay (survive, live) until I come, what is that to you? [What concern is it of yours?] You follow Me!" (v. 22).

It sounds to me as if Jesus was politely telling Peter to mind his own business, not compare himself with John. The Lord has an individual plan for each of us, and often we can't understand what He is doing or why He is doing it.

We look at other people as the standard for what should happen to us, but they cannot be the standard because God sets a new standard with each person. That we all have a different set of fingerprints is proof enough we are not to compete with one another and live in unfair comparisons.

It is unfair to compare ourselves with others. It is unfair to us, to them, and to God. It pressures relationships and says to God, "I want to limit You to this and nothing else." What if God ends up giving you something far greater than anyone you know?

We would be satisfied with what we see other people have, but God can go beyond that for the person who will trust Him. Galatians 5:26 teaches us not to be "envying" and "jealous" of one another, "competitive," in that regard.

Proverbs 14:30 says, "Envy, jealousy, and wrath are like rottenness of the bones." Depression feels just like that—"rottenness of the bones." Everything feels as if it has caved in.

Galatians 6:4 tells us to do "something commendable [in itself alone] without [resorting to] boastful comparison" with our neighbor. In other words our goal should be to be "the very best me I can be," to just do what we believe we are supposed to do without seeking to do something greater than someone else so we can feel better about ourselves.

When our value as an individual is firmly rooted in Christ, we are free from the agony of comparisons and competition. That kind of freedom releases joy. Depression is the result of looking at what we don't have and can't do. Joy is the result of being thankful for every little thing we have and counting ourselves blessed just to be alive and to know Jesus as our Lord.

Depression Begets Depression

Our associations are very important, for we can become like whomever we are around. Daniel was a great man of integrity and excellence, but I noticed that his friends were the same way. Daniel would not compromise, but neither would Shadrach, Meshach, and Abednego.

A depressed, gloomy, negative person is very unpleasant to be around. If those around the person are not careful, they will find themselves starting to feel the same way the depressed person does.

If you have to be around someone regularly that is depressed, keep yourself covered by faith with the blood of Jesus for protection against the spirit of depression. Be sure you are more aggressive against depression than it is against you.

Psalm 1:1 tells us not to sit inactive in the pathway of sinners. I firmly believe in trying to help people, and this would include depressed people, but sometimes they don't want help, they just want to be depressed.

I have dealt with individuals who were so negative, no matter what kind of good things I tried to point out, they would always come back with something sour and negative. I was that way myself for a good number of years, and it would actually make me mad when someone would try to cheer me up.

I can well remember how Dave would persist in being happy no matter how gloomy I was. His joy actually made me angry!

Depressed people want others to be depressed. Joy irritates them. Actually it irritates the evil spirit that is oppressing them. I am not saying that people who are depressed are all possessed by the devil. I am saying that depression is the result of an evil spirit oppressing us.

We know that all wicked and evil things come from Satan and his demons, so let's face it for what it is and not be offended.

If you are someone who is being attacked with bouts of depression and you sincerely want to overcome it, one of the things you can do is make sure you spend time with happy people. Dave's joy irritated me in my depressed days, but his stability and joy also made me hungry for what he had.

I learned from being around him how to handle situations. I saw how differently he handled things from the way I handled them, and I began to realize that his joy was not due to his never having any challenges in life—it was due to how he handled them, his attitude toward them.

Spirits and anointings are transferable. That is why we lay hands on people, which is a biblical doctrine. Seventy men were chosen to help Moses in the ministry to which God called him. First God said to bring them to the tent of meeting and let them stand there with him, then He would come and take of the Spirit upon Moses and put it upon them.

First they had to just get around Moses—just stand there with him—and God would see to it that the Spirit on him got on them. It's a powerful principle!

I needed a lot of change in my personality. One of the things I needed most was stability in my moods. God understood why I was the way I was. There were many things that had happened to me over the years that developed the moodiness in my emotional nature. But He also arranged for my healing. He surrounded me in my personal life with people who were extremely stable.

My husband was one, and so was a couple that has lived with Dave and me for eleven years and taken care of our home and ministry when we are traveling. Paul and Roxane are both very stable.

I talk with all three of these people almost daily, eat most of my meals with them, watch movies with them, shop with them, go to church with them, make plans with them, and so on. I was so surrounded by happy, stable people that I looked like a big spot or blemish until I changed. Their joy and stability convicted me and I am glad for it. That is what happy, joy-filled, stable people can do for you.

So if you're battling depression, remember that your associations are very important. Don't associate with depressed people if you need to get over depression yourself!

The last thing we need when we are experiencing bouts of depression is to get together with other discouraged, depressed people and talk about all of our problems. We need to laugh, sing, rejoice, shout occasionally, and think about happy things.

7

❧

LISTEN TO WHAT GOD SAYS ABOUT YOU

To the praise of the glory of his grace, wherein he hath made us accepted in the beloved.

Ephesians 1:6 (KJV)

God does not want us to feel frustrated and condemned. He wants us to realize we are pleasing to Him just as we are.

The devil keeps trying to tell us what we are not, but God keeps trying to tell us what we are—His beloved children who are well pleasing to Him.

God never reminds us how far we have fallen, He always reminds us how far we have risen. He reminds us of how much we have overcome, how well we are doing, how precious we are in His sight, how much He loves us.

The devil tells us we cannot possibly be acceptable to God because we are not perfect, but God tells us that we are accepted in the Beloved because of what He has already done for us (see Ephesians 1:6 KJV).

God wants us to know that His hand is upon us, that His angels are watching over us, that His Holy Spirit is right there in us and with us to help us in everything we do.

He wants us to know that Jesus is our Friend, and that as we walk with Him day by day good things are going to take place in our lives.

If you and I will listen to God rather than to the devil, He will cheer us up and make us feel good about ourselves. He will give us peace about the past, joy for the present, and hope for the future.

Remember: The joy of the Lord is our strength and our stronghold.

Conclusion

The principles that will change your life usually aren't complicated. By applying the principle of rejoicing at the onset of something that would cause you depression, your situation will change.

Part Two

───── ✧ ─────

Scriptures to Overcome Depression

When the righteous cry for help, the Lord hears, and delivers them out of all their distress and troubles. (Psalm 34:17)

I waited patiently and expectantly for the Lord; and He inclined to me and heard my cry. He drew me up out of a horrible pit [a pit of tumult and of destruction], out of the miry clay (froth and slime), and set my feet upon a rock, steadying my steps and establishing my goings. And He has put a new song in my mouth, a song of praise to our God. (Psalm 40:1–3)

My whole being follows hard after You and clings closely to You; Your right hand upholds me. (Psalm 63:8)

I wait for the Lord, I expectantly wait, and in His word do I hope. (Psalm 130:5)

A gentle tongue [with its healing power] is a tree of life, but willful contrariness in it breaks down the spirit. (Proverbs 15:4)

Arise [from the depression and prostration in which circumstances have kept you—rise to a new life]! Shine (be radiant with the glory of the Lord), for your light has come, and the glory of the Lord has risen upon you! (Isaiah 60:1)

The Spirit of the Lord God is upon me, because the Lord has anointed and qualified me to preach the Gospel of good tidings to the meek, the poor, and afflicted; He has sent me to bind up and heal the brokenhearted, to proclaim liberty to the [physical and spiritual] captives and the opening of the prison and of the eyes to those who are bound, to proclaim the acceptable year of the Lord [the year of His favor] and the day of vengeance of our God, to comfort all who mourn, to grant [consolation and joy] to those who mourn in Zion—to give them an ornament (a garland or diadem) of beauty instead of ashes, the oil of joy instead of mourning, the garment [expressive] of praise instead of a heavy, burdened, and failing spirit. (Isaiah 61:1–3)

For God Who said, Let light shine out of darkness, has shone in our hearts so as [to beam forth] the Light for the illumination of the knowledge of the majesty and glory of God [as it is manifest in the Person and is revealed] in the face of Jesus Christ (the Messiah). (2 Corinthians 4:6)

Do not fret or have any anxiety about anything, but in every circumstance and in everything, by prayer and petition (definite requests), with thanksgiving, continue to make your wants known to God. And God's peace [shall be yours, that tranquil state of a soul assured of its salvation through Christ, and so fearing nothing from God and being content with its earthly lot of whatever sort that is, that peace] which transcends all understanding shall garrison and mount guard over your hearts and minds in Christ Jesus. For the rest, brethren, whatever is true, whatever is worthy of reverence and is honorable and seemly, whatever is just, whatever is pure, whatever is lovely and loveable, whatever is kind and winsome and gracious, if there is any virtue and excellence, if there is anything worthy of praise, think on and weigh and take account of these things [fix your minds on them]. (Philippians 4:6–8)

Prayer to Overcome Depression

Father,

In the name of Jesus, I come to You bearing the burden of my depression. It is a burden I do not need, and I leave it at Your feet now, O Lord.

Replace these downcast feelings with Your joy. Your grace is sufficient for me.

I am coming into agreement with Your Word. I need to be in Your presence. It is in You that I live and move and have my being!

Thank you!

STRAIGHT TALK ON *Discouragement*

CONTENTS

INTRODUCTION

We have all been disappointed at one time or another. In fact, it would be surprising if we went through the week without encountering some kind of disappointment. We are "appointed" (set in a certain direction) for something to happen a certain way, and when it doesn't happen that way, we become "dis-appointed."

Disappointment not dealt with turns into discouragement. If we stay discouraged very long, we are liable to become devastated, and devastation leaves us unable to handle anything.

Many devastated Christians are lying along the roadside of life because they have not learned how to handle disappointment. The devastation they are experiencing now most likely began with a minor disappointment not dealt with.

Jesus healed all who were oppressed by the devil (see Acts 10:38 KJV). It is not God's will for us to live disappointed, devastated, or oppressed! When we become "disappointed," we must learn to become "re-appointed" to keep from becoming discouraged, then devastated.

When we learn to place our hope and confidence in Jesus the Rock (see 1 Corinthians 10:4) and resist the devil at the onset, we can live in the joy and peace of the Lord, free from discouragement.

Part One

FREE FROM OPPRESSION

1

⁂

THE GREATER ONE LIVES IN US

God anointed and consecrated Jesus of Nazareth with the [Holy] Spirit and with strength and ability and power; . . . He went about doing good and, in particular, curing all who were harassed and oppressed by [the power of] the devil, for God was with Him.

Acts 10:38

During His earthly ministry, Jesus' calling—we could even say "His job"—was to go about in the anointing of the Holy Spirit upon Him and deliver all those who were oppressed by the devil. That power is available to us today. It is not God's will for His children to be harassed or oppressed, and Jesus' power is available to deliver us from oppression today.

According to *Webster's* dictionary, to oppress is "to weigh heavily upon," especially "so as to depress the mind or spirits."[1] Other meanings are "to crush or overwhelm," to press down.

I believe the enemy, Satan, can oppress not only our mind or spirit but any part of our being, including our body and soul. Sometimes he does so without our even knowing what specifically is bothering us.

At times each of us has had something weigh heavily upon us. Most of us have experienced oppression to the point of it being hard to think and make decisions. At other times we have been oppressed physically.

We must keep in mind that Satan at various times will try to oppress different parts of our being in different ways for different reasons. We have the power available to us through Jesus to be aggressive against the devil. If we aren't aggressive toward him, he will be aggressive toward us.

Although the devil is the root of all evil, there are things we do in the flesh that can cause us to feel overwhelmed or bring a heaviness on us. We can feel overwhelmed by not dealing with little problems as they occur. People who gossip, complain, backbite, and judge can experience a feeling of heaviness.

In order for us to feel uplifted, as though there were a spring of living water flowing out of us, we must resist the devil who tries to oppress us, and all his ways. But we must also refuse to bring oppression and depression upon ourselves. And most important, we must aggressively tackle the things God tells us to do. When we obey God we will undertake some challenging projects. But the Lord gives us His Spirit to powerfully work in us to enable us to do what He has asked.

Again according to Webster, to be aggressive is to initiate forceful action, to be "energetic" or "boldly assertive"—"enterprising," which itself means to be imaginative.[2]

As it was originally created by God, the power of man to imagine is not meant to be some kind of wicked, evil thing. It is the creative imagination of man that keeps coming up with new ideas and bringing forth new processes through innovative thoughts. Think how creative Adam must have been to name all the animals in his holy state before he fell into sin. Some of us have trouble coming up with a name for our dog!

Led by the Spirit

By following the leading of the Holy Spirit and allowing the fruit of the Spirit (see Galatians 5:22–23) to be evident in our lives, we are initiators and innovators. We can purposefully bring forth the creative ability of God that is on the inside of us. Many people are bored because they are in an "oppressed" state rather than in a "godly aggressive" state. Exercising our God-given creativity eliminates boredom!

Some of us are naturally more creative, imaginative, innovative, and aggressive than others. But each of us can use the creativity, imagination, innovativeness, and aggression that God has placed within us to make our lives more satisfying, productive, and fulfilling.

Instead of waiting for something to come on us, we can initiate. For example, instead of waiting for others to be friendly toward us, we can initiate friendships.

Keep the Devil on the Run

The devil lies to us (see John 8:44). If we aren't aggressive against him and don't stop listening to his lies, he will run our life. He goes about *like* a roaring lion (see 1 Peter 5:8), but we have the Lion of Judah, Jesus, inside us. We are the ones who should be doing the roaring!

When the devil makes one move toward us, we should keep ourselves so spiritually attuned that we pick up exactly what he's trying to do and back him down. It should take only a few seconds.

The devil is always trying to come against us. As long as we back down, he keeps on coming. If we make one move against him in the authority Jesus made available to us, the devil has to back down.

We need to continue standing in our authority against him. If we stop, he will start moving against us, backing us up. The devil is a liar, a bully, a bluff, a deceiver. He comes *like* a lion, but he is not the lion. We believers in Jesus Christ have the power of the greater one on the inside of us. "Greater is he that is in you, than he that is in the world" (1 John 4:4 KJV).

Know the Word well enough that the minute a thought comes into your head that doesn't line up with God's Word, you can say to the devil, "*Liar!* No, I'm not listening to you."

You can spend your life backing up and hiding from the devil, or you can spend it forcing him to back up.

Choose Life

I call heaven and earth to witness this day against you that I have set before you life and death, the blessings and the curses; therefore choose life, that you and your descendants may live.

Deuteronomy 30:19

Happiness and joy do not come from the outside. They come from within. They are a conscious decision, a deliberate choice, one that we make ourselves each day we live.

In our ministry we have a young woman working for us who has many things she would like to see changed in her life. But despite those challenges, she is happy and joyous.

This young woman is filled with happiness and joy not because she doesn't have any problems but because of the decision she has made to enjoy her life and work in the midst of adversity.

Every day she has a choice: to be filled with misery or to be filled with the joy of the Lord.

That is the same choice each of us faces every day of our life.

Either we choose to passively listen to the devil and allow him to ruin our life and make us miserable, or we choose to aggressively withstand him so we can live in the fullness of life God has provided for us through His Son Jesus Christ.

Either way we will still get to heaven. But do we want to get to heaven and discover how much fun we could have had on the way? Let's choose life now and enjoy life in the way God desires.

2

❧

WATCH AND PRAY

All of you must keep awake (give strict attention, be cautious and active) and watch and pray, that you may not come into temptation. The spirit indeed is willing, but the flesh is weak.

Matthew 26:41

Suppose you knew that your house was surrounded by enemy agents and that at any moment they might break through the door and attack you. Do you think you would be inclined to stay awake and watch the door?

What would you do if for some reason you couldn't stay awake and watch? Wouldn't you make sure someone else in the family was aroused and alerted to the danger?

In this verse, Jesus tells us to keep awake, to give strict attention, to be cautious and active, and to watch and pray.

As believers, we are to be constantly alert, alive, and watchful. Then, if necessary, we must be ready to take up arms against the attack of the enemy.

Be a Fighter

Fight the good fight of the faith.

1 Timothy 6:12

To be aggressive is to be a fighter.

Just as the apostle Paul said that he had fought the good fight of faith (see 2 Timothy 4:7), so he instructed his young disciple Timothy to fight the good fight of faith.

In the same way, you and I are to fight the good fight of faith in our daily lives as we struggle against spiritual enemies in high places and in our own mind and heart.

One part of fighting the good fight of faith is being able to recognize the enemy, knowing when things are normal and when things are wrong. Let me give you an example.

Some time ago I was engaged in a conversation with a certain individual. As I was listening to this person, confusion began to set in. I realized that this happened every time I tried to talk to this person.

Usually I would just go off thinking, "I wonder what's wrong. I don't understand why this happens." I just wasn't comfortable with the person.

The more I thought about it, the more I came to see what the problem was. Every time we would meet and talk I would begin to worry about whether this individual misunderstood something I had done.

The next time we met the same feeling began to rise up in me. But this time I took a more aggressive approach. I just stopped and prayed, "In the name of Jesus Christ, I take authority over this spirit. I am not going to worry. If this person does not like what I did, that is between them and God.

"I have to be free. I can't go all my life making decisions based on what everybody else is going to think. Satan, I will not have this worry. In the name of Jesus, it's over!"

I took a stand, and freedom rushed in. As long as I was passive, Satan tormented me.

That's our problem. We are too passive. Too often we don't move against the enemy when he comes against us with worry or fear or doubt or guilt. We just draw back into a corner somewhere and let him beat us up.

You and I are not supposed to be punching bags for the devil; instead, we are supposed to be fighters.

Now the devil wants us to fight in the natural with everybody around us. But God wants us to forget all the junk that Satan stirs up within us to get us riled up against other people. Instead, He wants us to fight against the spiritual enemies who try to war over our lives and steal our peace and joy.

What Is Normal?

For wherever there is jealousy (envy) and contention (rivalry and selfish ambition), there will also be confusion (unrest, disharmony, rebellion) and all sorts of evil and vile practices. But the wisdom from above is first of all pure (undefiled); then it is peace-loving, courteous (considerate, gentle). [It is willing to] yield to reason, full of compassion and good fruits; it is wholehearted and straight-forward, impartial and unfeigned (free from doubts, wavering, and insincerity).

James 3:16–17

Confusion is not the normal state for a born-again believer, at least not as far as God is concerned. So anytime we feel confusion rising up within us, we need to attack it.

But too often we just go along thinking something is wrong with us rather than realizing the problem is that we are under spiritual attack.

Another mistake we make is trying to figure out everything instead of watching and praying as Jesus commanded us.

Anytime you begin to feel abnormal, anytime you begin to feel oppressed or heavy in spirit, watch and pray. That is how you move into praying without ceasing (see 1 Thessalonians 5:17). You are ready at any time you sense a need to pray.

But what is normal for the believer? In order to answer that question let's begin by looking at what is not normal.

It is not normal to worry. It is not normal to be tormented by reasoning, trying to figure out things for which we do not have the answers. It is not normal to be plagued by thoughts of what everybody is going to think of us. It is not normal to be depressed, to feel heavy, to think we are no good. It is not normal to feel we are a failure.

These things may have become normal to some people, but God never intended for these things to be normal. He never intended for

life to be that way—for us to live in a state of constant turmoil or
torment from our thoughts.

When these kinds of thoughts come upon us, we should be able
to recognize them for what they are—lies of the enemy.

In his book, *The Spiritual Man*, under the section entitled,
"Weights on the Spirit," Watchman Nee wrote that in those situations, "The spirit needs to be in a state of perfect freedom. It should
always be light as though floating in the air . . . A Christian ought to
realize what the weights laid on his spirit are. Often he feels it is
under oppression, as if a thousand pound load were pressing upon
his heart . . . It is employed by the enemy to harass the spiritual, to
deprive him of joy and lightness, as well as to disable his spirit from
working together with the Holy Spirit . . . A free spirit is the basis for
victory . . . Whenever the spirit suffers oppression the mind cannot
function properly."[1]

All our parts work together. We need to keep ourselves in a state
of freedom and a state of normalcy. To do that, we must keep ourselves under the leadership of the Lord Jesus Christ.

The Lordship of Christ

*[We] refute arguments and theories and reasonings and every
proud and lofty thing that sets itself up against the [true] knowledge of God; and we lead every thought and purpose away captive
into the obedience of Christ (the Messiah, the Anointed One).*

2 Corinthians 10:5

The Lord will give us the victory over the devil, but He will do that
only as we cry out to Him and ask Him to get involved in our problems.

Nothing is going to change about our situation if all we do is just
sit and wish things were different. We have got to take action.

The Lord is ready, willing, and able to do something for His people in the areas of passivity, apathy, laziness, lethargy, and procrasti-
nation—all the things that wrap themselves around us and drag us
down into depression, discouragement, and despair. But we have a
part to play also.

We are not a people called to function according to the way we feel. We are a people who are called to take hold of the Word of God and apply it to our lives daily. In order to do that we must stay spiritually alert—at all times.

3

❦

Six Things to Do Aggressively

From the days of John the Baptist until the present time, the kingdom of heaven has endured violent assault, and violent men seize it by force [as a precious prize—a share in the heavenly kingdom is sought with most ardent zeal and intense exertion].

Matthew 11:12

We need to take the kingdom of God—righteousness, peace, and joy (see Romans 14:17)—by force. As soon as you feel disappointed, aggressively stop the devil at the onset.

From my years of ministry as well as from my own personal Christian walk, I have learned there are six things we need to do aggressively.

1. Think aggressively.

What king, going out to engage in conflict with another king, will not first sit down and consider and take counsel whether he is able with ten thousand [men] to meet him who comes against him with twenty thousand? (Luke 14:31)

A general preparing for battle thinks. He plans and calculates how he can engage and defeat the enemy at the least risk to himself and his army.

You and I need to do the same thing in our Christian warfare as well as in our everyday life.

We need to think, *How can I get out of debt? How can I get my house cleaned up? How can I better provide for my family?*

But we also need to think, *How can I reach more people in my ministry? How can I affect my neighborhood for good? How can I be a blessing to the poor? How can I give more to God?*

Think about it. Ask yourself how you can become more involved and more active in the work of the Lord.

Of course, if you have a family, they must be your first priority and responsibility. You shouldn't get your priorities out of line if you have young children. You need to spend plenty of time with them, especially during their formative years.

But sometimes it is possible to handle both a family and a ministry. I have done it for years. I began my ministry, Life In The Word, when my son was just a year old.

You will find you can do anything that might at first look impossible, *if* you are called by God to do it and *if* you want to do it badly enough.

Think creatively. Don't just sit around wishing you could do more. Take the initiative and get started.

Think aggressively!

2. Pray aggressively.

> Let us then fearlessly and confidently and boldly draw near to the throne of grace (the throne of God's unmerited favor to us sinners), that we may receive mercy [for our failures] and find grace to help in good time for every need [appropriate help and well-timed help, coming just when we need it]. (Hebrews 4:16)

How are we to come before the throne of God? Fearlessly, confidently, and boldly.

That means aggressively!

You and I do not have to be bashful or timid with God. We can step forward in confidence and tell Him what we need. We can let Him know we are expecting Him to do for us what He has promised in His Word.

In Ephesians 3:20 we are told that God is able to "do super-abundantly, far over and above all that we [dare] ask or think [infinitely beyond our highest prayers, desires, thoughts, hopes, or dreams]."

Notice that word dare. You and I need to be confident, bold, aggressive, daring Christians.

When you approach the throne of God, do so aggressively!

3. Speak aggressively.

Whoever speaks, [let him do it as one who utters] oracles of God. (1 Peter 4:11)

As the children of God, you and I are to have an aggressive voice.

Now when I talk about speaking aggressively, I am not talking about being aggressive in the flesh. I am talking about being spiritually aggressive against the forces of evil.

Let me give you an example.

In one place the Bible teaches that we are to be as gentle as doves (see Matthew 10:16), but in another place it teaches that we are to be as bold as lions (Proverbs 28:1). I used to have a hard time reconciling those two images.

Then I thought about a person who is on the job when his boss who is not a Christian calls him in on the carpet and starts chewing him out unfairly. The worker knows that if he talks back he will get fired, so he just stands there and says nothing, waiting for the Lord to vindicate him.

Although he is gentle as a dove on the outside, on the inside he is as bold as a lion.

In the same way, you and I may sometimes have to stand passively in the flesh, but react aggressively in the spirit. We can allow harsh words to be directed at us physically, but we do not have to receive those words spiritually.

We can refuse to allow ourselves to come under condemnation. We can pray in the Spirit while we are being assaulted in the flesh.

Then once we are out of that situation we can speak forth aggressively from our own mouth, taking authority over the spiritual enemies who are bringing that abuse against us.

Whenever anyone starts coming against me in the flesh, I immediately start praying in the Spirit. I know I don't have to soak up all that abuse, so I protect myself spiritually.

For years I allowed other people to heap all their junk on me. Then later I tried to come against them in the flesh. I finally learned that neither of those tactics works. Since then I have discovered what does work.

I found out the hard way that we war not against flesh and blood but against principalities and powers and spiritual wickedness in high places. So I have learned how to wage spiritual warfare.

You may need to learn to do the same thing. Be as gentle as a dove and as bold as a lion. Develop an aggressive voice.

When you speak to people, don't hang your head and murmur or mumble or whine. Stand up straight, look them in the eye, and speak positively, definitively, clearly. Articulate and enunciate. Make yourself understandable.

Don't be mealy-mouthed, insecure, unsure. Be bold enough to open your mouth and say what you have to say with confidence and assurance.

If you are going to sing and worship God then do so aggressively.

Whenever you open your mouth to utter anything, do so as if you are speaking as the oracle of God. Do it enthusiastically, joyfully, graciously—and aggressively.

4. Give aggressively.

Give, and [gifts] will be given to you; good measure, pressed down, shaken together, and running over, will they pour into [the pouch formed by] the bosom [of your robe and used as a bag]. For with the measure you deal out [with the measure you use when you confer benefits on others], it will be measured back to you. (Luke 6:38)

When you and I give, we are to give generously and aggressively. Because the way we give is the way we receive.

When we look into our wallet or purse, we are not to pull out the smallest bill we can find. Instead, we are to give as God gives—abundantly.

Now I realize that no offering is too small and none is too great.

But at the same time we have got to learn to be as aggressive in our giving as we are in any other aspect of our Christian life.

I seek to be a giver. I desire to give all the time.

One time I was in a Christian bookstore and saw a little offering box for one of those ministries that feeds hungry children. There was a sign beside it that read, "For fifty cents two children can eat for two days."

I started to open my purse and make a donation when a voice inside said to me, "You don't need to do that; you give all the time."

I immediately got violent—spiritually violent! No one could tell on the outside, but I was aroused on the inside. I reached into my purse, pulled out some money, and placed it in the box just to prove I could give as an act of my free will!

You can do the same. Whenever you are tempted to hold back, give more! Show the devil you are an aggressive giver!

5. Work aggressively.

Whatever your hand finds to do, do it with all your might. (Ecclesiastes 9:10)

Whatever we put our hand to, we need to do it aggressively.

Don't face any task in your life dreading it and wishing you could escape from it. Stir yourself up in the Holy Spirit and boldly declare, "This is the work the Lord has given me to do, and with the help of the Holy Spirit I am going to do it with all my might to the glory of God!"

6. Love aggressively.

This is My commandment: that you love one another [just] as I have loved you. No one has greater love [no one has shown stronger affection] than to lay down (give up) his own life for his friends. (John 15:12–13)

As the children of God, we must love others as God loves us. And that means aggressively—and sacrificially.

Love is an effort. We will never love anybody if we are not willing to pay the price.

One time I gave a woman a nice pair of earrings. My flesh wanted to keep them for myself, but my spirit said to be obedient to the Lord and give them away.

Later that woman stood up in a meeting and told how she had been given the earrings she was wearing as "a free gift."

The Lord spoke to me and said, "Yes, it was a free gift to her, but it cost you, just as salvation is a free gift to you but it cost Jesus His life."

Love is the greatest gift of all. When you show forth the love of God, do it freely, sacrificially—and aggressively!

4

❦

DEALING WITH DISAPPOINTMENT

According to *Webster's*, to *disappoint* is "to fail to satisfy the hope, desire, or expectation of."[1]

In other words, when we set ourselves to hope, desire, or expect something and that hope, desire, or expectation is not met, then we become disappointed.

None of us is ever going to get to the place in life where we have no more disappointments. None of us has that much faith. Disappointment is a fact of life, one that must be faced and dealt with because it leads to discouragement, which ultimately leads to devastation if not confronted.

Too often people end up devastated and don't understand why. They don't realize the problem began a long time ago in simple disappointment, which can be an indication of more serious problems ahead.

Heed the Telltale Signs

If I wake up in the morning sneezing with a slight sore throat and feeling a bit of a headache, I recognize that I am catching a cold. I have found that if I will pray, take some extra vitamins C and A, and get more rest, many times I can head off the sickness.

Disease is often accompanied by early symptoms, signs that

something is not right and needs to be attended to before it gets worse.

Disappointment works the same way. It too is preceded by telltale signs that we need to take aggressive action against what we can sense is coming against us.

As we have said, as soon as we detect the first signs that we are under attack by Satan, we must resist him at the onset. It is much more effective to take a stand at the very beginning when we are experiencing disappointment than to wait until we are in the depths of depression and despair.

We all know it is much easier to forgive someone who has wronged us immediately after the offense than it is to forgive that person after we have given the devil time to work on us and cause us to become angry, bitter, and hard.

It is the same with disappointment. It is easier and more effective to deal with it right away than it is to wait until it has evolved into discouragement, depression, and devastation.

Causes of Disappointment

Suppose you plan a picnic or barbecue or some other outdoor activity like a wedding, and it rains.

You have invited all your family and friends, made elaborate preparations, and gone to a lot of time and expense to see that everything is just perfect. Then it ends up pouring down and you are left with a soggy mess.

That is a disappointment. But it is a minor disappointment, one that can be survived.

I have learned that in times like that instead of getting all worked up I have to just say, "Oh, well, that's disappointing, but it's not the end of the world. I'll just have to make the best of it."

Other disappointments are more serious and potentially damaging—especially if they involve people rather than inanimate things, like the weather.

Trust Few

But Jesus [for His part] did not trust Himself to them, because He knew all [men].

John 2:24

Besides the disappointments we all must bear because life is less than perfect, there are also the disappointments we have to endure because people themselves are imperfect.

Ultimately, all people, regardless of who they are, will disappoint us if we place too much confidence in them. That is not cynicism or being judgmental, it is just a fact of life. It is also why it is best not to rely excessively on others—even those who are closest to us.

Now that may sound strange, especially coming from someone who has spent years trying to learn to trust people.

But as we have seen in the life of Jesus, it is possible to trust people to a certain degree without opening up ourselves to them in an unbalanced, unwise manner.

Like Jesus, you and I should love everyone, but we are not required to trust everyone one hundred percent. Only a fool does that. Why? Because sooner or later, people will fail us, just as sooner or later we will fail others.

Fallibility is part of being human. And it is the wise person who guards himself against it—in himself and in others.

In many ways, the best solution for disappointment is to avoid it as much as possible. And the best way to do that is to be realistic in our hopes, desires, and expectations, especially as they relate to human beings—including ourselves.

A wise son makes a glad father, but a foolish . . . son is the grief of his mother. (Proverbs 10:1)

Sometimes children are a disappointment to their parents. Today it seems to many mothers and fathers that their children never hear a word they say, that it all goes in one ear and out the other.

I know what that is like. When my son, Danny, was growing up, he was just like that. I would try to talk to him about something important, and he would just look at me with a blank stare as if he didn't hear a word I was saying.

One time at school he had to stay in during lunch as punishment for something foolish he had done. When I asked why he had done it, he just shrugged his shoulders.

"That's not an answer," I said. "Now tell me, why did you do that?"

"I dunno," he mumbled.

No matter how much I questioned him about why he had done such a foolish thing, his answer was always the same, "I dunno."

So I gave him a little lecture about the importance of behaving himself and paying attention and learning all he could in preparation for his future life.

The very next day I sent him off to school, expecting to see a great improvement in his attitude and behavior. Instead, he came home with a note from the teacher saying Danny had had the worst day since school started.

That kind of thing is disappointing to a parent. And often it gets worse the older the child gets, because more is expected of him.

The greater the hope, desire, and expectation, the greater the disappointment. But even minor incidents can cause frustration and bitter disappointment that can lead to more serious problems if not dealt with promptly and properly.

The Little Foxes That Spoil the Vines

Take us the foxes, the little foxes, that spoil the vines.

Song of Solomon 2:15 (KJV)

Little disappointments can create frustration, which in turn may lead to bigger problems that can produce a great deal of damage.

Besides the huge disappointments that occur when we fail to get the job or promotion or house we wanted, we can become just as upset and frustrated by a series of minor annoyances.

For example, suppose someone is supposed to meet you for lunch and fails to show up. Or suppose you make a special trip downtown or to the mall to buy a certain sale item at a discount, then when you get there it is all sold out. Or suppose you get all dressed up for a special occasion and suddenly notice at the last minute that there is an unsightly rip in your clothes.

All these kinds of things are actually minor, but they can add up to cause a lot of grief. That's why we have to know how to handle them and keep them in perspective. Otherwise, they can get out of hand and be blown up all out of proportion. That in turn can open us up to serious problems when we are faced with a real challenge. Let me give you an example.

Imagine you start out your day behind time, so you are already frustrated. On the way to the office, the traffic causes you to be even later than you intended.

Then when you do finally get to work you find out someone on the job has been gossiping about you behind your back.

You go get some coffee to help you calm down and get a hold on yourself, and you spill it all over yourself—and you have an important meeting with the boss and no time to change!

All of those things pile up one on the other until you are in a real stew.

Then just about that time you get a report from the doctor that is not in line with your hope and prayers, and to top it all off your fiancé calls and threatens to break your engagement that has been announced to the whole world!

What is likely to be your reaction—faith or fury?

All those minor frustrations with the traffic and gossip and the coffee have set you up for a major calamity when you have to face some really serious problem like sickness or a failed relationship.

That's why we have to be on our guard against the little foxes that destroy the vines, because all together they can do just as much damage as the serious disappointments that often accompany or follow them.

We must learn to do as Paul did in the book of Acts when the serpent attached itself to his hand—he simply shook it off (see Acts 28:1–5)! If we practice dealing quickly with disappointments as they come, they will not pile up into a mountain of devastation.

5

CONFIDENCE IN JESUS

Why are you cast down, O my inner self? And why should you moan over me and be disquieted within me? Hope in God and wait expectantly for Him, for I shall yet praise Him, my Help and my God.

Psalm 42:5

You and I must have our hope in God because we never know what is going to come against us in this life.

In several places in the Bible Jesus is referred to as the Rock (see 1 Corinthians 10:4). The apostle Paul goes on to tell us in Colossians 2:7 that we are to be rooted and grounded in Him.

Nowhere are we taught to be rooted and grounded in other people, or in our job, or in our church, or in our friends, or even in ourselves.

If we get our roots wrapped around the Rock of Jesus Christ, we are in good shape. But if we get them wrapped around anything or anyone else, we are in trouble.

Nothing and no one is going to be as solid and dependable and immovable as Jesus. That's why I don't want people to get rooted and grounded in me or my ministry. I want to point people to Jesus. I know that ultimately I will fail them in some way, just as I know they will ultimately fail me.

That's the problem with us humans; we are always inclined to failure.

But Jesus Christ isn't.

Be rooted and grounded in Jesus. Put your hope wholly and unchangeably in Him. Not in man, not in circumstances, not in your bank account, not in your job, not in anything or anyone else.

If you don't put your hope and faith in the Rock of your salvation, you are headed for disappointment, which leads to discouragement and devastation.

People Are Faulty

Confidence in an unfaithful man in time of trouble is like a broken tooth or a foot out of joint.

Proverbs 25:19

Some time ago my daughter was engaged to be married. The ring had been picked out, the money saved, and the wedding plans made.

Then a short time after the engagement was announced, the whole thing was called off because of the infidelity and dishonesty of the groom.

It was really a sad situation, especially for the lovely, wonderful, sweet, young bride-to-be who had suffered many other hard disappointments in her short life.

But this time she got the jump on the devil. Rather than getting upset and feeling sorry for herself, she said, "Well, thank God I found out what kind of a man he really is now before the wedding and not somewhere down the road when it would have been too late to do anything about it."

I was so proud of her and so pleased with the way she handled that terribly disappointing situation.

Although she knew it was best that it happen before the wedding rather than afterward, she was still hurt. So her father and I encouraged her, counseled her, and prayed with her.

In addition, she began to listen to some of my teaching tapes and read books that encourage and uplift the spirit.

She came through that difficult, trying time because her faith and trust were not in faulty man but in the never-failing Jesus. She kept looking to Him as her example of perseverance in the face of disap-

STRAIGHT TALK ON *Discouragement*   219

pointment and discouragement. That is what each one of us needs to learn to do.

Today she is married to a wonderful man, and she and her husband both work in the ministry with us.

Keep on Looking to Jesus

Let us run with patient endurance and steady and active persistence the appointed course of the race that is set before us, Looking away [from all that will detract] to Jesus, Who is the Leader and the Source of our faith [giving the first incentive for our belief] and is also its Finisher [bringing it to maturity and perfection]. He, for the joy [of obtaining the prize] that was set before Him, endured the cross, despising and ignoring the shame, and is now seated at the right hand of the throne of God. Just think of Him Who endured from sinners such grievous opposition and bitter hostility against Himself [reckon up and consider it all in comparison with your trials], so that you may not grow weary or exhausted, losing heart and relaxing and fainting in your minds.

Hebrews 12:1–3

It does not take any special talent to give up, to lie down on the side of the road of life and say, "I quit." Any unbeliever can do that.

You don't have to be a Christian to be a quitter.

But once you get hold of Jesus, or better yet when He gets hold of you, He begins to pump strength and energy and courage into you, and something strange and wonderful begins to happen. He won't let you quit!

You may say, "Oh, Lord, just leave me alone. I don't want to go on anymore." But He won't let you give up, even if you want to.

I used to want to give up and quit. But now I get out of bed and start each day afresh and anew. I begin my day by praying and reading the Bible and speaking the Word, seeking after God.

The devil may be screaming in my ear, "That's not doing you one bit of good. You've been doing that for years, and look what it's got you, you still have trouble."

That's when I say, "Shut up, devil! The Bible says I am to look to

Jesus and follow His example. He is my Leader, the Source and Finisher of my faith."

That is what my daughter did to keep up her spirits and to keep going in spite of what had happened to her. She could have looked at her past record and said, "Well, it has happened to me again—more rejection. It happened once, then twice, and now it has happened the third time." Instead, she kept looking to Jesus.

You and I need to make a decision today that, come what may, we are going to keep pressing on no matter what.

Get Reappointed

Live in harmony with one another; do not be haughty (snobbish, high-minded, exclusive), but readily adjust yourself to [people, things] and give yourselves to humble tasks. Never overestimate yourself or be wise in your own conceits.

Romans 12:16

Recently I have been thinking about all the Lord has done for me in the course of my life and ministry. It is amazing now that I look back on it. But it was not always easy. There were many times when I wanted desperately to give up and quit.

I have shared with you how, when I would get down and discouraged, the Lord would say to me, "Joyce, when disappointment comes, you have got to get reappointed, because if you don't you will end up in discouragement and that will lead to devastation."

That's why we must learn to adapt and adjust, to change direction. That's what my daughter did, and it has led her into a totally new and different life.

Now, of course, it won't always be easy. It is a lot harder to adjust to a broken engagement than it is to adjust to a rained-out picnic. But the answer is still the same regardless of the circumstances that must be faced and dealt with.

Unless we learn to get reappointed, to adapt and adjust, to get a new direction, we will never discover or enjoy the wonderful new and exciting life God has in store for us.

6

MEDITATE ON THE THINGS OF GOD

Do not fret or have any anxiety about anything, but in every circum-
stance and in everything, by prayer and petition (definite requests),
with thanksgiving, continue to make your wants known to God. And
God's peace [shall be yours, that tranquil state of a soul assured of its
salvation through Christ, and so fearing nothing from God and being
content with its earthly lot of whatever sort that is, that peace] which
transcends all understanding shall garrison and mount guard over
your hearts and minds in Christ Jesus.

Philippians 4:6–7

If you don't want to be devastated by discouragement, then don't meditate on your disappointments.

Did you know your feelings are hooked up to your thinking? If you don't think that is true, just take about twenty minutes or so and think about nothing but your problems. I can assure you that by the end of that time your feelings and maybe even your countenance will have changed. You may have become depressed or angry or upset. Yet your situation will not have changed a bit.

That's why you can go to church and sing songs, hear sermons, then go away with the same negative attitude and outlook you had when you left home. It is because you sat there in church and medi-tated on your problems rather than focusing your mind and spirit on the Lord.

With Whom Do You Fellowship?

In one issue of my monthly magazine, I asked this question: "Do you fellowship with God or with your problem?"

The reason I asked that question of my readers is because that is what the Lord asked me one morning.

I got up that day with my mind thinking about my problem. Suddenly the Spirit of the Lord spoke to me. I could tell by the tone of His voice He was a little bit aggravated with me.

He said to me, "Joyce, are you going to fellowship with your problem or with Me?" Then He went on to say to me what I am saying to you, "Don't meditate on your disappointments."

When you get disappointed, don't sit around and feel sorry for yourself, because despite how you may feel you are no different from anyone else.

Sometimes that is a bit hard for us to realize because the devil tries hard to make us think we are the only one who has ever had a bad deal.

That's not true.

One time I encouraged my daughter greatly because I sat down with her and shared with her what my life was like from age eighteen through twenty-three. By the time I was done, she felt really blessed in her own life.

Like everyone else, she has had some unfortunate things happen to her from time to time, but for years and years my life was one long horrible disaster.

For example, I told her about the time I was eighteen or nineteen years old and found myself sitting in a rooming house in Oakland, California, three thousand miles from home, with no car, no television, no telephone, and no one to care about me. I told her how I would sit there every night and write sad poems and feel sorry for myself, and then get up the next morning and walk to work.

"Thank God you have a good family, a good job, a good home, and a good car," I told her, "because I had none of those things."

By the time I had finished telling her my life story, she was excited about her present situation and her future prospects.

That's the choice each of us has. We can get excited by thinking about what all we have or can have, or we can get discouraged by thinking about what all we don't have.

The fact is, if we don't have it, we don't have it, and sitting around wishing we did is not going to change anything. We might wish it did, but it doesn't.

If we want to overcome disappointment and avoid the discouragement and devastation it leads to, we have to be realistic and deal with the facts.

And the fact is, as bad as things may seem, we still have a choice. We can choose to fellowship with our problems or fellowship with God.

No matter what we have lost or how bad we may feel, we still have the ability to direct our thoughts away from the negative and toward the positive.

Think on These Things!

For the rest, brethren, whatever is true, whatever is worthy of reverence and is honorable and seemly, whatever is just, whatever is pure, whatever is lovely and lovable, whatever is kind and winsome and gracious, if there is any virtue and excellence, if there is anything worthy of praise, think on and weigh and take account of these things [fix your minds on them].

Philippians 4:8

In verses six and seven of this passage we are told that if we have a problem we are not to worry or fret but to take it to God in prayer. We are assured that if we will do that, the peace of the Lord will keep us from fear and anxiety and will mount a guard over our mind and heart.

But here in verse eight we see that there is something else we must do in order to receive and enjoy the marvelous joy and peace of the Lord. We must take control of our thought life. We have to direct our mind away from the negative toward the positive.

Now you may notice that the first thing we are told to do is to think on whatever is true. That does not mean we are to think on the bad things that have happened to us in the past because they did actually happen.

There is a difference between truth and fact. Things that happened in the past are fact, but Jesus and the Word are Truth, and they are greater than fact.

Let me explain by using an example from the life of a friend of ours.

Some time ago this friend's husband died and went to be with the Lord. He is now in heaven, and she will not see him again until she gets there.

That is fact.

But the truth is not that her life is over and now she has nothing to live for. The devil would like for her to believe that, but it is not so.

The fact is that the young man to whom my daughter was engaged lied to her and hurt her deeply. But the truth is that her life did not end with that disappointment. The truth is that she still had her whole life ahead of her, and it was filled with many blessings.

The fact is that she had lost a fiancé, but the truth is that she still had a future, a fine Christian home and family, her own car, a good job, caring friends, and the love of God.

This loss occurred just before her nineteenth birthday. That was quite a birthday present, wasn't it? But instead of becoming sad and bitter, she chose to take a different perspective and approach.

She said, "Tomorrow is my nineteenth birthday, and as far as I am concerned it is the first day of the rest of my life!"

I was so impressed by her attitude and outlook that I bought her a small diary and told her, "Write in this little book all the miracles God does for you this coming year. On your twentieth birthday, we will read them and celebrate together."

And that is just what we did.

That is what you and I must do too. Although we do not always have the power to keep disappointments from happening to us, we do have the power to choose how we are going to react to them.

We can allow our thoughts to dwell on them until we become totally discouraged and devastated, or we can focus our attention on all the good things that have happened to us in our life—and on all the good things God still has in store for us in the days ahead.

7

HOPE AND EXPECTATION

[For my determined purpose is] that I may know Him [that I may progressively become more deeply and intimately acquainted with Him, perceiving and recognizing and understanding the wonders of His Person more strongly and more clearly], and that I may in that same way come to know the power outflowing from His resurrection [which it exerts over believers], and that I may so share His sufferings as to be continually transformed [in spirit into His likeness even] to His death.

Philippians 3:10

In this verse Paul said he had done something that I think we all need to do: He had set a goal for himself.

You and I have got to have a goal. We have got to have hope and direction and expectation in life.

Sometimes when people have been disappointed over and over and over, they lose their direction and expectation. They become afraid to put their hope in anything or anyone for fear they will be disappointed again. They hate the pain of disappointment so much they would rather never believe at all than run the risk of being hurt.

The sad part is that in the game of life they are the losers not the winners because victory comes only with risk.

Hurt Breeds Suspicion

That if possible I may attain to the [spiritual and moral] resurrection [that lifts me] out from among the dead [even while in the body].

Philippians 3:11

When a girl has been hurt two or three times by a boy she cares about, she thinks, "I'll never trust anyone again."

That is exactly what the devil wants all of us to do.

If you and I have friends who fail us or let us down, Satan wants us to say, "That's it—I'll never trust anyone again."

When we do that, we are playing right into the devil's hands.

Someone once said, "If you get hurt, you get suspicious."

That may be true, but it is just another one of the devices the enemy uses to deceive us and keep us from reaching our God-given goal in life.

Satan wants us to believe that everybody is like the ones who have disappointed us.

But they aren't.

The devil always tries to take a few bad experiences and use them to convince us we should never trust anyone in life.

If you have been hurt, don't start thinking you can't trust anybody. If you do, you will allow Satan to rob you of many of God's greatest blessings.

The apostle Paul had a goal, a spiritual dream. He wanted to get to the place that no matter what happened to him in life, it did not affect him or keep him from living this earthly life to the fullest while fulfilling his God-given purpose.

In order to reach that goal, he had to take risks. He not only had to trust God, he also had to trust other people. He had to open himself up to the risk of harm and loss.

So do you and I. We have got to keep going despite everything the enemy may throw in our path to cause us to become discouraged, give up, and quit short of attaining our ideal.

Press On!

Not that I have now attained [this ideal], or have already been made perfect, but I press on to lay hold of (grasp) and make my own, that for which Christ Jesus (the Messiah) has laid hold of me and made me His own. I do not consider, brethren, that I have captured and made it my own [yet]; but one thing I do [it is my one aspiration]: forgetting what lies behind and straining forward to what lies ahead, I press on toward the goal to win the [supreme and heavenly] prize to which God in Christ Jesus is calling us upward.

Philippians 3:12–14

In verse twelve Paul says that although he has not yet reached his goal or attained his ideal, he is not quitting. Instead, he is pressing on.

Then in verse thirteen he goes on to say that there is one thing he does.

This one thing should be of interest and importance to us because it comes from the man who wrote two-thirds of the New Testament by revelation of the Holy Spirit.

What was that one principle by which the great apostle Paul operated in his life, the one principle he believed was responsible for bringing him into the fulfillment of his dreams and goals?

There are two parts to this principle: The first is forgetting that which lies behind in the past, and the second is pressing on toward that which lies ahead in the future.

That is an important lesson for all of us to learn.

For example, consider the woman who lost her husband. When we say she should forget that which lies behind in the past and press on toward what lies ahead in the future, we are not suggesting she should forget all about her husband and never remember him. We are just saying that if she focuses her mind too much on her old life, it will get her into trouble. She will be living in the past rather than pressing on toward the future.

I am reminded of a woman in our church whose son died of leukemia at the age of sixteen. We had all prayed and believed God for him to be healed, but it did not happen; he still went to be with the Lord. Yet in the midst of that tragic loss the Lord sustained this young mother.

One day after the memorial service, she was doing the laundry and came across one of her son's shirts. As she picked it up and hugged it, she began to weep uncontrollably. She said later that she could feel the grief taking hold of her.

Realizing what was happening to her, she suddenly began speaking the name of Jesus. Grabbing up one of her son's shirts, she boldly declared, "Satan, see this. I am going to use it as a garment of praise. I am not going to sink into grief, but I am going to rise up in praise!"

It is natural to grieve over what has happened in the past, but only to a point and only for a certain time. Sooner or later we must come to grips with our grief and loss and decide to put it behind us and get on with our life.

Paul is talking about our imperfections when he speaks of forgetting what lies behind and pressing on toward what lies ahead, but we can apply the principle to all of life.

If we are to accomplish what God has called us and anointed us and commissioned us to achieve in this life, then like Paul we must have a goal and keep pressing toward it.

8

※

A NEW THING

Do not [earnestly] remember the former things; neither consider the things of old. Behold, I am doing a new thing! Now it springs forth; do you not perceive and know it and will you not give heed to it?

Isaiah 43:18–19

In dealing with the past, the danger we must avoid is allowing it to keep us in grief for what has been rather than in gratitude for what is and in anticipation of what is yet to be.

To launch my own ministry I had to leave a position as associate pastor at a church. It was a very hard thing to do, and for a long time I grieved over the loss of relationships with the people in that church and the things we used to do together that I was no longer a part of.

I had to let go of the past in order to go on, but my mind and emotions were trying to hang onto it. Finally I won the victory. I became excited about the future, but at the same time I was still disappointed about losing the position and the close relationships with the people.

The disappointment was adversely affecting the joy of my new ministry. It was a confusing time for me, but through it I learned a lot about letting go of what lies behind and pressing on to what lies ahead.

Over and over God has to remind me, "You have to let go of what lies behind. The past is not your life anymore. Now I am doing a new thing."

I AM!

And God said to Moses . . . You shall say this to the Israelites: I AM has sent me to you! God said also to Moses, This shall you say to the Israelites: The Lord, the God of your fathers, of Abraham, of Isaac, and of Jacob, has sent me to you! This is My name forever, and by this name I am to be remembered to all generations.

Exodus 3:14–15

If you and I concentrate too long on the past, it will get us into trouble. That's why from time to time the Lord has to remind us, as He did Moses and the Israelites, that He is the I AM, not the I WAS.

We need to remember all the good things God has done for us in the past, just as He did for Abraham and Isaac and Jacob and all the other faithful men and women of the Bible. But we must not become so attuned to past joys and victories that we fail to appreciate and enjoy what God is doing for us now—and what He has in store for us in the future.

In John 8:58 we read, "Jesus replied, I assure you, most solemnly I tell you, before Abraham was born, I AM." Hebrews 13:8 tells us that "Jesus Christ (the Messiah) is [always] the same, yesterday, today, [yes] and forever (to the ages)."

That is the way our faith is to be—always, eternal, timeless, unchanging—now!

Don't Look Back!

Jesus said to him, No one who puts his hand to the plow and looks back [to the things behind] is fit for the kingdom of God.

Luke 9:62

God does not want us living in the past. He knows that even if we could go back and recreate everything just as it was in days gone by, it would still not be the same. Do you know why? Because that was then, and this is now.

Yesterday is gone; it is lost in the recesses of time. This is now.

We have got a now God, we are a now people, and we must live a now life—one day at a time.

So often people lose their joy because they had something in the past that made them joyful that is now gone. Many are pining away for the move of God that was, but is not any more.

It is too bad it no longer exists, but it doesn't, and there is nothing you or I can do about it. Instead, we must learn to live in the present. God is moving now—let's enjoy now!

We must put the past behind us and get on with what God is doing in our life where we are at the moment.

Thank God we can press on to what He has in store for us, but in the meantime we need to keep our hand to the plow and quit looking back to what once was and will never be again.

Turn Back or Press On?

Now those people who talk as they did show plainly that they are in search of a fatherland (their own country). If they had been thinking with [homesick] remembrance of that country from which they were emigrants, they would have found constant opportunity to return to it. But the truth is that they were yearning for and aspiring to a better and more desirable country, that is, a heavenly [one]. For that reason God is not ashamed to be called their God [even to be surnamed their God—the God of Abraham, Isaac, and Jacob], for He has prepared a city for them.

Hebrews 11:14–16

This passage is referring to the Israelites who were led out of their previous home but who had to go through some difficult, trying times to get to their new home.

It says that if they had been thinking with homesick remembrance of the country they had just left, they would have had ample opportunity to return to it. Instead, they were looking for a new homeland, one prepared for them by God, and so they kept pressing on despite obstacles and hardships.

That is the choice you and I must make. We can choose to look back with homesick remembrance, or we can choose to look ahead with joyful anticipation.

This passage does not mean to suggest that we are never to recall the good times from our past or never bring to mind our departed loved ones. It just means that we are not to keep our mind and heart constantly turned toward the past, because if we do we will miss what God has for us in the future.

That's why we need to make a vow that we are not going to waste our lives in looking back, but are going to press on to what lies ahead.

This is a *today* message. It is something we can and must do today and every new day we live.

I used to think this word about forgetting the past applied only to previous mistakes and failures. Then one day I realized I was making myself just as miserable by constantly reliving my past victories and successes.

When a thing is finished, we should let the curtain fall on it and go on to the next thing without making comparisons between them. We should not compare present mistakes or victories with past mistakes or victories. If we do, we will open ourselves up to either discouragement or pride.

We should completely enjoy our life as we are presently experiencing it. We can do that by not comparing it to experiences or segments of our life in the past.

That's why the Lord has told us in Isaiah 43:18–19 not to remember the former things, nor even consider the things of old. Why? Because they are gone, and now God is doing a new thing. It is springing up right before our eyes, and we need to perceive it and give heed to it if we want to be a part of it and benefit from it.

Sow in Tears, Reap in Joy

They who sow in tears shall reap in joy and singing.

Psalm 126:5

No matter what has happened to us in the past, or is happening to us now, our life is not over. And we must not let the devil convince us it is.

Our enemy will try to tell us that we made one mistake too many, and now it's too late for us.

We must not listen to him. Instead, we must tell him, "Satan, you are a liar and the father of all lies. This is a new day, and I am expecting a miracle."

The reason we go through life expecting a miracle at any time is because we never know when it is going to come. We never know when God is going to pass our way. That's what makes life so exciting.

The devil would like for us to think our time will never come and our miracle will never happen. But if we keep ourselves rooted and grounded in Jesus Christ, eventually our time *will* come, and our miracle *will* happen.

But we have to be prepared for it. To do that we must keep Satan from discouraging us so much that we quit and give up. If we do, then no matter what God has planned for us, it won't happen.

That's why God keeps urging us throughout the Bible not to become dismayed or discouraged or give up, because He knows that although "weeping may endure for a night . . . joy comes in the morning" (Psalm 30:5).

God Will Finish His Work

And I am convinced and sure of this very thing, that He Who began a good work in you will continue until the day of Jesus Christ [right up to the time of His return], developing [that good work] and perfecting and bringing it to full completion in you.

Philippians 1:6

God never starts anything He does not intend to finish. He is the Author and the Finisher (see Hebrews 12:2).

Too often the problem is not God, it is us. We are stuck in the past, in the old thing, so we fail to perceive and heed the new thing God is doing in the here and now. The reason we can't give heed to the new thing is because we are still hanging on to the old thing, as good as it may have been.

What God did for us yesterday is wonderful, but He has the capacity to do twice as much for us today and tomorrow.

The question we must ask ourselves is: Which do we want? The old thing or the new thing?

9

❧

NEW WINE, NEW WINESKINS

*He told them a proverb also: No one puts a patch from a new garment
on an old garment; if he does, he will both tear the new one, and the
patch from the new [one] will not match the old [garment]. And no one
pours new wine into old wineskins; if he does, the fresh wine will burst
the skins and it will be spilled and the skins will be ruined (destroyed).
But new wine must be put into fresh wineskins.*

Luke 5:36–38

In recent years the Lord has given me a whole new understanding
of this passage.

I used to think it applied only to salvation by grace rather than
salvation by keeping the law. Now I see it applies to the new lifestyle
and mind-set of those who have been made new creatures in Christ
Jesus.

You and I are always wanting to get the new but hold on to the
old. But Jesus says that is not possible. To illustrate His point, He
tells a proverb about not sewing a new patch into an old garment or
putting new wine in old wineskins.

The Sewing Proverb

Anyone who knows anything about sewing knows you cannot put a
new patch on an old garment.

If you have an old garment that has been washed and shrunk and faded, and you try to patch a hole in it by using a piece of new material, in time the new cloth will shrink and tear. Even if it doesn't, the new piece will not match the old garment because it has not yet become worn and faded by time and washing.

In this part of the proverb, Jesus is telling us not to try to take our new life and patch it into the old life. It just won't work.

Neither will it work to try to put new wine into old wineskins.

Which Is Better?

No one after drinking old wine immediately desires new wine, for he says, The old is good or better.

Luke 5:39

Do you know why a person says the old wine is better than the new wine? He says it for the same reason you and I prefer the old life to the new. Because the old is more comfortable.

Most of us prefer the old life to the new life because we are used to it. Even though there is a part of us that wants the new wine, the new thing, the new day, the new move, there is another part of us that wants to hang onto the old because it is what we are most comfortable with.

Rather than moving on with the Lord, we try to stay where we are because it is so much easier.

Moving on is hard.

It is hard to move to a new town, make new friends, find a new doctor and school and church. (Sometimes it is even hard for me to put a piece of furniture someplace new!) It is so much more appealing just to stay where we are and enjoy what we have and know.

But what we tend to forget is that as Christians we ourselves have been made new.

The New Has Come!

Therefore if any person is [ingrafted] in Christ (the Messiah) he is a new creation (a new creature altogether); the old [previous moral and spiritual condition] has passed away. Behold, the fresh and new has come!

2 Corinthians 5:17

You and I must realize and understand that we are new creatures in Christ Jesus. We have been called to a whole new life in Him. We must not be so afraid to let go of what we were and had in our old life that we cannot freely receive and enjoy what God has for us in our new life.

I came to see this when the Lord spoke to me and said, "Don't you realize, Joyce, that this is the foundation for the new creation reality: that old things are passed away and all things have become brand new?"

That is not true just when we answer an altar call and make a decision for Christ. It is an ongoing principle of the new creation lifestyle.

Out with the Old, In with the New!

Because God had us in mind and had something better and greater in view for us.

Hebrews 11:40

Have you realized yet that what you now have would not be so bad if you would simply quit comparing it with what you used to have?

When we go to minister in India, where the poverty and living conditions are absolutely horrible, the condition of the people there disturbs us more than it does them. Why? They have nothing else to compare to the way they live.

What the people in India we see have today is what they have always had. We of course have always lived in America, a land of abundance. Therefore, when we go to India, everywhere we look we see conditions that are almost unspeakably horrible *compared* to the conditions we have always known.

What's the sense of living day by day discouraged and depressed and downtrodden because of your old life that no longer exists?

Don't sit around and consider the old things. Don't remember the former things anymore. That is all gone now, replaced by something new and better, if you only knew it.

Press on to those things that lie ahead.

What are you to do when disappointment comes—which it will because it is a fact of life? It may be a little thing or a huge thing. It may be as insignificant as a rained-out picnic or as significant as a broken engagement.

Whatever form it may take, disappointment is going to come. When it does weigh upon you like a rock, you can either let it press you down so that you become discouraged and even devastated, or you can use it as a stepping-stone to higher and better things.

There is no way you can sit around and think negatively and have a positive life. It won't work. The more you think about your disappointments, the more discouraged you are going to get. And if you are discouraged long enough, you will become devastated. And when you get devastated, you are in big trouble.

But God has better things for you than that!

This is a new day. So the next time disappointment comes your way, get reappointed. Adapt and adjust. Forget what lies behind and press on to what lies ahead.

Remember that the Lord is doing a new thing in your life. So forget the past and live in the fullness and joy of the new life He has planned and prepared for you.

Conclusion

May Christ through your faith [actually] dwell (settle down, abide, make His permanent home) in your hearts! May you be rooted deep in love and founded securely on love.

Ephesians 3:17

I encourage you to be careful about where you place your hope and confidence.

In Ephesians 3:17 we are told to be rooted and grounded in love. We are to be rooted and grounded in the love of Christ Jesus—in Him—not other people, our children, our friends, our job, etc.

Jesus is called the Rock. He is a rock that is never going to move.

If you get your roots wrapped around the Rock, when minor disappointments come along you will be able to say, "Oh, well," and get on with your life. When major disappointments come, you can receive emotional healing from the Lord and through His power you can decide to go on.

If you are rooted and grounded in anything else, you will end up disappointed, discouraged, depressed, and devastated, because nothing else and no one else is rock solid—only Jesus!

Learn to adapt and adjust. You can do it! Why should you do it? For your own sake.

Count it a privilege to adapt and adjust to different people and situations.

Don't meditate on the disappointment that comes into your life. Let it go and let God take care of you. Face the disappointment at its onset and be quick to make any adjustments required to remedy the situation.

Instead of concentrating on your problems and getting discouraged, focus on God. Meditate on His promises. Confess His Word and submit yourself and your situation to Him in prayer.

Take an inventory of what you have left, not just what you have lost. This keeps your mind in the present where God is. Remember, Jesus called Himself, "I AM," not "I WAS" or "I WILL BE." He is here for you right now. Today you can begin enjoying life!

SCRIPTURES TO OVERCOME DISCOURAGEMENT

[What, what would have become of me] had I not believed that I would see the Lord's goodness in the land of the living! Wait and hope for and expect the Lord; be brave and of good courage and let your heart be stout and enduring. Yes, wait for and hope for and expect the Lord. (Psalm 27:13–14)

I have seen that everything [human] has its limits and end [no matter how extensive, noble, and excellent]; but Your commandment is exceedingly broad and extends without limits [into eternity]. (Psalm 119:96)

Confidence in an unfaithful man in time of trouble is like a broken tooth or a foot out of joint. (Proverbs 25:19)

For I know the thoughts and plans that I have for you, says the Lord, thoughts and plans for welfare and peace and not for evil, to give you hope in your final outcome. (Jeremiah 29:11)

But as for me, I will look to the Lord and confident in Him I will keep watch; I will wait with hope and expectancy for the God of my salvation; my God will hear me. (Micah 7:7)

Live in harmony with one another; do not be haughty (snobbish, high-minded, exclusive), but readily adjust yourself to [people, things] and give yourselves to humble tasks. Never overestimate yourself or be wise in your own conceits. (Romans 12:16)

Beloved, never avenge yourselves, but leave the way open for [God's] wrath; for it is written, Vengeance is Mine, I will repay (requite), says the Lord. (Romans 12:19)

God is faithful (reliable, trustworthy, and therefore ever true to His promise, and He can be depended on); by Him you were called into companionship and participation with His Son, Jesus Christ our Lord. (1 Corinthians 1:9)

What eye has not seen and ear has not heard and has not entered into the heart of man, [all that] God has prepared (made and keeps ready) for those who love Him [who hold Him in affectionate reverence, promptly obeying Him and gratefully recognizing the benefits He has bestowed]. (1 Corinthians 2:9)

But thanks be to God, Who in Christ always leads us in triumph [as trophies of Christ's victory] and through us spreads and makes evident the fragrance of the knowledge of God everywhere. (2 Corinthians 2:14)

And let us not lose heart and grow weary and faint in acting nobly and doing right, for in due time and at the appointed season we shall reap, if we do not loosen and relax our courage and faint. (Galatians 6:9)

For He foreordained us (destined us, planned in love for us) to be adopted (revealed) as His own children through Jesus Christ, in accordance with the purpose of His will [because it pleased Him and was His kind intent]—[So that we might be] to the praise and the commendation of His glorious grace (favor and mercy), which He so freely bestowed on us in the Beloved. (Ephesians 1:5–6)

Now to Him Who, by (in consequence of) the [action of His] power that is at work within us, is able to [carry out His purpose and] do superabundantly, far over and above all that we [dare] ask or think [infinitely beyond our highest prayers, desires, thoughts, hopes, or dreams]. (Ephesians 3:20)

And as for you, brethren, do not become weary or lose heart in doing right [but continue in well-doing without weakening]. (2 Thessalonians 3:13)

Prayer to Overcome Discouragement

Father,

Your Word is a lamp to my feet and a light to my path.

Keep me, I pray, from hanging my hopes and expectations on people like me, because we are all very capable of disappointing one another.

Let me release forgiveness toward those who have failed me in the past and let go of the painful memories of those disappointments.

Increase in me, Lord, that I may be more and more like You, and less and less like me.

These things I ask in Jesus' holy name, amen.

STRAIGHT TALK ON *Insecurity*

CONTENTS

—— ∞ ——

INTRODUCTION

Are you tired of playing games, wearing masks, trying to be someone other than who you are? Wouldn't you like the freedom just to be accepted as you are, without pressure to be someone you really don't know how to be?

Would you like to learn how to succeed at being yourself?

God wants us to accept ourselves, to like who we are and to learn to deal with our weaknesses because we all have plenty of them. He doesn't want us to reject ourselves because of them.

Jesus understands our weaknesses (see Hebrews 4:15).

The Holy Spirit bears us up in our weakness (see Romans 8:26).

God chooses weak and foolish things of the world to confound the wise (see 1 Corinthians 1:27).

If I look at my weaknesses and tell you what I believe my value is, it will be less than nothing. But our worth is not based on anything we do but in what God has already done.

God accepts us as we are, but the devil tries very hard to keep us from really understanding that. He brings pressure on us from many different sources to try to keep us feeling we don't measure up to the standard of where we should be. He doesn't want us to find out we can accept and like ourselves just as we are because he knows if we ever do that, something wonderful will begin happening to us.

The opinion we have of ourselves affects all our relationships—with people and with God. Because it affects our relationship with God, it affects our prayer life.

We can pray and pray, basing our prayers on the promises God gives us in the Scriptures and using all the right words, without the prayer being effective. One reason the prayer may not bear fruit is if we have such bad feelings about ourselves we don't believe God ought to do for us what we are asking. We have a hard time praying and believing God will do the great thing we are praying about because we don't expect Him to do it! We base our own value on our performance, letting our weaknesses, flaws, and failures negatively affect our opinion of ourselves.

People are extremely performance oriented. We learn from the time we are little, the better we perform the more love we receive. In our relationship with God, our thinking often continues in this pattern. We think God will love us and bless us more, the better we perform. But because we aren't able to behave right all the time, we start working and striving, trying to overcome all our weaknesses. We think God will then love us enough to do for us what we need.

Our worth is not in what *we* do, but in what God has made us through what *He* has done. Every Christian knows this principle—it is the basis of salvation. We are made righteous, or put in right standing with God, through what Jesus did by dying on the cross. We cannot earn salvation by what *we* do—it is a free gift from God because of what *Jesus* did (see 1 Corinthians 1:30; Ephesians 2:8). We just need to accept it.

But even though every Christian received salvation by believing we are made right with God through what He did, usually only very mature Christians continue in this truth and learn to approach all of life on the same basis (see Galatians 3:3). As we saw, this type of thinking is contrary to the way most people were brought up to think. We must change our thinking by renewing our mind with the Scriptures that teach our right standing with God is through Jesus— not through our own works.

Our worth is not based on how acceptable we can make ourselves to God. God is looking for people with a right heart attitude toward Him, not a perfect performance record. Second Chronicles 16:9 says, "For the eyes of the Lord run to and fro throughout the whole earth, to shew himself strong in the behalf of them whose heart is perfect toward him" (KJV).

"Whose heart is perfect toward him," means to have a right heart attitude toward God—to love God as much as we know how to love Him; to want what He wants; to want His will; to want to do His will.

God has made the provision for us to be in right standing with Him (if we will accept it). He loves us and is looking for people who are open to His will so that He can show Himself strong in their behalf and bless them.

We don't earn God's love; we don't earn His blessings. We can go to Him at any time and have our needs met. Hebrews 4:16 says, "Let us then fearlessly and confidently and boldly draw near to the throne of grace (the throne of God's unmerited favor to us sinners), that we may receive mercy [for our failures] and find grace to help in good time for every need [appropriate help and well-timed help, coming just when we need it]."

However, the ongoing lifestyle we choose affects our ability to receive all God has for us. A life of serving and obeying God allows Him to place us in a position for Him to open several avenues to use in consistently blessing us. Faithfulness releases blessings (see Proverbs 28:20).

A lifestyle of disobedience will definitely affect what God is able to do in our lives because the Bible teaches if we plant bad seeds, we will reap a bad harvest (see Galatians 6:8).

People who live and walk in intentional disobedience, but want God to bless them anyway, may think we don't have to make an effort to overcome our weaknesses to win God's approval. They believe if we are weak in an area, we have an excuse to sin. The truth is this: God will use us in spite of our weaknesses and will help us overcome them; we don't have to struggle to overcome them on our own, but we must be progressing toward overcoming them.

The Lord told Paul: "My strength and power are made perfect (fulfilled and completed) and show themselves most effective in [your] weakness" (2 Corinthians 12:9). Second Corinthians 13:4 (KJV) tells us we are "weak in him, but we shall live with him by the power of God."

When Paul was teaching the Romans the message of grace he said, "Are we to remain in sin in order that God's grace (favor and mercy) may multiply and overflow? Certainly not! How can we who died to sin live in it any longer?" (Romans 6:1–2).

In other words, should we see how much we can sin because sinning will give God an opportunity to give us grace? Paul's response in so many words was, "For crying out loud—how can you sin if you're dead to sin?"

Paul's point was to teach them who they were in Christ. They and we are acceptable because God made us acceptable (see Romans 6:5–16).

God wants us to come to terms with ourselves and learn our value is not in what we do but in who we are. He wants us to be willing to be who we are, weaknesses and all.

It's wonderful not to start the day by waking up and hating yourself for half an hour before you ever get out of bed! Or wake up to hear the devil rattling in your ears a list of all the mistakes you made the day before, telling you you're a failure and can't expect God to do anything good for you. Many people are beat down before they ever get their feet on the floor in the morning!

The devil's plan is to deceive us into continuing to base our worth on our performance, then keep us focused on our faults and shortcomings. Satan wants us to have a low opinion of ourselves and be insecure so that we live ineffectively for God, being miserable and unreceptive to God's blessings because we don't think we deserve them.

Once we come into peace with ourselves, we will begin to come into peace with other people. If we ever learn to accept and like ourselves, we will begin to accept and like others. I know from personal experience the more able I am to accept and like myself in spite of my weaknesses and flaws, the more able I am to accept and like others in spite of theirs.

Every one of us is imperfect, and God loves us just the way we are.

By applying the Bible-based principles in this section of the book you will overcome the sense of personal insecurity and will prepare yourself to fulfill God's marvelous plan for your life.

Part One

——— ❧ ———

ACCEPTED

1

ELIMINATE THE NEGATIVE

If you want to increase your self-acceptance and your opinion of yourself, decide right here and now that not one more negative thing about you will ever come out of your mouth.

Acknowledge the Good Things

That the communication of thy faith may become effectual by the acknowledging of every good thing which is in you in Christ Jesus.

Philemon 1:6 (KJV)

The communication of our faith is made effectual by acknowledging every *good thing* which is in us *in Christ Jesus*, not by acknowledging every *wrong* thing with *us*.

The devil wants us to acknowledge every bad thing we see in ourselves because he doesn't want the communication of our faith to be effectual. He wants us to spend every waking moment acknowledging in our mind and out of our mouth how awful we are because, as the accuser of the brethren (see Revelation 12:9–10), he continually tries to redirect our focus from who we are in Christ back onto our shortcomings.

The devil wants to bombard us with opportunities to think negative thoughts about ourselves so we will return to that pattern of thinking most of us learned growing up. We will again fall into the deception that our worth is based on our performance, and that because of our faults, we are worthless.

One reason it is so important not to speak negatively about ourselves is that we believe what we say more than what anybody else says. But once we truly understand who we are in Christ and see how much He has done for us through shedding His blood to make us worthy, we will realize we are actually insulting our heavenly Father by excessively meditating on our faults, flaws, and failures. Acts 10:15 says: "What God has cleansed and pronounced clean, do not you defile and profane by regarding and calling common and unhallowed or unclean."

In Right Standing with God

One of the first revelations God gave me out of the Word was regarding righteousness. By "revelation" I mean one day you suddenly understand something to the point that it becomes part of you. The knowledge isn't only in your mind; you no longer need to renew your mind to it because you don't wonder or hope it's true—you *know*.

I *knew* I was righteous in Christ because God gave me an understanding of 2 Corinthians 5:21:

> For our sake He [God] made Christ [virtually] to be sin Who knew no sin, so that in and through Him we might become [endued with, viewed as being in, and examples of] the righteousness of God [what we ought to be, approved and acceptable and in right relationship with Him, by His goodness].

Righteousness Is God's Gift

Romans 4:24 tells us, "[Righteousness, standing acceptable to God] will be granted and credited to us also who believe in (trust in, adhere to, and rely on) God, Who raised Jesus our Lord from the dead."

I understood that righteousness is something given to us. It is "imputed" (KJV) to us—"granted and credited" to us by virtue of our believing in what God did for us through His Son Jesus Christ. Jesus, Who knew no sin, became sin so that we might be made the righteousness of God in Jesus.

Above all else, the devil does not want us to walk in the reality that we are in right standing with God. He wants us always vaguely contemplating what is wrong with us instead of thinking about what is right with us through Jesus' blood.

I had been walking in this revelation of righteousness for a few years and teaching the Word for quite a while, when something happened that showed me how important it is not to speak negatively about ourselves. When we receive a revelation, we are held responsible for it, and I was held responsible for saying negative things about myself.

The Importance of Speaking in Line with God's Word

Dave and I planned and prayed to have our son Daniel. He wasn't an accident—we wanted him. But after he was born, I let the change in my lifestyle affect me negatively.

I wasn't used to spending so much time in the house. I had put on a few pounds and my skin had gone through changes, normal with having a baby. But I thought I was ugly and fat and would stay that way forever. I fell into a permanent lousy mood.

One morning before Dave left for work, he was trying to encourage and cheer me up. In the process he told me I really should not be acting as I was, that I knew better. I got mad at him. Then he said something else, and I said something else, and at last I had an excuse to do what I had wanted to do for days—blow up.

My background was very negative. I had a negative mouth and a very negative attitude about everything and everybody including myself. When I made mistakes or did things wrong, it was normal for me to think, "I can't ever do anything right—I'm just a big jerk— everything I do is wrong, all the time."

After Dave left and I was alone in the house nursing Daniel at the kitchen table, thinking about what had just happened, I started speaking bad things to myself: "That's right, Joyce, you're just a big jerk. You're a mess. You think studying the Word is going to help you? Nothing's going to help you. You've been a mess as long as you've been on the earth, and you're going to always be a mess. Just forget it; you're never going to straighten up."

All of a sudden I felt an evil, suffocating presence coming across the room at me. It was so strong I could almost see it. From my knowledge of the Word of God, I immediately knew a demonic power was about to attach itself to me because of what I had been saying about myself.

Thank God for the Word we plant in ourselves because without even thinking, I automatically started speaking it out: "I am the righteousness of God in Christ. I *am* the righteousness of God in Christ. I am the *righteousness* of God in Christ. I am the righteousness of God in *Christ*. His blood covers me."

In the same way it came in, the evil presence backed off and the atmosphere in the room became clear again. Needless to say, that experience put a holy fear in me about the importance of speaking in line with the Word—especially about myself!

In human beings there is a natural tendency to think negatively. "The imagination (the strong desire) of man's heart is evil and wicked from his youth" (Genesis 8:21). This negative tendency will continue until we turn the process around in our life.

God has worked with me since I have been in the Word to change me from being negative and thinking negative thoughts about myself all the time into not thinking or talking like that anymore.

For as he [a person] thinks in his heart, so is he.

Proverbs 23:7

I exhort you to never think or say bad things about yourself. Your opinion of yourself will make a major difference—in answered prayer, in what you can receive from God, and in how much God can use you. God is capable of using you, but you have to let Him. Let Him by believing He has made you worthy to receive the good things He wants to give you. Let Him by believing you are capable of doing what He asks you to do because He will enable you, and only speak things about yourself in line with those beliefs.

God's Love Drives Out Insecurity

"We love Him, because He first loved us" (1 John 4:19). If we don't let God love us, we are hardly going to be able to love Him back. If we don't come to some terms of peace with ourselves, we won't be able to go out and love other people, as the Bible tells us to do: "You shall love your neighbor as yourself" (Mark 12:31).

More than anything, people need a revelation of God's love for them personally. God's love for us is the foundation for our faith, for our freedom from sin, and for our ability to step out in ministry to others without fear in the form of insecurity.

God made all of us with a craving, longing, and desire in our heart to be loved. And the Word teaches us that God loves us as much as He loves Jesus (see John 17:23)!

People who think their right standing with God is based on how much progress they make toward overcoming their flaws think they have worn out God with their failures and messes. We can't wear out God. Love can't be worn out, and we can't cause God not to love us. Love isn't something God does—it is Who He is (see 1 John 4:8)!

Many people develop a shame-based nature as a result of unfair and unkind treatment from different people—parents, schoolteachers, friends, strangers. Our attitudes and our opinions of ourselves are programmed into us over a period of time. If we do not know we are beloved in Christ, we may become insecure. Don't allow the way other people treat you to determine your value.

People who lack confidence have a private little war going on within themselves about themselves most of the time. If we focus on the natural world, it isn't difficult to get up every day and start listing the many things wrong with ourselves. The devil puts lies in our heads for us to use in creating a view of ourselves based on what other people say.

Satan Has an Attitude, and He Wants You to Have It!

There is an attitude Satan wants us to have centering on self-dependence. It takes two equally troublesome forms. I don't think he cares which one people choose because both attitudes keep us from the will of God and prevent us from operating in the power available to us as God's children. Both attitudes generate from the belief that our worth is based on self—on us and not God.

A haughty, prideful, self-reliant, self-confident, self-dependent attitude says, "No matter what comes along, I can handle it; I don't need God." Many of us don't think we have this attitude. We say we need God, but this attitude is revealed subtly in our actions. We don't act as though we need God.

As believers we are not to be self-confident but God-confident. The Bible says repeatedly that we are not supposed to have confidence *in ourselves*. Instead, we are to have confidence in God—that He will work *through* us.

People with the other attitude the devil wants us to have condemn themselves. They are angry with themselves over their mistakes and faults. They hate themselves and think they are useless, worthless, and ugly. Some people think too highly of themselves and others think too lowly of themselves.

Many people dislike the way they look. They think they are unattractive or are convinced they are ugly when actually they are attractive. The devil is a liar (see John 8:44). The weapon he has to try to keep us distracted from seeing the truth of who we are and what God has for us is deception. He wants to keep us from fully enjoying the life God has for us and diminish or destroy our effectiveness for God.

One time when I was holding a meeting, the Lord prompted me to ask to come to the front for prayer all those in the audience who felt ugly! I was certainly surprised when He asked me to do that. That was the only time I have ever done that in all the years I have been in ministry.

I said, "Everyone who thinks you're ugly, come up here." The response was enormous!

One girl in the line looked like a fashion model. She was gorgeous. I went to her first because I thought she had misunderstood the altar call.

"Did you understand the invitation was for people who think they're ugly?" I asked.

Tears started streaming down her face as she answered, "All my life I've thought that I was horrible looking." When something happens like that you think, "Do they need glasses or what?" This is a perfect example of the way Satan will deceive. If the devil doesn't keep you busy enough raking yourself over the coals for your weaknesses, he will try to use something that isn't wrong with you or something good about you and make you think it's bad!

God Approves

Before I formed you in the womb I knew [and] approved of you [as My chosen instrument], and before you were born I separated and set you apart, consecrating you.

Jeremiah 1:5

God did not create you and me, then say, "Now I think I'll get to know you." The Bible says that before He ever formed us in the womb, He knew us and *approved* of us.

In Ephesians 1:6 we are told that God has made us acceptable in the Beloved. That means we are made acceptable to God through the sacrifice of Jesus Christ.

God approved of us before anybody else ever got a chance to disapprove. If God approves of us and accepts us as we are, why worry about what anyone else thinks of us? *If God* be for us, who can be against us that will make any difference? (see Romans 8:31).

Perfection: The Impossible Pursuit

Let no foul or polluting language, nor evil word nor unwholesome or worthless talk [ever] come out of your mouth, but only such [speech] as is good and beneficial to the spiritual progress of others, as is fitting to the need and the occasion, that it may be a blessing and give grace (God's favor) to those who hear it.

Ephesians 4:29

My son Danny was playing golf with my husband Dave and me by the time he was nine years old. He was already a good golfer at that age, but he had one serious problem. He had a tendency to be happy when he was playing really well, but if he hit a bad shot he would get upset and start calling himself names. He would say things to himself like, "Oh, stupo Danny, you do everything wrong!"

He felt if he couldn't do everything perfectly, then he was no good at all. If he didn't do everything just right, he began making negative remarks about himself. The devil tried to strap the self-condemnation attitude on Danny at that early age!

Dave and I began working with him, teaching him that was a dangerous habit.

"Danny," we would say, "saying things like that about yourself does not do you any good at all. Nor does it benefit anybody who is with you when you say such things."

This applies to all of us. Not only do we feel bad when we speak negatively about ourselves, but other people hearing someone talk negatively about themselves feel bad. In the verse following the one in which Paul warns us not to allow polluting language or worthless talk to come out of our mouth, he states, "And do not grieve the Holy Spirit of God" (Ephesians 4:30). Obviously, such negativism grieves the Holy Spirit. It also grieves our own spirit. God has not built us to speak or receive negativism. That's why none of us wants to be around somebody who is always negative.

If a person who makes a mistake says, "I'm not happy about making the mistake, but I'm learning; I'll do better next time; thank God I'm doing as well as I am able," then everybody is edified. The person feels right about himself, and so do others around him. He is taking responsibility for his wrong action without being negative or feeling condemned. That's the attitude and action we should take.

To teach Danny not to speak negative things about himself, the next time I hit a bad shot, I thought, Well, now I'm going to act the way he's been acting and see if he realizes how silly it is to be that way.

I started saying, "Oh, stupo Joyce, you know, you just never do anything right." Danny didn't even hear me. I tried to say it again, but it was distasteful to me even though I didn't really mean it. Just speaking those words out of my mouth and hearing them in my ears saddened my spirit.

The Power Is in Our Mouth

For by your words you will be justified and acquitted, and by your
words you will be condemned and sentenced.

Matthew 12:37

If we speak badly about ourselves, we will feel condemned. Let's actively apply what Jesus taught in the Scripture above to speak positively about ourselves as the first step to overcoming insecurity, and *never speak negatively about yourself.* Speak words that empower you—not words that weaken you.

Press Toward the Mark

I do not consider, brethren, that I have captured and made it my
own [yet]; but one thing I do [it is my one aspiration]: forgetting
what lies behind and straining forward to what lies ahead, I press
on toward the goal to win the [supreme and heavenly] prize to
which God in Christ Jesus is calling us upward.

Philippians 3:13–14

God is not concerned about whether we reach perfection but whether we are pressing toward the mark of perfection. Speak and act with the knowledge that Jesus is alive and working in your life, and no matter how big a mistake you make Jesus' shed blood covers it.

2

⟡

CELEBRATE THE POSITIVE

The second key to overcoming insecurity is related to the first: *Meditate on and speak positive things about yourself.*

We have learned how destructive thinking and saying negative things about ourselves can be. Now let's look at the power of thinking and saying positive things about ourselves that line up with the Word.

As we have seen, our thoughts and words about ourselves are tremendously important. We need to meditate on good things about ourselves—on purpose. We need to look for good things about ourselves, think on those things, and speak them to ourselves.

If we talk about ourselves in a negative way, we begin to see ourselves in a negative way. Soon we begin to convey that negativism to all those around us. It is literally true that others' opinions of us will never rise above the opinion we have of ourselves.

If I am around people who are confident and convey that confidence, I find I automatically have confidence in them. But if they convey to me that they don't believe in themselves, I find it very hard to have confidence in them.

That same principle applies to us. If we want others to have confidence in us, we must show them we have confidence in ourselves.

Giants or Grasshoppers?

There we saw the Nephilim [or giants], the sons of Anak, who come from the giants; and we were in our own sight as grasshoppers, and so we were in their sight.

Numbers 13:33

In the book of Numbers there is an account of twelve spies sent out into the promised land to scout out the land. Ten came back with an evil report, and two came back with a good report. The ten who came back with the evil report saw giants in the land and were frightened: "We were in our own sight as grasshoppers, and so we were in their sight." In other words, the enemy saw them the same way they saw themselves.

These ten spies ran home defeated. Why? Because they did not have the ability to overcome the giants in the land? No. They ran home defeated because of the way they saw themselves, because of the negative attitude they had toward themselves.

The Power of Positive Confession

Caleb quieted the people before Moses, and said, Let us go up at once and possess it; we are well able to conquer it.

Numbers 13:30

Here we see the response of one of the two positive spies, Caleb. In the face of seemingly overwhelming odds, his report was, "We are well able." The reason he said that was because he knew that God had told them to go into and take possession of the land.

In order to overcome the negative thinking and speaking that have been such a natural part of our lifestyle for so long, we must make a conscious effort to think and speak good things about ourselves to ourselves by making positive confessions.

Perhaps you think you would rather not go around talking to yourself, but you do. Even if you don't talk out loud, you have what is called "self-talk" going on inside you all the time.

I encourage you to begin speaking positively in private, for example when you are taking a shower or driving in the car alone. Begin to speak, on purpose, good things about yourself.

Confess in Line with the Word of God

But we have the mind of Christ (the Messiah) and do hold the thoughts (feelings and purposes) of His heart.

1 Corinthians 2:16

When I say we should make positive confession about ourselves, I mean we need to get our mouth in line with what the Word says about us. For example, the Word of God says we have the mind of Christ. So that is what we should be saying about ourselves.

The Bible also says we have a call on our life, that every one of us is called into the ministry of reconciliation and intercession (see 2 Corinthians 5:18–20; 1 Timothy 2:1–3). That does not mean that we all stand in the office of an intercessor, but we all have the call on our life to be used by God—and we should say so.

Speak Scriptural Confessions

Speak and publish fearlessly the Word of God.

Philippians 1:14

Many years ago God put in my heart to make a list of confessions about my life. By the time I was done there were over a hundred.

I found Scriptures to back up each confession I put on my list. It took me time to do that. But if you will make an effort to dig around in the Word for yourself, you will find gold in there.

When I began speaking these confessions, the things I started saying were not happening. They were not reality in my life at that moment.

For example, at that time I was living under a cloud of guilt and condemnation. But several times every day I would say, "I am the righteousness of God in Jesus Christ. I have been set apart and made holy by the Lamb. There is a call on my life, and God is going to use me."

I had such a bad attitude about myself, I had to convince myself I was okay before God could really do anything through me.

For six months, I was diligent to read that list at least once or twice every day. I still remember a good portion of those positive confessions. Those words are now built into me.

Believe in Yourself—in What God Can Do through You

We are not able to go up against the people [of Canaan], for they are stronger than we are.

Numbers 13:31

God needs you. But if you don't believe in yourself, if you don't believe in the ability God has placed on the inside of you, you will discount yourself. You will sit on the sidelines and watch other people be used by God in your place.

God deliberately chooses the weak and foolish things of the world to do His work to confound the wise, so that no mortal can ever have reason to glory or to boast in his own flesh (see 1 Corinthians 1:27–29).

God is not as concerned with your weaknesses as you are. The problem with the spies in Numbers 13 is they looked at the giants instead of looking at God. Yes, there were giants in the land, but the Israelites needed to look at God and not the giants.

There are some giants in my life. But I don't need to stare at those giants. I need to stare at God. I need to keep my gaze firmly fixed on God and believe that He can do what He says He can.

The same is true for you. Your spirit wants to produce tremendous things in your life. But if you always keep that spirit man pushed down by negative attitudes, thoughts, and words, he will never rise up to bring you into the place God wants you to occupy, into the land He wants you to possess.

God Gives Life to the Dead

*As it is written, I have made you the father of many nations. [He
was appointed our father] in the sight of God in Whom he believed,
Who gives life to the dead and speaks of the nonexistent things that
[He has foretold and promised] as if they [already] existed.*

Romans 4:17

Abraham knew it was not a sin to do or be something if it was in line
with the Word of God.

Before Abraham ever had a child God told him that he was to be
the father of many nations. Yet how could that be? Abraham was an
old man, and his wife Sarah was barren.

But God "gives life to the dead." He proved that by quickening
Sarah's dead womb and sparking up Abraham's dead body. And God
"speaks of the nonexistent things that [He has foretold and prom-
ised] as if they [already] existed."

Based upon this Scripture we should get our mouths in line with
anything that God has promised in the Word. That does not mean
that we are to go around speaking any off-the-wall thing we want to.
We must speak only those things promised us in the Word of God.

Confessing the Word Brings Results

*So shall you find favor, good understanding, and high esteem in the
sight [or judgment] of God and man.*

Proverbs 3:4

I used to have major problems in my life. Now I am walking in victory because the Word of God has worked in my life. But I did not
just fall out of bed one morning and begin to experience immediate
and total victory. Nor did I just drop into a meeting once every three
weeks and listen to a tape occasionally. I have had my nose in the
Word ever since I became baptized in the Holy Spirit. I began to experience victory by continually exalting the Word of God in my life.

I expect favor because I have quoted Scriptures on favor to myself for a long time. The Bible says repeatedly that we have favor with
God and that God will give us favor with man. I expect to get favor

with men. That is not a bad, prideful attitude; it is not improper. Why? Because it is a promise to me in the Bible.

If you will speak about yourself what the Word of God says about you, you will receive positive results, but it will take time and effort.

When God first started teaching me these things I am sharing with you in this book I had a weight problem. I had always been about twenty to twenty-five pounds overweight. I remember standing in front of a full-length mirror looking at myself and saying, "I eat right, I look good, I feel good, and I weigh 135 pounds."

At that time, *none* of that was true. I did not eat right, I did not look good, I did not feel good, and I *certainly* did not weigh 135 pounds. But I felt that was a good weight for me, so I began confessing it to myself.

I did not go tapping other people on the shoulder saying, "Hey! I look good, I feel good, I eat right, and I weigh 135 pounds." These were private confessions about myself that I made to myself.

As Goes the Mouth, So Goes the Life

For we all often stumble and fall and offend in many things. And if anyone does not offend in speech [never says the wrong things], he is a fully developed character and a perfect man, able to control his whole body and to curb his entire nature.

James 3:2

Positive confession of the Word of God should be an ingrained habit of every believer.

If you have not yet begun to develop this important habit, start today. Begin thinking and saying good things about yourself: "I am the righteousness of God in Jesus Christ. I prosper in everything I lay my hand to. I have gifts and talents, and God is using me. I operate in the fruit of the Spirit. I walk in love. Joy flows through me. I eat right, I look good, I feel good, I weigh exactly what I should weigh."

Even though God wants to help us, the Bible teaches that we get our lives straightened out by getting our mouth straightened out. It teaches we can appropriate the blessings of God in our lives by believing and confessing the positive things God has said about us in His Word.

3

~⚭~

AVOID COMPARISONS

The next step to overcoming insecurity is simple: *Never compare yourself with anyone else.*

If you lack confidence, this is an important point. You may think you are perfectly all right until you look around and see somebody else who seems to be doing what you are doing a little better than you are.

Take prayer as an example. Many times even personal communion with God can be a source of condemnation. Compared to someone else you may feel you are not praying long enough, good enough, or "spiritually" enough.

Comparison Invites Condemnation

Do you have faith? Have it to yourself before God. Happy is he who does not condemn himself in what he approves.

Romans 14:22 (NKJV)

There was a time in my life when I was praying about half an hour a day. I was just as happy as I could be doing that because there was an anointing on me to pray thirty minutes each day. I was perfectly content and satisfied with my daily half-hour fellowship with the Lord.

Then one day I heard a minister preach about how he prayed

four hours every day and got up at some awful hour to do it. (At least it seemed awful to me—I think he started at four or five o'clock in the morning.) When I compared myself to him, I felt like a wretch even though I had been honestly and truly happy about my prayer life up to that point. After hearing that message I felt as though I hardly even loved God.

Sometimes I would hear people preach about how God would get them up in the middle of the night to pray. I would think, "Lord, what's the matter with me? I go to bed and sleep!"

Why was I put under condemnation? Because I really was not secure in who I was in Christ.

As a minister I have learned to be careful about what I say because many of those to whom I preach are not secure. There is a danger they will take my testimony and compare themselves to me. So for the most part I keep to myself how long I pray and how I pray and what I pray about.

We Are All Unique

For he who serves Christ in these things is acceptable to God and approved by men.

Romans 14:18 (NKJV)

We can feel perfectly fine about ourselves until we start comparing ourselves with somebody else. Then all of a sudden, we think we are an awful mess.

I really want to encourage you to stop comparing yourself with other people: how you look compared to how they look, what position you occupy compared to what position they occupy, how long you pray compared to how long they pray, how often you prophesy compared to how often they prophesy.

Likewise, you cannot compare your tribulation to someone else's tribulation. You cannot compare your suffering to someone else's suffering. Some situations may seem hard to you. But you cannot look at somebody else and say, "Why is all this happening to me and everything comes up roses for you?"

For example, perhaps two young women in the same neighborhood get born again. Ten years down the road both are still believing for their husbands' salvation but neither has been saved. Then a woman across the street gets born again. She believes God for her husband to get saved and two weeks later, he is born again, filled with the Spirit, and ready to start running around the world preaching.

God Knows What He Is Doing

For I know the thoughts and plans that I have for you, says the Lord, thoughts and plans for welfare and peace and not for evil, to give you hope in your final outcome.

Jeremiah 29:11

If you don't understand that God has an individual plan for your life, you will begin to look around and compare yourself with other people and say, "What's wrong with me? I have been praying ten years and haven't gotten an answer; you've been praying two weeks and look what God has done for you."

People tell me all the time how they work in the church, tithe, love God, and are trying as hard as they know how. Yet it seems as though nothing ever works out for them while others around them seem to get everything they desire. Why is that?

I don't have a pat answer to that question, but I do know this: We have to believe above everything else that God knows what He is doing. It is amazing the peace that comes with that belief.

Walking by Faith, Not Sight

For we walk by faith . . . not by sight or appearance.

2 Corinthians 5:7

Sometimes when people have a call on their life, they go through things that others may never go through.

Because of the things I went through for a period of four or five years in particular, I have deep, heartfelt understanding and compassion for hurting people when they come to me for ministry. There are some things that cannot be received by the laying on of hands. They come only through personal experience. The experience I had helped prepare me for my ministry.

In the beginning of my ministry I would cry out, "Why, God, why? I'm believing You. I don't understand why this is happening to me."

Many times we do not understand something until we get on the other side of it, when it is all over and we are rejoicing in victory. Perhaps a year or more after the experience is over, our eyes are opened and we are able to say, "Now I understand."

Or we may never understand. But when we learn to trust God even if we don't understand, our faith will grow.

Don't Compare, Just Follow!

He said this to indicate by what kind of death Peter would glorify God. And after this, He said to him, Follow Me! But Peter turned and saw the disciple whom Jesus loved, following—the one who also had leaned back on His breast at the supper and had said, Lord, who is it that is going to betray You? When Peter saw him, he said to Jesus, Lord, what about this man?

John 21:19–21

Just as we must guard against comparing our gifts and talents with the gifts and talents of others, so we must not compare our trials and tribulations with their trials and tribulations.

Jesus revealed to Peter ahead of time some of the suffering he would go through. Peter immediately wanted to compare his suffering and his lot in life with somebody else's by saying, "What about this man?"

"Jesus said to him, If I want him to stay (survive, live) until I come, what is that to you? [What concern is it of yours?] You follow Me!" (John 21:22).

That is His answer to us also. We are not called to compare, only to comply.

Don't Covet the Blessings of Others

You shall not covet.

Exodus 20:17

When you are having a hard time, never look at others and say, "God, I don't understand. Why am I having such a hard time while they just seem to be so blessed?" That kind of question only brings torment. Why? Because it is a sign of covetousness.

When your brothers or sisters are blessed, be joyful for them; when they hurt, share their pain with them (see Romans 12:15). But don't compare yourself to others. Instead trust God. Believe that He has an individualized, specialized plan for your life. Be secure in the knowledge that no matter what is happening to you or how things may appear for the moment, He cares about you very much and is working out everything for the best (see 1 Peter 5:7; Romans 8:28).

4

❦

Focus on Potential, Not Limitations

This is the fourth point in how to succeed at being yourself, how to build confidence and overcome insecurity: *Focus on potential instead of limitations*. In other words, focus on your strengths instead of your weaknesses.

Concentrate on Potential

Having gifts (faculties, talents, qualities) that differ according to the grace given us, let us use them.

Romans 12:6

The well-known actress Helen Hayes was only five feet tall. In the early days of her career she was told that if she was just four inches taller, she could be a great stage star. Although she could not actually grow to increase her height, she worked to improve her posture and bearing, to stand tall, so that on stage she appeared taller.[1]

Instead of concentrating on the fact that she was only five feet tall, she began concentrating on her great acting potential, and she didn't give up. Later on in her life, she was chosen to portray Mary, Queen of Scots, one of the tallest queens who has ever lived.[2]

Focus on your potential instead of on your limitations.

You Can Do What God Has Called You to Do

I can do everything God asks me to with the help of Christ who gives me the strength and power.

Philippians 4:13 (TLB)

Recently I saw a sign on a church that said, "Trust in God, believe in yourself, and you can do anything." That is not correct.

There was a time in my life when I would have seen that sign and said, "Amen!" But not anymore. You and I really cannot do *anything* we want to do. We cannot do anything or everything that everyone else is doing. But we can do everything *God has called us to do.* And we can be anything *God says we can be.*

We must get balance in this area. We can go to motivational seminars and be told with a lot of emotional hype, "You can do anything. Think you can do it; believe you can do it; say you can do it—and you can do it!" That is true only to a degree. Carried too far, it gets off into humanism. We need to speak about ourselves what the *Word* says about us.

We can do what we are *called* to do, what we are gifted to do. There are ways we can learn to recognize the grace gifts that are on our life.

I have learned this regarding myself: When I start getting frustrated, I know it is a sign that either I have gotten off into my own works and am no longer receiving God's grace, or I am trying to do something for which there was no grace to begin with.

Don't Frustrate the Grace of God

I do not frustrate the grace of God.

Galatians 2:21 (KJV)

God has not called us to frustration.

Each of us is full of gifts and talents and potentials and abilities. If we really begin to cooperate with God, we can go for the very best that God has for us. But if we get high-minded ideas and set goals that are beyond our abilities and the grace gifts on our life, we will become frustrated. We will not attain those things, and we may even end up blaming God for our failure.

Strength for All Things in Christ

I have strength for all things in Christ Who empowers me [I am ready for anything and equal to anything through Him Who infuses inner strength into me; I am self-sufficient in Christ's sufficiency].

Philippians 4:13

If we just pull that Scripture out of the Bible, it certainly looks like we ought to be able to do anything we want to do, doesn't it? If we pick out the verses we want, we can make the Bible say anything we want it to say. But let's read this passage in context and see what it really says. Let's begin at verse ten:

I was made very happy in the Lord that now you have revived your interest in my welfare after so long a time; you were indeed thinking of me, but you had no opportunity to show it.

The people in the Philippian church had sent Paul an offering, which pleased him. He was writing to say, "Friends, I am happy you have revived your interest in me after such a long time." Then he went on to add in verses eleven and twelve:

Not that I am implying that I was in any personal want, for I have learned how to be content (satisfied to the point where I am not disturbed or disquieted) in whatever state I am. I know how to be abased and live humbly in straitened circumstances . . .

(That means there were times when Paul did *not* have everything he wanted, times when his circumstances were *not* the way he would have liked them to be.)

. . . and I know also how to enjoy plenty and live in abundance. I have learned in any and all circumstances the secret of facing every situation, whether well-fed or going hungry, having a sufficiency and enough to spare or going without and being in want.

Paul's message was not that he could do anything he set his mind to, but that he had learned the secret of making the best of whatever situation he found himself in. It is in that context that he makes the statement we hear quoted so often about the ability to "do all things in Christ."

The Truth About "Doing All Things"

I have strength for all things in Christ Who empowers me [I am ready for anything and equal to anything through Him Who infuses inner strength into me; I am self-sufficient in Christ's sufficiency].

Philippians 4:13

When we read verse thirteen in context we realize what Paul is actually saying: "God has done a work in my life. I have learned the secret of staying at peace whether I have everything I want or not. If my circumstances are exciting I know how to handle that situation and stay humble. If my circumstances aren't too good, I have the inner strength to deal with that situation, also. I am able to handle all the varying situations of life through Christ Who gives me strength."

If Philippians 4:13 is taken out of its context, we might believe we can do anything we feel like, anytime we want to, anywhere we want to. That is not true. We must stay with the anointing that only comes with the will of God.

Stay with the Anointing

But it is God Who confirms and makes us steadfast and establishes us [in joint fellowship] . . . in Christ, and has consecrated and anointed us [enduing us with the gifts of the Holy Spirit].

2 Corinthians 1:21

You may have experienced deep confusion at some time in your life by trying to do something for which God has not consecrated and anointed you. You thought it was God's will, then discovered it was not. If so, you are not the only one who has done this. I have done the same thing and so have many others. But then how can you ever know that something is truly of God?

If you believe God has spoken something to you—it has a scriptural basis, and you really have peace about it—then move toward it. But if you discover that no matter what you do, nothing works, don't spend your life banging your head against a brick wall trying to force something that God is not helping you with. If there is no anointing, it will never work.

Some people spend all their lives trying to ride a dead horse. I heard someone say recently, "The horse has been dead seven years— it's time to dismount."

Do your part. Do what you believe is right, follow God's leadership to the best of your ability, then leave the outcome in His hands. In this way you are doing all you can, but you are not spending your life trying to do what you can't do, which is God's part.

Leave It in God's Hands

And, having done all . . . stand.

Ephesians 6:13

Remember, if God has called you to do something, do your part and then stand firm. When you have done all you can do, leave the situation in God's hands and go on about your business. If He does not do His part, then it is not time, it is not right, or it is not for you.

People often ask me, "How can I do what you're doing? God has called me to preach like you. Tell me how you got started." I tell them, "It's not that easy. I can't just give you three easy lessons on how to begin a ministry. But if God calls you, He opens the doors. He apprehends you, prepares you, provides the money, gives you favor, and makes it happen."

It is okay to confess that you are going to have a ministry similar to another person's if you believe God has called you to do so. Just be sure to make that confession in the privacy of your home, not in public. Keep it mainly between you and God until God makes it public. If that desire is of God, you will see it come to pass. But if it is not of God and nothing happens, that still should not affect your sense of self-worth.

You have to believe in yourself. It is okay to look at somebody who is successful in ministry or in business and say, "I believe if God wants me in that position, He will make me able to do it. I have potential, and I have ability." Just make sure it is God's will for you and not your own selfish desire. If it is God's will, you will find joy in it.

Do What You Love, Love What You Do!

If God has called you to do something, you will find yourself loving it despite any adversity that may beset you.

Sometimes Dave and I have to leave someplace at three o'clock in the morning with only three hours of sleep. Often I have had to sleep in the back of the van—that's like trying to sleep while riding a horse. Some of the bathrooms we have to use when on the road are not very nice. Some of the restaurants we eat in are not very good. Some of our hotel accommodations are awful, and I wake up in the morning feeling like I am about a hundred years old. Sometimes I have to study on the bed in a motel because there is no desk.

Like Paul, my husband and I face undesirable conditions again and again. But I love what I am doing. How could I love it if it was not of God? In spite of all the hardships and inconveniences, we truly enjoy traveling all over the country doing the work of the Lord.

If God has called you to do something, He enables you to do it. If you are struggling all the time saying, "I hate this," something is wrong!

God Gives Promotion

For not from the east nor from the west nor from the south come promotion and lifting up. But God is the Judge! He puts down one and lifts up another.

Psalm 75:6–7

Often we humans ask other people, "What's your occupation?" When they answer, sometimes we imply by our attitude that they should have a desire for a higher position than the one they presently occupy.

It is okay to believe God for a greater position or responsibility, but it is equally acceptable to remain in the position we are in if that is where we feel God wants us.

God can enable us to fill a position and do a job that, in the natural world, we are not qualified for. But there are some insecure people who think they can gain worth and value through a higher position. They step out on their own without God's leading, their motive is wrong, and they fall flat on their face.

I have discovered that it is unwise to try to get a position that God is not giving to us. We can labor in the flesh and make things happen, but we will never be at peace with the results.

> Therefore humble yourselves [demote, lower yourselves in your own estimation] under the mighty hand of God, that in due time He may exalt you. (1 Peter 5:6)

God does things in our lives when He knows we are truly ready. Set high goals, but let your focus be on doing the very best you can where you are, knowing that if and when God wants to promote you, He is certainly well able to do so.

Focus on Potential

> *All these [gifts, achievements, abilities] are inspired and brought to pass by one and the same [Holy] Spirit, Who apportions to each person individually [exactly] as He chooses.*
>
> 1 Corinthians 12:11

Gifts and talents are distributed by the Holy Spirit according to the grace that is on each person to handle them. God is not displeased with us if we have only one gift while somebody else has five gifts. But He does not like it if we do not develop the one gift we do have (see Matthew 25:14–30).

In the book of Numbers we saw that twelve spies were sent in to scout out the promised land they had been commanded by God to possess. Ten of them came back saying, "There are giants in the land, so we can't take it." But two of them said, "Yes, there are giants there, but we are well able to take it because *God* has said to do so."

Ten of the Hebrew spies looked at their limitations; two looked at their potential. Ten of them looked at the giants; two looked at God.

If you are going to like yourself, if you are going to succeed at being yourself, you are going to have to focus on your potential—what God has created you to be—not on your limitations.

5

⚜

Exercise Your Gift

Here is the fifth point in overcoming insecurity: *Find something you like to do and that you do well, then do it over and over.* Do you know what will happen? You will begin to succeed because you will be doing what you are gifted to do. And you will start to feel better about yourself because you won't be constantly failing.

Locate Your Gift

[He whose gift is] practical service, let him give himself to serving; he who teaches, to his teaching.

Romans 12:7

That Scripture does not say, "If you are a teacher, teach, but at the same time try real hard to be a worship leader."

There was a time in my life when I was really mad at myself because all I could do was teach. I wanted to do all the other things I saw everybody else doing. I struggled and prayed and "tore down strongholds." I told the devil, "I'm going to do more!" But I came to a place where I had to be satisfied preaching the Word.

I spent a year of my life trying to grow tomatoes and make my husband's clothes because my next-door neighbor did that. I compared myself with her and concluded there was something wrong with me because I didn't act like a "normal" housewife. Frankly, I did not want to grow tomatoes. And I *really* didn't want to make my husband's clothes. But I got all hung up in trying to do what others were doing.

Don't Keep Doing What You Don't Do Well

Except the Lord builds the house, they labor in vain who build it.

Psalm 127:1

I spent a year trying to do something I did not do well. Day in and day out I had continual defeat. I was so discouraged. I might spend all day sewing on a shirt, then hem it on the wrong side and have to spend hours picking the hem out. I continually felt defeated.

Don't spend all your time trying to do something you are not good at. Instead, let God show you what you are good at. Generally, the things you are good at are the things you are going to enjoy.

God wouldn't make us do something we hated all of our life. Why are we always trying to do something we can't do? Why not just find something we do well and go for it? It is amazing how much better it makes us feel.

Look for the Anointing

But as for you, the anointing (the sacred appointment, the unction) which you received from Him abides [permanently] in you; [so] then you have no need that anyone should instruct you.

1 John 2:27

A lot of people in ministry try to do things they are not anointed to do just because other people do them.

In my travels, I see ministers all over the country who are struggling. Often the reason is that they are trying to do what some other church or ministry is doing even though God has not anointed them to do it. They feel if they cannot do what someone else is doing, they are not as good as that person.

We can only do what God has gifted us and anointed us to do. If we try to do otherwise, we will feel pressured continually.

Don't Exceed God's Grace

John answered, A man can receive nothing [he can claim nothing, he can take unto himself nothing] except as it has been granted to him from heaven. [A man must be content to receive the gift which is given him from heaven; there is no other source.]

John 3:27

A man can receive how much? A man can claim how much? He can take unto himself how much? Only as much as is granted to him from heaven.

As Christians we must be *content*. If I can never preach as well as some other preacher, I am just going to have to be content to preach the best I can. If my ministry never gets as big as Brother So-and-So's or Sister So-and-So's, I must be content with what I have.

You and I cannot go beyond the grace of God in our life. We cannot receive a gift from God just because we want one. The Holy Spirit gives us gifts according to His will for us, and we must be satisfied with what we receive from Him.

Sometimes even though God wants to confer a gift upon us, it is not yet time for it to be bestowed. Until God leans over the banister of heaven and says, "Now!" we can struggle and fume and fuss and fight and complain and quarrel, but we will still not get it.

Do you know when we are going to get what God wants us to have? When He gets ready to give it to us. We are not going to get it until then, so we may as well learn to be content with such things as we have (see Hebrews 13:5). We must remember that "Father knows best!"

Use Your Gift

Having gifts (faculties, talents, qualities) that differ according to the grace given us, let us use them: [He whose gift is] prophecy, [let him prophesy] according to the proportion of his faith; [He whose gift is] practical service, let him give himself to serving; he who teaches, to his teaching; He who exhorts (encourages), to his ex-

hortation; he who contributes, let him do it in simplicity and liberality.

Romans 12:6–8

Don't waste time trying to figure out what your gift is. Just start functioning in what you are good at.

I remember a woman who led worship in a church we visited in Maine. She was an exhorter. When I had finished preaching she chased me down the back stairs. "Oh, come here, come here," she said, and began praying for me.

Then she began speaking to me. "Oh, honey, that was wonderful, that was marvelous. Oh, you're so anointed."

She just carried on! By the time I left I felt *great*, like I was floating on air!

Sometimes I work really hard and feel that I have fallen flat. Then here come the exhorters in the church. The more they say to me, the more I believe I am able to start all over again.

But what does the devil say to an exhorter? "That's nothing, just being able to cheer people up." He is not about to tell that person that exhortation is an important ministry in the church.

If you have the gift of exhortation, Satan will tell you that you ought to preach or teach or become a pastor or build a church! But the Bible says if your gift is exhorting, then begin to exhort. If you are to teach, then begin teaching. If you are to give yourself in serving, then start serving. If you are to help others, then start helping.

The Ministry of Helps

He who gives aid and superintends, with zeal and singleness of mind.

Romans 12:8

If you are to give aid in the Body of Christ, then make it your business to give. If God calls you to be a giver, He is obviously going to provide you the means to do that.

The phrase "he who gives aid" refers to the helpers. There are many people in the Body of Christ who are called as servants, as helpers, as those whose job it is to assist a ministry.

God calls strong leaders, people upon whom He bestows a powerful anointing for leadership. It is a gift to lead large numbers of people while keeping things in proper order. If an individual does not have the gift to do that, he will soon get himself into big trouble.

But even if he is gifted for the position, the leader can't do everything, so God anoints other people to help him, to hold up his hands, to pray for him. No one can exercise any kind of successful ministry without those who have been called and anointed to help.

If that is your calling and anointing, do it with all your might because it is vitally important.

Some people say, "Well, I'm just in helps." No, they are not *just* in helps. They are in one of the greatest ministries in the Bible. There are more people in helps than in any other ministry of the Church.

If you believe you are called into the ministry of serving, I hope you will never again feel insulted because "all you are is in helps." After all, that is the ministry of the Holy Spirit.

The Holy Spirit Is the Helper

And I will ask the Father, and He will give you another Comforter (Counselor, Helper, Intercessor, Advocate, Strengthener, and Standby), that He may remain with you forever.

John 14:16

The helps ministry is a great, marvelous, wonderful, powerful ministry. The Holy Spirit is in the ministry of helps. He leads it. He is *the* Helper. He is the One Who walks alongside each believer waiting to provide whatever assistance may be needed.

Some people are insulted because they have been called into the ministry of helps. They struggle with themselves trying to be something else. They simply do not realize that they exercise the same ministry the Holy Spirit exercises.

Be a Blessing Where You Are

He who does acts of mercy, with genuine cheerfulness and joyful eagerness.

Romans 12:8

There are certain things you and I like to do as a result of our gifts from God. We may not think those things are important—but they are, as we will discover if we will just begin to do them.

You can be a blessing to people no matter how simple your gifts may be. If you are a good cook or love to bake, use your gifts and talents to bless somebody other than yourself.

One night a friend brought my husband and me a pot of soup. It was the best soup I had ever tasted in my whole life; I just loved it. We talked for days about how wonderful the soup was.

Later our friend told us she kept thinking as she was making the soup, "I need to take Joyce some of this." But she dismissed the idea thinking it was silly. "She's not going to want my soup."

How many times does the devil cheat us out of being a blessing? Do you know the greatest thing you can do is be a blessing? Stop trying to figure out what your gift is and begin to function in something you like to do—just get busy and do it.

If you like to cheer people up, make it your business to cheer them up. If you love to give, find something and give it away. If you love to help, then help everybody you can. Just bless people.

We don't always have to do some *great* spiritual thing. Actually some of the things we don't think are really spiritual are more important to God than the things we think are so great.

Stir Up Your Gift

Wherefore I put thee in remembrance that thou stir up the gift of God, which is in thee. . .

2 Timothy 1:6 (KJV)

So many times we look for some great "spiritual" experience. We go to bed at night and the devil says, "Well, you didn't do a thing worthwhile today." But if we touched somebody else's life, if we made someone else happy, if we put a smile on someone's face, we *did* do something worthwhile. That ability is a gift from God.

The great apostle Paul tells his young disciple Timothy to stir up the gifts within him. That is good advice for all of us. Sometimes we get lazy with our gifts. We need to stir up those gifts on purpose. We need to "get with the program" again.

If you want to overcome a sense of worthlessness and insecurity, stir up your gift. Start using what God has put in you. Get busy and do what you can with what you have.

Do what you like to do. Then do it over and over.

6

❧

HAVE THE COURAGE TO BE DIFFERENT

If you are going to overcome insecurity and be the person you are called to be in Christ, *you must have the courage to be different.*

Even though each of us *is* different, we still try to be like each other. That is what causes unhappiness.

Don't Be Like Everyone Else

Now am I trying to win the favor of men, or of God? Do I seek to please men? If I were still seeking popularity with men, I should not be a bond servant of Christ (the Messiah).

Galatians 1:10

If you are going to be a success at being completely and fully you, you are going to have to take a chance on not being like everyone else.

Why not ask yourself the question Paul asked? Are you trying to win the favor of men, or of God?

Men-pleasers or God-pleasers?

Not with eyeservice, as menpleasers; but as the servants of Christ, doing the will of God from the heart.

Ephesians 6:6 (KJV)

Becoming men-pleasers is one of the easiest things we can do but one that can ultimately make us very unhappy. When we begin pleasing other people we begin to hear comments that make us feel good about ourselves. That is okay as long as we do not derive our sense of worth from it. As believers, our sense of worth has to be rooted and grounded not in the opinions of men but in the love of God.

We are worth something because God sent His only Son to die for us. We are worth something because God loves us, not because of what everybody else thinks about us or says about us.

We become "men-pleasers" when we no longer do the things we want to do, but what everybody else wants us to do because we think that will gain us acceptance and approval.

That was not the attitude the apostle Paul had or advocated.

Don't Let Others Manipulate You

Moreover, it is [essentially] required of stewards that a man should be found faithful [proving himself worthy of trust]. But [as for me personally] it matters very little to me that I should be put on trial by you [on this point], and that you or any other human tribunal should investigate and question and cross-question me. I do not even put myself on trial and judge myself.

1 Corinthians 4:2–3

That is a very liberating attitude—not to be concerned with public opinion or even self-opinion.

How far do you think Jesus would have gotten if He had worried about what people thought? Philippians 2:7 (KJV) says Jesus purposely "made himself of no reputation." As I was pondering that verse one day, Jesus said, "I got that over with right away." Eventually so did I. Now I no longer feel I have to run around trying to please people all the time.

I must admit I don't like it when people are unhappy with me. I don't even like it if one of my own children gets upset with me. But I know I cannot let people manipulate me with their demands.

As followers of Christ, we are to be led by the Spirit, not controlled by people. In the same manner, we should not try to control others, but allow them to be led by the Spirit just as we are.

Walk in Love

And walk in love . . . as Christ loved us and gave Himself up for us.

Ephesians 5:2

The point is, if we know we are doing the best we know how, we should not let other people's opinions of us bother us.

Still we must walk in love. We cannot just do anything we want to, anytime we want to. We cannot say, "Whoever doesn't like it, that's tough, that's their problem." Love does not behave that way.

Yet we must not allow people to manipulate and control us to the point we are never free to be who we are. If we do, we will always be trying to become whatever we think others expect us to be.

Be Transformed, Not Conformed

Do not be conformed to this world (this age) [fashioned after and adapted to its external, superficial customs], but be transformed (changed) by the [entire] renewal of your mind [by its new ideals and its new attitude], so that you may prove [for yourselves] what is the good and acceptable and perfect will of God, even the thing which is good and acceptable and perfect [in His sight for you].

Romans 12:2

The world is continually trying to conform us to its image. When I say "the world," I mean those we know and deal with on a daily basis. It may be family, friends, people in the neighborhood, or even the church.

The word *conform* means "to be similar in form or character; to comply; to behave in accordance with prevailing modes or customs."[1]

People will always try to get us to fit into their mold, partly due to their own insecurity. It makes them feel better about what they are doing if they can get someone else to do it too.

Very few people have the ability just to be who they are and let everybody else be who they are. Can you imagine how nice the world would be if we would all do that? Each person could be secure in who he is and would let others be who they are. We would not have to try to be little clones of one another.

Be Different—Become an Innovator

Behold, I am doing a new thing! Now it springs forth; do you not perceive and know it and will you not give heed to it?

Isaiah 43:19

All the great reformers in the Church, like Martin Luther, and in the world have been people who stepped out of the mold and did things differently. The same is true of the great men and women in the Bible.

Jeremiah was very young to be called as a prophet of God. The excuse he gave God was, "I'm too young."

Timothy also said, "I'm too young." Paul had to encourage Timothy over and over: "Don't worry about your youth, Timothy. God has called you and anointed you. Keep your eyes on that call."

What if John the Baptist or the apostle Paul or even Jesus had not had the courage to be different? We look at the great men and women in the Bible and think how wonderful they were. But they paid a price. They had to step out and be innovators. They had to be different. They had to avoid being ruled and controlled by what everybody thought they should be.

Operate in the Fruit of the Spirit

But the fruit of the [Holy] Spirit [the work which His presence within accomplishes] is love, joy (gladness), peace, patience (an even temper, forbearance), kindness, goodness (benevolence), faithfulness, Gentleness (meekness, humility), self-control (self-restraint, continence). Against such things there is no law [that can bring a charge].

Galatians 5:22–23

Even if we decide we are going to be innovative and different, we still need to operate in the fruit of the Spirit. We must not go around with a sarcastic, rebellious attitude. At the same time we cannot live our lives being conformed to the world because God wants to use us. He has something He wants to do through us.

God Wants to Use Us

While they were worshiping the Lord and fasting, the Holy Spirit said, Separate now for Me Barnabas and Saul for the work to which I have called them.

Acts 13:2

God wants to take us with all our weaknesses and inabilities and transform us, by working from the inside out, to do something powerful in this earth.

Satan will use the world and the world system to try to keep us out of God's will, out of God's best for us. Satan will try to get us to conform to what the world wants by telling us if we don't, we will be rejected.

If we are going to stand up and overcome insecurity, if we are going to succeed at being ourselves, we cannot continue to be afraid of what everybody else may think.

If we are seeking to be popular, there is a real good chance we are going to miss the will of God for our life.

Say Yes to the Call of God

Also I heard the voices of the Lord, saying, Whom shall I send? And who will go for Us? Then said I, Here am I; send me.

Isaiah 6:8

I would be miserable right now if I had said no to the call of God on my life. I might have stayed home and tried to grow tomatoes and sew my husband's clothes because that's what I thought would cause me to fit into the neighborhood. But I would have been miserable all of my life. Get hold of this truth today for your own life.

When God began showing Dave and me teachings about healing and the baptism of the Spirit and the gifts of the Spirit, we were going to a church where such ideas and practices were not popular or even acceptable. We ended up having to leave that church and all of our friends.

We were involved in everything in that church. Our whole life revolved around it. But we were told, "If you are going to believe the things you say you believe, then we can no longer have anything to do with you." What those people were really saying was, "Joyce, look, we've got a system here, and what you and Dave are doing doesn't fit into it. If you want to stay here, you must forget that stuff and fit into our mold."

The decision to leave that church was a difficult one. But if I had conformed to their demands, I would have missed the will of God for my life.

You Will Come Out Victorious

Jesus said, Truly I tell you, there is no one who has given up and left house or brothers or sisters or mother or father or children or lands for My sake and for the Gospel's who will not receive a hundred times as much now in this time—houses and brothers and sisters and mothers and children and lands, with persecutions—and in the age to come, eternal life.

Mark 10:29–30

After we left that church, I went through times of intense loneliness. But now I have more friends than I had before.

If God calls you to step out, the world will demand that you conform. Decide for God. You will go through trials—that's part of the challenge. You will go through a period of loneliness. There will be other problems. But you will come out on the other side victorious. You will be able to lie down at night and have that peace inside knowing that, even if you may not be popular with everybody else, you are pleasing to God.

Please God, Not Men

You are My Son, My Beloved! In You I am well pleased and find delight!

Luke 3:22

Jesus must have felt good when that voice came out of heaven at His baptism saying, "This is my beloved Son, in whom I am well pleased" (Matthew 17:5 KJV). But until that time in His life, there were few people who understood Him or liked what He was doing.

As we have seen, Paul refused to be judged by others or by himself. If he had succumbed to judgment, Satan would have defeated him.

Paul's message to those who questioned his qualification for ministry was to say: "From now on let no person trouble me [by making it necessary for me to vindicate my apostolic authority and the divine truth of my Gospel], for I bear on my body the [brand] marks of the Lord Jesus [the wounds, scars, and other outward evidence of persecutions—these testify to His ownership of me]!" (Galatians 6:17).

Stand Your Ground

And the king assigned for them a daily portion of his own rich and dainty food and of the wine which he drank. They were to be so educated and so nourished for three years that at the end of that time they might stand before the king.

Daniel 1:5

After the fall of Judah to Babylon, Nebuchadnezzar, the king of Babylon at that time, decided to bring in some young Hebrew men and train them as his attendants. His purpose was to conform them to the lifestyle of his court.

But Daniel, one of the devout young men of Judah who loved the Lord, "determined in his heart that he would not defile himself by [eating his portion of] the king's rich and dainty food or by [drinking] the wine which he drank" (Daniel 1:8).

Daniel was determined he would be a God-pleaser and not a man-pleaser. He refused to conform to the king's image of what he ought to be.

Daniel stood his ground and won favor with the king and his court. As a result of his fearless stand, God ended up using him in a very powerful way.

Exalted in the Kingdom

Then the king made Daniel great and gave him many great gifts, and he made him to rule over the whole province of Babylon and to be chief governor over all the wise men of Babylon.

Daniel 2:48

Daniel went through a period of testing and trial, but, in the end, the same king who tried to get him to conform had such respect for him that he exalted him to a high position in the kingdom.

The same thing happened to me years ago in the work world. My boss wanted me, in a roundabout way, to help him steal some money. I was a bookkeeper, and he wanted me to write off a customer's credit balance. The customer had paid a bill twice, and my employer didn't want that fact reflected on the client's statement.

I refused to do it.

Some years down the road, I ended up having great favor in that company. I was made second in command in charge of the office, the warehouse, all the inventory, and all the truck drivers. I was called upon to solve problems I didn't even understand.

As a young woman I had a major position of leadership in the company. I didn't really have the education or even the training for the position.

How did that happen? It came about because, like Daniel, I refused to conform to a lower standard. I was respected in the company and was exalted to a higher position of honor.

Those who try to get you to conform will not respect you if you do conform. In fact, they will despise your weakness. They will know they are controlling you and that what they are doing is wrong. But if you will stand your ground, you will be the one who ends up with the respect. For a while they may treat you as though you were the lowest life on earth. But when all is said and done, you will gain their respect.

Obey God

> [Then] Nebuchadnezzar said to them, Is it true, O Shadrach, Meshach, and Abednego, that you do not serve my gods or worship the golden image which I have set up?
>
> Daniel 3:14

This same king made a new rule and issued a new decree. He set up a golden image in the middle of the town and everybody was required to bow down before it and worship it. Anybody who refused to do so would be thrown into a fiery furnace.

Shadrach, Meshach, and Abednego, three of Daniel's close friends, refused to bow down. They had the same Spirit on them that Daniel did. The king said to them, "If you don't do as I say, I'm going to burn you alive."

Isn't that basically what the world says to you and me? If we refuse to conform to its standards, the world threatens us by saying, "If you do not bow down and do what we want you to do, if you do not fit into our mold, we are going to burn you alive."

That's when we need to do as the Hebrew children and trust the Lord.

Trust God

Shadrach, Meshach, and Abednego answered the king, O Neb-
uchadnezzar, it is not necessary for us to answer you on this point.
If our God Whom we serve is able to deliver us from the burning
fiery furnace, He will deliver us out of your hand, O king. But if
not, let it be known to you, O king, that we will not serve your gods
or worship the golden image which you have set up!

Daniel 3:16–18

Do you know what I like about Shadrach, Meshach, and Abednego?
Their absolute refusal to be frightened or intimidated. They told the
king: "We believe God is going to deliver us, but even if He *doesn't*,
we're not conforming to your image of what you think we ought to
be. We're going to do what God is telling us to do. You can do what
you want to with your furnace. But whatever happens to us, we will
have peace."

That is the attitude we ought to have toward those who would
try to pressure us into disobeying what we know to be the will of
God for us.

Boldly Do What God Has Commanded

Now when Daniel knew that the writing was signed, he went into
his house, and his windows being open in his chamber toward
Jerusalem, he got down upon his knees three times a day and
prayed and gave thanks before his God, as he had done previously.

Daniel 6:10

Here is one final example from the book of Daniel.

Later on another royal decree was issued forbidding anyone to
pray to anyone but the king. The law was a trick used by Daniel's enemies to try to destroy him. But Daniel boldly went into his room
and prayed to the Lord with the windows open toward Jerusalem just
as he did every day.

If that had happened to us, would we have closed the windows
hoping not to get caught? Would we have closed the windows and

just prayed once? Would we have done just enough to hope God would not get mad at us? Would we have tried to please both God and the king?

If we believe we are doing the will of God, and we run into opposition, we need to boldly continue doing what we know God has told us to do.

Dare to Be Different

So this [man] Daniel prospered in the reign of Darius and in the reign of Cyrus the Persian.

Daniel 6:28

In every single account of Daniel, we find he was pressured to conform to what others wanted him to do and to be. He refused to yield to pressure. After a period of trial and tribulation, God exalted him and he was put in charge of the entire kingdom.

Have the courage to be different. It will change your life, and God will exalt you in the process.

7

LEARN TO COPE WITH CRITICISM

If you are going to overcome insecurity, you are going to have to learn to cope with criticism.

Be Led by the Holy Spirit

But you have received the Holy Spirit and he lives within you, in your hearts, so that you don't need anyone to teach you what is right. For he teaches you all things, and he is the Truth.

1 John 2:27 (TLB)

Are you a self-validating person or do you need outside validation? By outside validation I mean somebody to tell you that you are okay, that what you are doing is all right. By self-validation, or inward validation, I mean taking action as you are led by the Holy Ghost, doing what you believe God is telling you to do.

One day I decided to redecorate my house. I got books of wallpaper samples and picked out patterns I thought would really look good, then showed them to other people and said, "I'm going to put this here and this here and this here. What do you think?"

Because I was insecure in that area I was looking for outside validation. I needed to hear what everybody thought about what I was doing.

Well, I didn't find one person who thought what I thought. Everyone I asked had a different opinion. Confusion came over me, and I hardly knew what to do.

We are all different; we are all individuals. I should not have expected anyone else to like what I liked. The real issue was whether I was satisfied with the outcome. I was the one who was going to have to live with it.

Don't waste your time asking other people whether your clothes are all right or whether your hair is okay or if they like your car. Become self-validating.

Make Your Own Decisions

But when it pleased God, who separated me from my mother's womb, and called me by his grace, To reveal his Son in me, that I might preach him among the heathen; immediately I conferred not with flesh and blood.

Galatians 1:15–16 (KJV)

Paul said when he was called by God to preach the Gospel to the Gentiles, he did not confer with anyone else about the matter.

Many times when we receive a message from God, we confer too much with flesh and blood. We go around looking for someone to assure us we are doing the right thing. John tells us that since we have the Holy Spirit, the Spirit of Truth, within us, we have no need to consult with other human beings.

Of course, there is another side to this question. The writer of Proverbs says that "in the multitude of counselors there is safety" (Proverbs 11:14).

The answer is to be obedient to the Spirit without refusing counsel from others who are wiser or more knowledgeable about the subject than we are.

By listening to what people said to me about decorating, I learned some valuable principles, things I didn't even know before. But I did not let their opinions determine my final decision.

We must not allow ourselves to be unduly influenced by others simply because we are afraid to make our own decisions. If we are going to be self-validating people, we must learn to cope with criticism.

What if I had decorated my whole house according to the opinions of others and then someone else had come in and said, "Oh, I don't think I would have done it this way"? I would have been caught in a dilemma.

Some people seem to think it is their job in life to give their personal opinion on everything to everybody. One of the greatest lessons we can learn is not to offer—or receive—unsolicited opinions or advice.

Don't Come Under Bondage

Stand fast therefore in the liberty wherewith Christ hath made us free, and be not entangled again with the yoke of bondage.

Galatians 5:1 (KJV)

Be secure enough to know how to cope with criticism without feeling there is something wrong with you. Don't come under bondage thinking you have to conform to other people's opinions.

Suppose someone came into my newly redecorated house and said to me, "You know, I don't know if you're aware of this or not, Joyce, but if you put that flower arrangement on a little bit taller table, it would look better than it does on that shorter table."

If I were secure in myself and my own viewpoint, I could listen to that person's opinion without feeling I had to do what she suggested. If I had some humility about me, I could at least consider what she said.

"You know, I think you're right."

Sometimes I know something doesn't look right, but I don't know how to fix it. If someone who knows more about it has a suggestion, I can say, "Yes, I think you may be right; I'll try it."

Have enough confidence in who you are in Christ that you can listen to others and be open to change without feeling you have to agree with their viewpoint or meet with their approval if you don't feel their suggestion is right for you.

Learn to cope with criticism.

8

❧

DETERMINE YOUR OWN WORTH

Determine your own worth—don't let other people do it for you.

The Need for Affirmation

You are My Beloved Son; in You I am well pleased.

Mark 1:11

A child needs affirmation from his parents. It is the job of parents to teach their children they are loved despite their weaknesses and flaws.

If children are instilled with that knowledge from a young age, they will grow up with solidity to their personality. They will not always be on a "works trip" trying to manifest perfection, thinking that the only way they will be accepted is by their good deeds.

A lot of times parents don't know how to give that affirmation. Often they have problems because they did not receive affirmation from *their* parents.

I read a story about a man who had never been able to get affirmation from his father. The father had never said, "I love you and am pleased with you."

This man was successful, yet he was very unhappy and would find himself weeping and crying for no apparent reason. So he began to go to therapy where he discovered the root cause of his problem. He learned he was constantly trying to prove himself to his father through works, which left him worn out all the time.

Several times during these counseling sessions this man made trips across the country to his father's house still trying to get his father to affirm him. He longed to hear his father say, "Son, I love you and think you're great. I'm proud of what you've accomplished in life."

So many times we just want somebody to say, "I'm proud of you. I'm pleased with you." But sometimes we must come to realize we may never receive that affirmation we desire from certain people.

One day the man left his father's house saying to himself, "My father is never going to give me what I'm trying to get him to give me—he doesn't know how." When he said that, it was as though something broke in him. From that moment on he experienced a liberty of spirit he had never known before.

Accepted in the Beloved

For He foreordained us (destined us, planned in love for us) to be adopted (revealed) as His own children through Jesus Christ, in accordance with the purpose of His will [because it pleased Him and was His kind intent]—[So that we might be] to the praise and the commendation of His glorious grace (favor and mercy), which He so freely bestowed on us in the Beloved.

Ephesians 1:5–6

Part of our struggle may simply be trying to get affirmation from somebody who is never going to give it to us because he simply doesn't know how.

The Bible teaches us that we have been made acceptable to God in the Beloved (His Son Jesus Christ), and that anyone who comes to the Father through Jesus He will in no wise cast out (Ephesians 1:6 KJV; John 6:37 KJV).

We need certain things from our loved ones, but if they do not know how to give those things to us, God does. He will be our mother, our father, our husband or wife, whatever we need Him to be.

The Lord will give us and build in us those things that others are not able to give us.

Take Responsibility for Your Own Actions

And so each of us shall give an account of himself [give an answer in reference to judgment] to God.

Romans 14:12

In the earlier years of my marriage I had many problems in my life and in my personality. After several years of marriage, Dave said to me, "You know what? If I determined my worth and my manhood by the way you treat me, I sure wouldn't have a very good opinion of myself."

Is there someone in your life you are not treating right? Are you trying to blame that person for your own faults? Is there someone who is making you miserable because of his own failure or unhappiness?

A woman in Chicago told me of her husband's arrest for public indecency.

"I can't forgive him for that," she said. "He got caught up in pornography, and I know what a trap that is. But the one thing that I'm having a hard time with is, he's blaming it on me. He says he did it because I didn't meet his needs."

I told her, "Even if you weren't 'meeting his needs,' that's no excuse for his sin. You can't let somebody else put his problems off on you."

Often people who have problems don't want to take the responsibility for those problems. They look for a scapegoat. They look for somebody to blame.

I used to do that to my own family. Everything I did wrong was somebody else's fault: If Dave hadn't done a particular thing, I wouldn't have acted in a particular manner; if my kids helped me more in the house, I wouldn't complain all the time; if Dave didn't watch so much football, I wouldn't be constantly on his case. I always found a way to blame someone else for my negative attitude and behavior.

I am so glad my husband was secure in who he was in Christ. I am so glad he had a firm spiritual foundation and was able to love me through that period of time. I am so glad he refused to let me make him feel guilty or unhappy.

Our Worth Is Based on the Blood

To Him Who ever loves us and has once [for all] loosed and freed us from our sins by His own blood.

Revelation 1:5

We need to come to the place where we are secure enough in who we are in Christ that we will not allow our sense of worth to be based on the opinions or actions of others.

Don't try to find your worth in how you look. Don't try to find your worth in what you do. Don't try to find your worth in how other people treat you. You are worth something because Jesus shed His blood for you.

You may have faults, there may be things about you that need to be changed, but God is working on you the same as He is on everybody else. Don't let somebody else dump his problems off on you. Don't allow someone else to make you feel worthless or useless just because he doesn't know how to treat you right and love you as you deserve to be loved as a blood-bought child of God.

Recognize What Is Right with You

I have been crucified with Christ [in Him I have shared His cruci-fixion]; it is no longer I who live, but Christ (the Messiah) lives in me; and the life I now live in the body I live by faith in (by adherence to and reliance on and complete trust in) the Son of God, Who loved me and gave Himself up for me.

Galatians 2:20

God wants us to stop thinking all the time, "What's wrong with me?" He wants us to dwell on what is *right* with us.

Certainly we should recognize our faults and weaknesses. We need to keep those areas open before God all the time. We need to confess, "Father, I know I'm not perfect; I know I have faults and weaknesses. I want You to work with me and change me. Show me my faults and help me to overcome them, Lord."

But we must not let other people grind us into the ground because of *their* weaknesses and problems.

Don't spend all your life trying to win somebody else's acceptance or approval. Remember that you have already been accepted and approved by God. Make sure that your affirmation, your validation, your sense of self-worth come from Him.

9

~ ❧ ~

KEEP YOUR FLAWS IN PERSPECTIVE

If you are ever going to really succeed at being yourself, you must *keep your flaws in perspective.*

Don't Focus on Imperfections

Look not to the things that are seen but to the things that are unseen.

2 Corinthians 4:18

My secretary Roxane is very attractive. She has light blonde hair and beautiful cream-colored skin. If she even gets the least bit embarrassed her cheeks turn bright rosy red. She is one of those people who will probably still look twenty years old when she is forty. She is tiny (she weighs ninety-three pounds), yet she is not skinny. She is just really cute.

Roxane told me she went through years and years of major frustration about her body. In particular she thought her thighs were too big. She said she was so paranoid about them, she wouldn't wear certain kinds of clothes. She hardly ever wore a bathing suit.

I went out with her a couple of times to buy clothes. She would try on things that looked darling on her, but I could tell she was not happy with them. Finally she shared with me how uncomfortable she was about her thighs.

I couldn't believe it! When a person weighs ninety-three pounds, *nothing* can be too big!

I use that as an example because no matter how good we look, the devil will have us find some part of our body that we happen to think is imperfect, and he will cause us to focus on that one part even though we may be the only one who notices it.

I had my hair done one time and it wasn't cut in the back exactly the way I like it. No one else noticed that my hair looked any different. As a matter of fact, when I mentioned it to Dave, he said, "You know that's really funny because I've been thinking the last few days how nice the back of your hair has looked recently."

It's just a matter of getting our eyes off the one imperfection and looking at everything in perspective.

If we are ever going to overcome feeling insecure about ourselves, we must learn to put our flaws into perspective. All of us have flaws, but we don't have to stare at them in the mirror twenty-four hours a day.

If we told our closest friends some of the things we think are flaws, they would probably just laugh at us. In fact, they might think those things we consider to be our greatest flaws are some of our best qualities.

Be Satisfied with Your Looks

Will what is formed say to him that formed it, Why have you made me thus?

Romans 9:20

The devil puts such junk in our minds. Who decides what a perfect body is anyway? Who draws out the model and says, "Now everybody who doesn't look like this is wrong"?

God created every one of us. According to Ephesians 2:10 we are His own handiwork, His workmanship. Therefore, He must like what He has made. To be pleasing to God we don't all have to look like a fashion model or a muscle man!

Each one of us has to come to a place where we are satisfied with how we look. That doesn't mean we don't need to exercise or perhaps lose some weight. I am not talking about failing to make an effort to stay trim and healthy. I am talking about all these foolish things we get caught up in, things that so often we cannot change about ourselves.

Do you want to overcome insecurity in your life? Learn to keep your flaws in perspective.

10

⸎

DISCOVER THE TRUE SOURCE
OF CONFIDENCE

The final and most important step to becoming more secure is to *discover the true source of confidence.*

Put No Confidence in the Flesh

For we [Christians] are the true circumcision, who worship God in spirit and by the Spirit of God and exult and glory and pride ourselves in Jesus Christ, and put no confidence or dependence [on what we are] in the flesh and on outward privileges and physical advantages and external appearances.

Philippians 3:3

In what do you place your confidence? That question must be settled before you can ever have God's confidence. Before your confidence can be in Him, you must remove your confidence from other things.

Don't place your confidence in the flesh—in appearance, education, finances, position, or relationship.

One time my daughter Sandy and her boyfriend broke up. I told her, "That's a shame, he really lost out."

If somebody doesn't want to have a relationship with you, why do you feel you are the one to blame? Maybe the other person is the one who is at fault.

If the devil thinks he can get you on the run with negative thoughts, he will chase you around from now until Jesus comes. Sooner or later you must come to the place where your confidence is not in the flesh or outward appearance but in Christ Jesus.

A young woman told me how much value she placed in her grades at school. She had a learning disability similar to dyslexia, and she studied hard so that nobody could tell from her grades that she had a problem. But she was studying *so* hard it was actually stealing her joy.

I told her, "You need to put those grades on the altar." I watched as fear came all over her.

"My grades really mean a lot to me," she said. "Not a little bit, but a lot."

Her real problem was not her learning disability, it was her confidence disability. She was trusting in grades rather than in God.

I have seen my daughter try so hard to get her hair to look good that I was surprised she had hair left when she was done. Sometimes her hair would look better *before* she combed it than it did after she had spent an hour fussing with it. But in her mind she could not face the world unless every hair was in its place.

That is another example of misplaced confidence.

Misplaced Confidence

For the Lord shall be your confidence, firm and strong.

Proverbs 3:26

Parents sometimes place their confidence in the accomplishments of their children, which can sometimes lead to serious problems for both of them. One father, for example, wanted his daughter to be a doctor, so she began to value her worth in terms of that goal. What her father did not know was that God had already picked his daughter to be my secretary!

Is God dealing with you about where you have placed your confidence? Is it in marriage? A college degree? Your job? Your spouse? Your children?

As Christians, we should not place our confidence in our education, our looks, our position, our property, our gifts, our talents, our abilities, our accomplishments, or in other people's opinions. Our heavenly Father is saying to us, "No more; it is time to let go of all those fleshly things to which you have been holding so firmly so long. It is time to put your trust and confidence in Me, and Me alone!"

But too often, like some of the Old Testament prophets, we allow ourselves to be influenced by what others think and say, and by how they look.

You Are What God Says You Are

Then the word of the Lord came to me [Jeremiah], saying, Before I formed you in the womb I knew [and] approved of you [as My chosen instrument], and before you were born I separated and set you apart, consecrating you; [and] I appointed you as a prophet to the nations. Then said I, Ah, Lord God! Behold, I cannot speak, for I am only a youth. But the Lord said to me, Say not, I am only a youth; for you shall go to all to whom I shall send you, and whatever I command you, you shall speak. Be not afraid of them [their faces], for I am with you to deliver you, says the Lord.

Jeremiah 1:4–8

Jeremiah was afraid to preach. He said, "I cannot speak." God said, "You get out there and do what I tell you to do. Speak to the people the message I give you. Don't look at their faces. I am with you to deliver you from all their wrath because you are My chosen vessel."

If God says we are something, then we are, whether anybody else agrees or not.

People told me I couldn't preach. Actually it was funny because they told me I couldn't preach after I was already doing it!

Some people said, "You can't preach because you are a woman."

I said, "I can't?"

"No, you can't."

"But I am preaching," I said. "I already am!"

Certainly there were temptations to quit because of all the criticism I received. But I never gave in to those temptations because I knew I was doing what God had told me to do. Like Paul, I found my confidence in the Lord, not in religion.

Religion Can Interfere with God

Though for myself I have [at least grounds] to rely on the flesh. If any other man considers that he has or seems to have reason to rely on the flesh and his physical and outward advantages, I have still more! Circumcised when I was eight days old, of the race of Israel, of the tribe of Benjamin, a Hebrew [and the son] of Hebrews; as to the observance of the Law I was of [the party of] the Pharisees, As to my zeal, I was a persecutor of the church, and by the Law's standard of righteousness (supposed justice, uprightness, and right standing with God) I was proven to be blameless and no fault was found with me.

Philippians 3:4–6

Paul was not only a Pharisee—perhaps the most pious of the Jews of his day—he was a chief of the Pharisees. He was so religious he kept all of the stringent religious rules of his sect. But he discovered that none of his religious piety mattered at all, so he was quite willing to give it all up in order to gain Christ.

Give Up Rules for Christ

But whatever former things I had that might have been gains to me, I have come to consider as [one combined] loss for Christ's sake. Yes, furthermore, I count everything as loss compared to the possession of the priceless privilege (the overwhelming preciousness, the surpassing worth, and supreme advantage) of knowing Christ Jesus my Lord and of progressively becoming more deeply and intimately acquainted with Him [of perceiving and recognizing and understanding Him more fully and clearly]. For His sake I have

> *lost everything and consider it all to be mere rubbish (refuse, dregs), in order that I may win (gain) Christ (the Anointed One).*
>
> Philippians 3:7–8

What kind of rules are you trying to keep in order to find a sense of self-worth? Maybe your rules are praying a certain amount of time or reading so many chapters of the Bible each day.

Religious rules tell us, "Do this, do that, don't eat this, don't touch that" (see Colossians 2:20–21). But God wants us to do what Paul did—get rid of all those rules and regulations so we can gain Christ and be known and found in Him.

Be Found and Known in Christ

> *And that I may [actually] be found and known as in Him, not having any [self-achieved] righteousness that can be called my own, based on my obedience to the Law's demands (ritualistic uprightness and supposed right standing with God thus acquired), but possessing that [genuine righteousness] which comes through faith in Christ (the Anointed One), the [truly] right standing with God, which comes from God by [saving] faith.*
>
> Philippians 3:9

This verse has an anointing on it that must not be missed. In it Paul says he wants to achieve one thing in life—to be found and known in Christ.

This needs to be our attitude also. We cannot always manifest perfect *behavior,* but with God's help we can always reflect a perfect *Savior.*

Do you know why God will never let us achieve perfect behavior? If we ever did, we would derive our sense of worth from our perfection and performance rather than from His love and grace.

If you and I behaved perfectly all the time, we would think God owed us an answer to our prayers because of our obedience to all the rules and regulations. So do you know what God does? He leaves us some weaknesses so we have to go to Him constantly to ask for His help—so we have to depend on Him whether we like it or not.

God is not going to let us work our way into a sense of peace and fulfillment. But He will allow us to work ourselves into a fit and frenzy. Why? So we will realize that works of the flesh produce nothing but misery and frustration (see Romans 3:20).

If that is so, what are we supposed to do? Just relax and enjoy life. We need to learn to enjoy God more. That will not only help us, it will also take the pressure off the people around us. We need to quit demanding that everyone be perfect all the time. We need to start enjoying them just as they are.

In essence Paul said he wanted to be able to stand before God and say, "Well, here I am, Lord, as big a mess as ever! I don't have a perfect record; but I do believe in Jesus."

You and I have to live like that every day or we will never enjoy peace and contentment. We cannot enjoy life if everything is based on our good works. We must learn to acknowledge our dependence on God.

Three Steps to Dependence on God

Trust (lean on, rely on, and be confident) in the Lord and do good; so shall you dwell in the land and feed surely on His faithfulness, and truly you shall be fed.

Psalm 37:3

There are three steps to a position of dependence on God.

First, learn what you are not. Accept the fact that you are not going to achieve success in life based upon your works. Instead, like it or not, you must trust God: "Commit your way to the Lord [roll and repose each care of your load on Him]; trust (lean on, rely on, and be confident) also in Him and He will bring it to pass" (Psalm 37:5).

The second step to staying in a position of dependence on God is to learn Who God is: "To you it was shown, that you might realize and have personal knowledge that the Lord is God; there is no other besides Him" (Deuteronomy 4:35).

The third step is to learn that as God is so are you: "We may have confidence . . . because as He is, so are we in this world" (1 John 4:17).

Not by Bread Alone

You shall [earnestly] remember all the way which the Lord your God led you these forty years in the wilderness, to humble you and to prove you, to know what was in your [mind and] heart, whether you would keep His commandments or not. And He humbled you and allowed you to hunger and fed you with manna, which you did not know nor did your fathers know, that He might make you recognize and personally know that man does not live by bread only, but man lives by every word that proceeds out of the mouth of the Lord.

Deuteronomy 8:2–3

I once went through a set of circumstances concerning my ministry that was confusing and upsetting. On some days there would be all kinds of mail and money for the ministry. The next day I would go to the post office and find only two or three pieces of mail. One week I would have a meeting with a large crowd, then the next week there would only be half as many in attendance. Satan would say to me, "Well, the people didn't like what you said last week so they didn't come back."

When circumstances conveyed to me I was doing well, my emotions were up. When circumstances indicated I was not doing very well, my emotions were down. The devil had me on the run. Every good experience elated me; every bad circumstance deflated me. (I call this "yo-yo" Christianity.)

This situation went on for years. Dave would try to tell me I was just under attack from the devil, but I couldn't see it. I saw the situation with my head, but I did not understand it in my heart.

One day as I was driving in my hometown I said to God, "Why is this happening?" The Spirit of the Lord said to me, "I am teaching you that man does not live by bread alone, but by every word that proceeds out of the mouth of God."

Bread was the daily sustenance for the children of Israel. Bread kept them going. When the Lord spoke to me about bread, He was saying, "I am trying to teach you that you cannot live by all these other things that keep you going. You must look to Me for your daily strength."

After delivering them from their oppressors in Egypt, God kept the Israelites out in the wilderness for forty years teaching them that very lesson. They were slow learners. Deuteronomy 1:2 says, "It is [only] eleven days' journey from Horeb by the way of Mount Seir to Kadesh-barnea [on Canaan's border; yet Israel took forty years to get beyond it]."

God as Deliverer and Sustainer

He brought [Israel] forth also with silver and gold, and there was not one feeble person among their tribes.

Psalm 105:37

When the Israelites came out of Egypt, they were a blessed people. They had seen the miracles of God and all the things He had done to Pharaoh on their behalf. Because the Lord was with them, they came out of the land of bondage with much of the Egyptians' material wealth, and with great physical health and stamina.

But God wanted them to know it was He Who brought them out, and not they themselves. He wanted them to learn that if they were to stay out of trouble, they had to keep depending on Him.

I used to think the size of the crowds in my meetings was dependent on my good preaching. I did not yet understand that it was not Joyce Meyer who got the people to the meetings. I had to learn that if they came, God had to bring them. I had to learn total dependence on God. It took me almost forty years also. Hopefully reading this book will save you some time.

The Key to Joy and Peace in God

And beware lest you say in your [mind and] heart, My power and the might of my hand have gotten me this wealth.

Deuteronomy 8:17

I now realize my joy has to be in God, not in my ministry. My peace has to be in the Lord, not in my works.

Not everything that comes into our lives is from God. But God will use the things of life—both bad and good—to teach us to depend upon Him.

I no longer have thoughts that bigger crowds are a result of my efforts. Now when I finish preaching I say, "Well, Lord, what happens next time will be up to You. You got the people here this time. If You want them to return, You will have to bring them back. I am just going to get up and preach the best I know how and leave the rest to You."

If you truly want to live in peace and security, that is the attitude you must have. You must do your best and then leave the results to God.

Allow the Lord to shake loose from you all those earthly things from which you are trying so hard to derive a sense of confidence, worth, security, and well-being. You may as well let Him have them, because He will not give up until He has His way—and His way is always best.

Conclusion

It is so important to have a positive sense of self-esteem, self-value, and self-worth—to be secure in who we are in Christ, to truly like ourselves. We learn to like ourselves by learning how much God loves us. Once we become rooted and grounded in God's love, we can come to terms of peace with ourselves.

Ten Steps to Building Confidence

Following is a list of the ten steps to building confidence. I urge you to copy it and put it up somewhere where you can see it every day.

1. Never speak negatively about yourself.
2. Celebrate the positive.
3. Avoid comparisons.
4. Focus on potential, not limitations.

5. Exercise your gift.
6. Have the courage to be different.
7. Learn to cope with criticism.
8. Determine your own worth.
9. Keep your flaws in perspective.
10. Discover the true Source of confidence.

SCRIPTURES ON CONFIDENCE

There is no fear in love; but perfect love casts out fear, because fear in-volves torment. But he who fears has not been made perfect in love.

1 John 4:18 (NKJV)

Satan enjoys tormenting people in a variety of ways. Insecurity, self-rejection, self-punishment, and a poor self-image are some of his ways. Insecurity is nothing but a diminished version of the spirit of fear.

Let these Scriptures minister the love of God to you, and your in-securities will fade away.

For you are a holy and set-apart people to the Lord your God; the Lord your God has chosen you to be a special peo-ple to Himself out of all the peoples on the face of the earth. The Lord did not set His love upon you and choose you be-cause you were more in number than any other people, for you were the fewest of all people. (Deuteronomy 7:6–7)

And you shall be secure and feel confident because there is hope; yes, you shall search about you, and you shall take your rest in safety. You shall lie down, and none shall make you afraid. (Job 11:18–19)

You number and record my wanderings; put my tears into Your bottle—are they not in Your book? (Psalm 56:8)

For God so greatly loved and dearly prized the world that He [even] gave up His only begotten (unique) Son, so that whoever believes in (trusts in, clings to, relies on) Him shall not perish (come to destruction, be lost) but have eternal (everlasting) life. (John 3:16)

May you be rooted deep in love and founded securely on love, That you may have the power and be strong to apprehend and grasp with all the saints [God's devoted people, the experience of that love] what is the breadth and length and height and depth [of it]; [That you may really come] to know [practically, through experience for yourselves] the love of Christ, which far surpasses mere knowledge [without experience]; that you may be filled [through all your being] unto all the fullness of God [may have the richest measure of the divine Presence, and become a body wholly filled and flooded with God Himself]! (Ephesians 3:17–19)

For God did not give us a spirit of timidity (of cowardice, of craven and cringing and fawning fear), but [He has given us a spirit] of power and of love and of calm and well-balanced mind and discipline and self-control. (2 Timothy 1:7)

My trust and assured reliance and confident hope shall be fixed in Him. (Hebrews 2:13)

And we know (understand, recognize, are conscious of, by observation and by experience) and believe (adhere to and put faith in and rely on) the love God cherishes for us. God is love, and he who dwells and continues in love dwells and continues in God, and God dwells and continues in him. (1 John 4:16)

We love Him, because He first loved us. (1 John 4:19)

Prayer for Confidence

Glorious Father,

I am made in Your own image, therefore I am not insecure. My security is in You. You are my righteousness and my peace.

I turn away from the fear of man and the feeling that I just don't measure up. Help me stop comparing myself to others. Help me see myself as You see me—complete, secure, and whole. Help me remember that through Christ Jesus I am able to overcome all of my insecurities and walk in quiet confidence all the days of my life!

In Jesus' name, amen!

STRAIGHT TALK ON *Worry*

CONTENTS

INTRODUCTION

———— ❧ ————

God wants to make a trade with you. He wants you to give Him all your cares, your problems, your failures—your "ashes"—and He will give you beauty. He will take your cares, and for them, He will care for you.

> Humble yourselves therefore under the mighty hand of God, that he may exalt you in due time: Casting all your care upon him; for he careth for you. (1 Peter 5:6–7 KJV)

> The Spirit of the Lord God is upon me, because the Lord has anointed and qualified me . . . to grant [consolation and joy] to those who mourn in Zion—to give them an ornament (a garland or diadem) of beauty instead of ashes ["beauty for ashes" KJV]. (Isaiah 61:1, 3)

God wants to take care of us, but in order to let Him, we must stop taking the care. Many people want God to take care of them while they are worrying or trying to figure out an answer instead of waiting for God's direction. They are actually wallowing around in their "ashes," but still want God to give them beauty. In order for God to give us the beauty, we must give Him the "ashes."

We give Him our cares by trusting that He can and will take care of us. Hebrews 4:3 says: "For we who have believed (adhered to and trusted in and relied on God) do enter that rest."

We enter into the Lord's rest through believing. Worry is the opposite of faith. Worry steals our peace, physically wears us out, and can even make us sick. If we are worrying, we are not trusting God, and we are not entering God's rest.

What a great trade! You give God ashes, and He gives you beauty. You give Him all your worries and concerns, and He gives you protection, stability, a place of refuge, and fullness of joy—the privilege of being cared for by Him.

Part One

———— ⬥ ————

DWELLING IN THE SECRET PLACE

1

❦

ABIDING IN PROTECTION

He who dwells in the secret place of the Most High shall remain stable and fixed under the shadow of the Almighty [Whose power no foe can withstand].

Psalm 91:1

God has a secret place where we can dwell in peace and safety.

The secret place is the place of rest in God, a place of peace and comfort in Him. This secret place is a "spiritual place" where worry vanishes and peace reigns. It is the place of God's presence. When we spend time praying and seeking God and dwelling in His presence, we are in the secret place.

The word *dwell* means "to make one's home; reside; live."[1] When you and I *dwell in Christ—in the secret place—*we do not just visit there occasionally, we take up permanent residence there.

In the New Testament, one of the Greek words translated *dwell* is the same Greek word translated *abide* in John 15:7 (NKJV) where Jesus says, "If you abide in Me, and My words abide in you, you will ask what you desire, and it shall be done for you."

If you and I abide in God, it is the same thing as dwelling in God. As a matter of fact, *The Amplified Bible* translates John 15:7, "If you live in Me [abide vitally united to Me] and My words remain in you and continue to live in your hearts, ask whatever you will, and it shall be done for you."

In other words, we need to be firmly planted in God. We need to know the Source of our help in every situation and in every circumstance. We need to have our own secret place of peace and security. We need to rely on God and trust Him completely.

In the Secret Place

He who dwells in the secret place of the Most High shall remain stable and fixed.

Psalm 91:1

The psalmist says that he who dwells in the *secret place* will be settled and secure.

The secret place is a hiding place, a private place, or a place of refuge. It is the place we run to when we are hurting, overwhelmed, or feeling faint. It is the place we run to when we are being mistreated or persecuted, when we are in great need, or when we feel we just cannot take it anymore.

I remember when I was a child we lived in a large, roomy house. (My mother cleaned that house; that was how we paid our rent.) It was a huge, very ornate building with a number of wood carvings, and it had some neat little secret places in it. One day I found one of those little secret places. It was a small bench carved out underneath one of the stairwells with a stained glass window by it.

Even now I can still picture myself sitting on that bench just pondering. I don't know what I was pondering as a small child, but I do know I had quite a few hurts and problems.

My home life was marked by many upsetting and disturbing domestic situations. That carved-out place with a bench in the stairwell was like a hiding place for me. It was where I would go when I was afraid or needed comfort.

This verse tells us that God wants to be our hiding place.

Some people in the world use alcohol as their hiding place. Some use drugs and others television. Some just get depressed and pull the covers up over their head. There are a lot of people out there hiding from a lot of things.

Instead of looking to the world to hide us, God wants us to find our hiding place in Him. That is what is meant by the phrase "the secret place of the Most High." When we have problems, when we are in trouble, God wants us to take refuge under the protective shadow of His wings. He wants us to run to Him!

Under the Shadow of the Almighty

Under the shadow of the Almighty [Whose power no foe can withstand].

Psalm 91:1

If we are in the secret place of the Most High, where will we be found? According to the psalmist, we will be abiding "under the shadow of the Almighty." This is the place God wants His people to live.

Our heavenly Father does not want us just to visit Him once in a while or run to Him when we feel overwhelmed; He wants us to dwell under the shadow of His wings, to abide there, to live there. When we do that, we remain stable and fixed because no foe can withstand the power of the Almighty. If we remain in that place, the devil can do us no harm.

There was a time in my life when I just ran in and out of the secret place, but I have since found that when I go there and stay, when I abide there, I don't feel so overwhelmed.

We need the Lord all the time—not just occasionally. In John 15:5 Jesus says, "Apart from Me [cut off from vital union with Me] you can do nothing."

What exactly does it mean to abide under the *shadow* of the Almighty? First of all, a *shadow* implies "shade," a place of protection from the hot sun or from the heat of the world. A shadow, as we know, always has a border. If we intend to stay under the shadow of God's wings, there are definite borders within which we must stay.

A *border* is an intermediate area or boundary between two qualities or conditions. In the case of a shadow, a border is where the shade stops and the sunshine starts.

Suppose it is noon, the sun is out in full force, and we see a big tree. If we go and stand under that tree, we are going to be a lot more comfortable in its shade than if we continue to stand out in the sun.

When people work outdoors in the sun and begin to sweat, they like to find a shade tree to get under when break time comes. Some people plant shade trees around their house because it lowers the temperature of the interior of the house and makes it even cooler. So the shade is a desirable place to be, especially on a hot day.

If we decide to stay in the shade under the shadow of God's wings, life is going to be more comfortable. It is not going to be so hot, and we are not going to be "sweating it out," so to speak. Instead of worrying about our problems, we will be resting in God.

If we decide to stand in the sun, we are going to be uncomfortable, sweaty, miserable, thirsty, and dry. It is up to each of us to decide where we are going to stand—in the shade (trusting God) or in the sun (sweating it out); in Jesus, or in the world with all its problems.

Where will you decide to stand? I want to stay in the shade. But, as we all tend to do from time to time, I sometimes wander out of the shade and end up back out in the heat where the conditions are not too nice. Then when I am about to expire, I run back to the shade to get rested up again. Then eventually, I once more venture back out into the heat of the sun.

Romans 1:17 (KJV) says we can live from faith to faith. However, sometimes we live from faith to doubt to unbelief and then back to faith.

What if we really want to stay within the protection of the shadow but sometimes find ourselves outside of it? How will we know when we are getting out from under God's protection? We will know by the signposts the Lord has placed along our way.

2

⟨⟨⟩⟩

READ THE SIGNPOSTS: TRUSTING GOD

Imagine you are driving down a road. This road is the road of life. In the middle of the road are lines. Sometimes there are double yellow lines that warn, "If you cross these lines, you are going to be in trouble; you run a high risk of a head-on collision."

Sometimes there are broken white lines meaning, "You can cross into the other lane and pass the car in front of you if you would like. If you cross these lines, you will probably be okay, but you can get into trouble if you do not watch the oncoming traffic to make sure the way is clear."

There are also roadside signposts that provide a specific direction or warning: "Soft Shoulder," "Falling Rocks," "Deer Crossing," "One Way," "Detour," "Under Construction," "Curve Ahead." If you heed the instructions on these signposts, they will help you keep your car on the road. You will avoid going too far to the left and getting into a collision or too far to the right and running into a ditch.

In the same way, in life there are spiritual signposts as well. In order to stay under God's protection, we must heed these signposts along the way that tell us to trust Him and not to worry, fear, or be anxious, that tell us to cast our care on Him. Then instead of excessively trying to reason out a solution, we need to turn our thoughts to things that are "true," "honest," "just," "pure," "lovely," of "good report," of "any virtue," or of any "praise" (Philippians 4:8 KJV).

If we will heed these signposts and stay within the borders of the road, we will be able to remain on course. We will be protected and will experience in our lifetime the fulfillment of all the wonderful, marvelous promises of God's Word.

Heed the Signpost!

And your ears will hear a word behind you, saying, This is the way; walk in it, when you turn to the right hand and when you turn to the left.

Isaiah 30:21

Suppose you are driving along the road of life, and you begin to veer off the road to the right. You notice that the road seems a little bumpier than it had been, and you begin to pay closer attention to where you are driving. Just then, you remember a signpost a few miles back that said, "Trust God and Don't Worry."

If you decide to continue on your course, you will go even farther off the shoulder of the road and could end up in the middle of the ditch. Then you will have to call a tow truck to come get you out.

So it is when we decide to worry rather than trust God. We get out from under His protection so the enemy is able to get at us more easily. When that happens, we inevitably lose our peace.

Straight Paths

And cut through and make firm and plain and smooth, straight paths for your feet [yes, make them safe and upright and happy paths that go in the right direction].

Hebrews 12:13

When you make a wrong decision, when you decide to worry rather than trust God, you will begin to get uncomfortable and start to lose your peace. You may even begin to get a sense that things are not working out right anymore and that you have missed the way somewhere.

As soon as you lose your peace, you need to stop and say, "Wait a minute. What am I doing wrong?"

Sometimes as I am going down life's road I suddenly realize that deep down inside I am not at peace. When that happens I stop and say, "Lord, where did I go wrong?" I know that when I lose my peace, it is an indication I have traveled out from under the protection of the shadow of His wing.

Usually it will be because I have started worrying. Sometimes it will be because I have done something wrong and have not repented or because I have mistreated somebody and have not been sensitive to my mistake.

In that situation I simply ask Him, "Lord, show me why I have lost my peace." Once I know that, I can take the necessary steps to get the situation back in order.

If you find you are having a worry attack as you follow through on what the Lord has shown you to do, I suggest you read aloud the words of Jesus in Matthew 6:25–32.

Stop Worrying

Therefore I tell you, stop being perpetually uneasy (anxious and worried) about your life, what you shall eat or what you shall drink; or about your body, what you shall put on. Is not life greater [in quality] than food, and the body [far and above and more excellent] than clothing?

Matthew 6:25

If you are on a diet, perhaps you should start by reading the first part of that verse—the part about eating and drinking! If you are like me, when you are dieting, it seems that all you can think about is food!

I remember when I used to go on a diet. All day long I would be thinking about when and what I was going to eat and how I was gong to fix it. I would be mentally weighing it out and calculating how many calories were in it. Often it would even make me hungrier because all I was doing was thinking about food!

Actually, we probably worry less about what we are going to eat and drink than we do about what we are going to do in a particular situation: what if this happens or what if that happens? Most of us have enough clothes, adequate food, comfortable houses, and serviceable cars. But when things get tough, and we are faced with situations that seem impossible, we have voices within our mind that scream, "What are you going to do now?" And we begin to worry.

Look at the Birds

Look at the birds of the air; they neither sow nor reap nor gather into barns, and yet your heavenly Father keeps feeding them. Are you not worth much more than they?

Matthew 6:26

Have you ever seen a bird sitting in a tree having a nervous breakdown? Have you ever seen a bird pacing back and forth saying to himself, "Oh, I wonder where my next worm is coming from? I need worms! What if God quits making worms today? I don't know what I would do. Maybe I would starve to death! What if God keeps making worms, but they aren't juicy this year or what if He doesn't send any rain, and no worms come out of the ground? What if I can't find any straw to build my nest?" What if, what if, what if!

Jesus said, "Look at the birds!" They aren't having a nervous breakdown. Every morning they are flying around outside just singing and having a good time.

I wonder how much peace you and I could enjoy if we would just take off an hour or so and go watch the birds!

What Does Worry Accomplish?

And who of you by worrying and being anxious can add one unit of measure (cubit) to his stature or to the span of his life?

Matthew 6:27

Of course, the answer is no one. But we can surely shorten our life span if we insist on continuing to make worry a habit!

Instead of worrying, we need to be more like the birds of the air who are totally dependent upon the Lord to feed them and yet who sing all day long as though they didn't have a care in the world.

Consider the Lilies

And why should you be anxious about clothes? Consider the lilies of the field and learn thoroughly how they grow; they neither toil nor spin. Yet I tell you, even Solomon in all his magnificence (excellence, dignity, and grace) was not arrayed like one of these . . . But if God so clothes the grass of the field, which today is alive and green and tomorrow is tossed into the furnace, will He not much more surely clothe you, O you of little faith?

Matthew 6:28–30

What Jesus was saying was that the flowers of the field do not get all "hung up" in works of the flesh. They don't work at being lilies; they just are. And God dresses them very nicely.

Do we really think we are any less important to God than birds and flowers?

Don't Be Anxious

Therefore do not worry and be anxious, saying, What are we going to have to eat? or, What are we going to have to drink? or, What are we going to have to wear? For the Gentiles (heathen) wish for and crave and diligently seek all these things, and your heavenly Father knows well that you need them all.

Matthew 6:31–32

The problem with worry is that it causes us to start *saying* things like: "What are we going to have to eat? What are we going to have to drink? What are we going to have to wear?" In other words, "What are we going to do if God doesn't come through for us?"

We begin to fret and fuss with the words of our mouth. Instead of calming our fears and removing our worries, that just makes them even more deeply ingrained.

The problem with this way of doing things is that it is the way people act who don't know they have a heavenly Father. But you and I do know we have a heavenly Father, so we need to act like it. Unbelievers may not know how to rely on Him, but we should.

Jesus assures us that our heavenly Father knows all the things we need before we ask Him. So why should we worry about them? Instead, we need to focus our attention on the things that are much more important—the things of God.

Seek First Things First

But seek (aim at and strive after) first of all His kingdom and His righteousness (His way of doing and being right), and then all these things taken together will be given you besides.

Matthew 6:33

For many years I would pace around before going in to minister in one of my meetings, getting myself all worked up. I would be praying, "Oh, God, help me!" There is nothing wrong with praying for God's help, but I was praying more out of anxiety than out of faith.

Now while preparing to minister, I simply study and prepare the best I can. Then just before the meeting begins I spend time in quiet prayer and meditation, worshipping the Lord and fellowshipping with Him.

Never once has He told me to seek a big meeting. Never once has he told me to seek a big offering. All I do is seek Him, and He takes care of the size of the crowd, the amount of the offering, and everything else.

Too often we spend all of our time seeking God for answers to our problems when what we should be doing is just seeking God.

As long as we are seeking God, we are staying in the secret place, under the shadow of His wing. ("Under His wings shall you trust and find refuge," Psalm 91:4.) But when we start seeking answers to all the problems and situations that confront us, trying to fulfill our desires rather than God's will, we get out from under the shadow of His wing.

For many years I sought God about how I could get my ministry to grow. The result was that it stayed just the same as it was. It never grew. Sometimes it even went backwards. What I didn't realize was that all I needed to do was to seek the kingdom of God, and He would add the growth.

Do you realize that you don't even have to worry about your own spiritual growth? All you need to do is seek the Kingdom, and you will grow. Seek God, abide in Him, and He will cause increase and growth.

A baby just drinks milk and grows. All you and I have to do is desire the sincere milk of the Word, and we will grow (see 1 Peter 2:2).

We can never experience any real measure of success by our own human effort. Instead, we must seek first the kingdom of God and His righteousness; then all these other things we need will be *added* to us.

We are not to seek God's presents, but His presence.

Spend Time in the Shade

One thing have I asked of the Lord, that will I seek, inquire for, and [insistently] require: that I may dwell in the house of the Lord [in His presence] all the days of my life, to behold and gaze upon the beauty [the sweet attractiveness and the delightful loveliness] of the Lord and to meditate, consider, and inquire in His temple. For in the day of trouble He will hide me in His shelter; in the secret place of His tent will He hide me; He will set me high upon a rock. And now shall my head be lifted up above my enemies round about me; in His tent I will offer sacrifices and shouting of joy; I will sing, yes, I will sing praises to the Lord.

Psalm 27:4–6

Sometimes we live our lives backwards. This is exactly what I was doing some years ago. I was seeking a big ministry. I was seeking all kinds of changes in myself because I didn't like myself. I was seeking for my husband to change. I was seeking for my children to change. I was seeking healing and prosperity. I was seeking everything under the sun, and I was not spending any time in the shade.

Then the Lord stepped in and showed me what I was doing wrong. He used Psalm 27:4–6 to emphasize to me that I must first seek Him and His presence all the days of my life.

At that time, I was asking for a lot of things, none of which had much to do with God's presence. Yet as I began to seek Him, that is exactly what I began to desire more of. Then when troubles came, He hid me, as it were, in the secret place of His tent. When the enemy came against me to try to destroy me, I lifted up shouts of joy and sang praises to the Lord.

The devil could not get to me because I was in the secret place of the Most High. I was inaccessible to him. Satan could not cause me to have a nervous breakdown because I was in the shade where I was anxious for nothing.

Be Anxious for Nothing

Be anxious for nothing, but in everything by prayer and supplication, with thanksgiving, let your requests be made known to God; and the peace of God, which surpasses all understanding, will guard your hearts and minds through Christ Jesus.

Philippians 4:6–7 (NKJV)

A long time ago, God told me that when I came to Him in prayer I was to give to Him whatever the devil had tried to give to me.

That is what prayer is. The devil comes to us and hands us a problem. We say, "I can't carry this because it's too heavy for me. Here, God, I give it to You."

In Philippians 4:6–7 the apostle Paul tells us in essence, "Pray and *don't* worry." He doesn't say, "Pray *and* worry." When we pray and give our problems to God, that is a sign to the Lord that we are trusting Him. That is what prayer is supposed to be.

I have to do this quite often where my teenaged son Danny is concerned. He is still at home, and because the ministry my husband and I are in requires that we travel, it grieves my heart sometimes to have to leave Danny behind. Before he graduated, he once told me on the telephone that he had experienced some struggles in school and that he missed us when we were gone, especially in the morning when he got up and when he went to bed at night.

Through the years, Dave and I have developed a really good relationship with our son. We love him, and he loves us. (Our next youngest was ten years old when God spoke to us to have Danny, so he is our baby!) We were concerned about him as he faced high school and the pressures and influences we knew he would encounter there.

All of us are faced with daily challenges that must be dealt with. Falling into the trap of feeling sorry for ourselves, walking around with our head hanging down because everything in our life is not working out perfectly, will not get us anywhere. We must change our focus and do what the Bible says—pray!

Every time I started to worry about Danny while we were away from him ministering, I prayed:

> Father, I thank You that You are taking care of Danny. Thank You, Lord, that You have a good plan for his life and that You are watching over him and working out everything for the best for him. Thank You that he is covered by the blood of Your Son Jesus.

When you and I start praying that way, the devil will leave us alone. He will see that we will not be shaken and that we are determined to trust God.

Stay in the Positive

> *Only it must be in faith that he asks with no wavering (no hesitating, no doubting). For the one who wavers (hesitates, doubts) is like the billowing surge out at sea that is blown hither and thither and tossed by the wind. For truly, let not such a person imagine that he will receive anything [he asks for] from the Lord.*

> James 1:6–7

If we take our concerns to the Lord in prayer and then continue to worry about them, we are mixing a positive and a negative force. Prayer is a positive force, and worry is a negative force. If we add them together, we come up with zero.

I don't know about you, but I don't want to have zero power, so I try not to mix prayer and worry.

God spoke to me one time and said, "Many people operate with zero power because they are always mixing the positives and the negatives. They have a positive confession for a little while, then a negative confession for a little while. They pray for a little while, then they worry for a little while. They trust for a little while, then they worry for a little while. As a result, they just go back and forth, never really making any progress."

Why not make a decision to stay in the positive by trusting God and refusing to worry?

3

❦

EVERYTHING'S GOING TO BE ALL RIGHT

The second signpost deals with anxiety. It says, "Fear Not and Don't be Anxious." This signpost has a warning that is similar to the first, "Trust God and Don't Worry," but the consequences of disobeying it are a bit more drastic. Instead of going in a ditch, as you would if you were to veer to the right, you run the risk of having a head-on collision. It is like crossing over that center double yellow line while taking a curve.

Anxiety, unlike worry, is an uneasy feeling that lingers even after we think we have dealt with it. It is almost like a double portion of worry. Once we go in this direction we step out of faith and into fear, especially fear of tomorrow and fear of the unknown. The result is anxiety.

Signs of Anxiety

Anxiety in a man's heart weighs it down.

Proverbs 12:25

Anxiety brings a heaviness to a person's life.

Webster's says that *anxiety* is "a state of being uneasy, apprehensive, or worried."[1] Sometimes this uneasiness is really vague, something we just cannot put our finger on. We may not even know exactly what it is. All we know is that we are uneasy, sometimes even around other people.

According to *Webster's, apprehension* is "an anxious feeling of foreboding; dread."[2] In other words, apprehension is a bad case of anxiety.

I remember a bad case of anxiety I once had. I had experienced so many bad things in my life that I finally got to the point that I expected bad things to happen. But I really didn't understand what I was experiencing until the Lord revealed it to me in Scripture.

Evil Forebodings

All the days of the desponding and afflicted are made evil [by anxious thoughts and forebodings], but he who has a glad heart has a continual feast [regardless of circumstances].

Proverbs 15:15

One morning, many years ago, I was fixing my hair in front of the mirror. I sensed a vague feeling that something bad was going to happen to me. I didn't understand what it was at the time because I had only been filled with the Holy Spirit and studying the Word of God for a short while. All I knew was that I had a vague feeling of being threatened.

So I decided to ask the Lord, "What is this thing that hangs around me all the time? It has been with me as far back as I can remember." The Lord told me it was "evil forebodings."

Never having heard that term, I thought to myself, "What in the world is a 'foreboding'?" So I went and looked it up in the dictionary. I discovered that a *foreboding* is "a sense of impending misfortune or evil."[3]

I learned that a foreboding has nothing to do with anything that is happening right at the moment; it is a negative feeling about the outcome of some event in the future.

At the time, I didn't know that term was in the Bible. Later, however, I came across it in Proverbs 15:15 which speaks of "anxious thoughts" and "evil forebodings."

God wants us to get rid of evil forebodings so we can enjoy life.

But that is easier said than done because Satan, our adversary, wants us to believe that nothing is ever going to turn out right for us. He wants us to believe that we will always be misunderstood and unappreciated, that nobody will ever like us or want to be around us, that nobody will ever care anything about us. He wants us to feel humiliated about the past, helpless about the present, and hopeless about the future. He wants to heap so much worry and anxiety upon us that we will be drawn away from our relationship with God and distracted from accomplishing the work He has set before us.

Each of the meanings of the word *anxious*—"worried and distressed about an uncertainty," "attending with, exhibiting, or producing worry"—confirms this fact.[4]

If You're Redeemed, Say So!

Let the redeemed of the Lord say so, whom He has delivered from the hand of the adversary.

Psalm 107:2

Once you realize that the devil is trying to distract you, don't just sit around and let him beat you up with worry and negative thoughts. Open your mouth and say something he doesn't want to hear, and he will leave. Begin to confess your authority in Christ.

Sometimes while I am preparing to speak at a church or seminar, negative thoughts will begin to bombard me.

Some years ago I was wondering how many people had registered in advance for a ladies' meeting I was scheduled to lead. When I asked my assistant, she said that not many had registered but that the organizers of the meeting believed there would be as many in attendance as the previous year.

All of a sudden the thought flashed across my mind, "What if nobody comes? What if my team and I travel all of that distance and only a few people show up?" Then I encouraged myself with my own mouth and said out loud, "Everything is going to be all right."

Sometimes we have to do that because if we don't, those evil forebodings will continue to hang around to cause us worry and anxiety.

Once I recognized those anxious thoughts and evil forebodings and took authority over them, God began to bring some deliverance to my life so I could start to enjoy it.

Satan places anxious and worried thoughts in our minds, sometimes actually bombarding our minds with them. He hopes we will receive them and begin saying them out of our mouths. If we do, he then has material to actually create the circumstances in our lives he has been giving us anxious thoughts about.

Words have creative power in the spiritual realm. Genesis 1:3 says, "God *said,* Let there be . . . and there was"!

Jesus said, "Therefore take no thought, *saying,* What shall we eat? or, What shall we drink? or, Wherewithal shall we be clothed?" (Matthew 6:31 KJV). If we take a negative thought and start saying it, then we are only a few steps away from real problems. "Take therefore no thought for the morrow: for the morrow shall take thought for the things of itself" (v. 34 KJV).

Enjoy Life!

> *A gentle and peaceful spirit . . . [is not anxious or wrought up, but]*
> *is very precious in the sight of God.*
>
> 1 Peter 3:4

Anxiety also means "care; concern; disquietude; a troubled state of mind."[5] Peter tells us that the type of spirit God likes is a peaceful spirit, not one that is anxious or wrought up.

When we are wrought up, we are all tense inside, and we feel as though our stomach is tied in knots. Everything becomes a burden to us—a big, intense, overwrought deal—so that we are not able to relax and enjoy life as God intends.

In my case, I was always tense and upset because my childhood had been stolen through abuse. (At a very early age, I was already feeling like an adult.) Because I never really got to be a child, I didn't know how to let go and be childlike. So when I got married and had children of my own, I didn't know how to truly enjoy them.

For years I couldn't even enjoy my husband because I was too intense about trying to change him. I was continually trying to perfect him—and everybody else.

I had children, but I didn't enjoy them. Each day before they left for school, I made sure every hair was in place, that there was not a wrinkle in their clothes, and that their lunch was securely packed away in their lunch box. I loved my children, but I didn't enjoy them.

I had a nice house, I kept it spotlessly clean with everything in its place, but I didn't enjoy it. Nobody else enjoyed the house either. We couldn't live in it. All we could do was look at it.

My children had nice toys, but they didn't enjoy them because I wouldn't let them. I didn't want them to get their toys out and play with them.

I never knew what fun was. Whatever it was, I didn't think it was anything my family was entitled to. I figured, "You don't *need* to have fun. All you *need* is to put in a good day's work."

I remember telling my kids, "Get out of here and go play." Then when they did so, I would come right along behind them saying, "Pick up that mess! Get that stuff cleaned up right now! All you ever do around here is make messes!"

What I needed to realize at that point in my life was that if things did not turn out exactly the way I wanted them to, it was not the end of the world. I needed to learn to relax and enjoy life.

The Bible says in Psalm 118:24, "This is the day the Lord has made; we will rejoice and be glad in it" (NKJV).

In John 16:33, Jesus said, "I have told you these things, so that in Me you may have [perfect] peace and confidence. In the world you have tribulation and trials and distress and frustration; but be of good cheer [take courage; be confident, certain, undaunted]! For I have overcome the world."

In Philippians 4:4 the apostle Paul says, "Rejoice in the Lord always [delight, gladden yourselves in Him]; again I say, Rejoice!"

Don't be so intense. Lighten up a little. Give God a chance to work. Make the decision to enjoy life.

Changed from Glory to Glory

And all of us, as with unveiled face, [because we] continued to behold [in the Word of God] as in a mirror the glory of the Lord, are constantly being transfigured into His very own image in ever in-

creasing splendor and from one degree of glory to another; [for this comes] from the Lord [Who is] the Spirit.

2 Corinthians 3:18

Do you realize that if the only time you decide to enjoy yourself is when everything is perfect, you are never going to have much fun?

Don't make the mistake of waiting to enjoy yourself until you and everyone around you are all perfected and have arrived at the finish line.

The Bible says that you and I are being changed into God's own image and are going from glory to glory. That means we are going to go through a lot of different stages. We need to learn how to enjoy the glory of the stage we are in right now while we are moving into the next one. We must learn to say, "I'm not where I need to be, but, thank God, I'm not where I used to be. I'm somewhere in the middle, and I'm going to enjoy each stage."

When our children are babies they do cute things like smile and coo, but they also do things that are not so cute like cry in the middle of the night, cut teeth, and get diarrhea. We catch ourselves saying, "I'll be glad when they get through this stage so I can really enjoy them."

Somehow they make it through that stage, then they enter the next one. At this point, they are talking and saying cute expressions, but they are also walking and throwing any object they can get their hands on. Again we find ourselves wishing they were through this stage.

Soon they are in kindergarten, and we find ourselves saying, "I'll be glad when they're in the first grade, then they'll go to school all day." But as soon as they are in elementary school, we start saying, "I'll be glad when they start high school." Then when they graduate from high school, we say, "I'll be glad when they're grown and married."

Then one day that happens, and suddenly we realize that we never enjoyed any stage of their lives. We were always waiting to be glad *when*.

That is the way I used to spend my entire life. I was always going to be glad some other time.

When I used to hold meetings of fifty people, I would think, "I'll be so glad when hundreds of people start coming to my meetings." The truth is that when that finally happened, it didn't make me any happier.

Every phase we go through brings with it a certain amount of joy, but it also comes with its own little set of problems. What we need to do is to learn to be glad in spite of any circumstance.

Be Glad in Spite of Circumstances

For You, O Lord, have made me glad by Your works; at the deeds of Your hands I joyfully sing.

Psalm 92:4

Some years ago I finally found the doorway to happiness. It is found in the presence of God.

I used to be happy if God was doing something that made me glad. But I didn't know how to be glad *because* of Him. I knew how to seek His hand, but I didn't really know how to seek His face.

Don't think you are going to be glad when God does the next thing for you that you want Him to do. As soon as He does, there is going to be something else you are going to want that you think you can't be glad until you get. Don't spend all your life waiting until some other time to be happy.

One day after I had received this breakthrough, I was going to a meeting, and I was singing that once popular spiritual song, "You have made me glad, You have made me glad; I will rejoice for You have made me glad." It was then that the Holy Ghost spoke to me and said, "For the first time, you're singing that song right."

Because God hears our hearts more than our words, that song sounded different to Him. Before, what He heard was, "The things You have done for me have made me glad, the things You have done for me have made me glad; I will rejoice for all the things You have done for me have made me glad."

When the Lord was doing what I wanted Him to do for me, I was glad, but when He wasn't doing what I wanted Him to do for me, I was not glad. So I lived an up-and-down life. It was like riding a roller coaster. I was getting worn out from going up and down all the time. If my circumstances suited me, I was up, and if they didn't, I was down.

If we are to live in the fullness of joy, we must find something to be glad about besides our circumstances.

Be Glad in Spite of People

Be glad in the Lord and rejoice, you [uncompromisingly] righteous [you who are upright and in right standing with Him]; shout for joy, all you upright in heart!

Psalm 32:11

Even if every one of our circumstances suits us, we will eventually find that the world is full of people who don't suit us. As soon as we shape up the ones who don't suit us, still others will come along who don't suit us. It is an unending cycle.

In our ministry, we have a large number of people on our staff. Even though they are some of the most wonderful people I have ever met, there are times when they don't all make me glad.

Even being around Christian people will not make us glad all the time. The only One Who can make us glad all the time, every time, is Jesus—and even He cannot do that for us unless we allow Him to do so.

The Martha Syndrome

Now while they were on their way, it occurred that Jesus entered a certain village, and a woman named Martha received and welcomed Him into her house. And she had a sister named Mary, who seated herself at the Lord's feet and was listening to His teaching. But Martha [overly occupied and too busy] was distracted with much serving; and she came up to Him and said, Lord, is it nothing to You that my sister has left me to serve alone? Tell her then to help me [to lend a hand and do her part along with me]!

Luke 10:38–40

No one knew the Source of happiness, peace, and joy better than Mary, the sister of Martha. When their guest, Jesus, arrived in their home, she positioned herself at His feet so she could hear everything he was going to say without missing a word. She was excited that He had decided to visit them that day and wanted to really enjoy the time they would have together. So she sat right down and fixed her eyes on Jesus.

Then there was her sister—dear old Martha. She had already spent all day running around cleaning and polishing and cooking, trying to get everything ready for Jesus' visit.

(The reason I find it so easy to picture Martha in this situation is because I used to be just like her.)

Everything had to be in order when Martha's guest arrived. Once He did arrive, she busied herself in the kitchen getting all the food prepared and putting the last-minute touches on the table setting.

Eventually Martha got upset and came to Jesus saying in so many words, "Master, why don't You make my sister Mary get up and help me do some of the work around here?" Hoping to get some sympathy and perhaps a little recognition for all she had done, she was shocked when He said, "Martha, Martha, you are anxious and troubled about many things; There is need of only one or but a few things. Mary has chosen the good portion . . . which shall not be taken away from her" (Luke 10:41–42).

I am sure things got a bit quiet around the house after that comment. But the truth is, Martha needed to hear it.

I remember one time when God said something similar to me. He said, "Joyce, you can't enjoy life because you're too complicated." And He was right! I could complicate a simple barbecue!

I remember one time when I saw some of our friends and on the spur of the moment invited them to come visit. I remember saying something like, "Hey, why don't you guys come over Sunday? We'll throw some hot dogs on the grill and open a bag of potato chips and a can of pork and beans. I'll make some tea, and we'll just sit around the patio and have a good time, or maybe we can play some ball or some games or something."

After I said this, I was feeling good thinking about how much fun we were going to have. I got in my car and started to drive home. By the time I got back to the house, the hot dogs had turned into steaks, and the potato chips had turned into potato salad! After all, I wouldn't want my friends to think I could only afford hot dogs or that I didn't know how to make potato salad.

It wasn't long before I decided that the barbecue grill needed to be painted and the old lawn furniture needed to be replaced. Of course, the lawn needed to be mowed and the house thoroughly cleaned. After all, I had to make a good impression on my guests.

After a while, I started thinking about not only the six people I had invited but the fourteen who would get offended if they knew the six were there and I had not asked them also. So now, all of a sudden, this simple get-together had become a nightmare. I was giving in to the fear of man.

Then the Martha syndrome sank in a little more. I began madly cleaning the house and mopping the floors. I was sending everybody out to the store to get this and that. Invariably, I got mad at Dave and the kids and said something like, "I just don't understand why it is that I have to do *all of the work* around here while everybody else just has fun!" By that time, I had "Martha" written all over my face, and I knew that, unlike Mary, I had not chosen the best portion.

Live in the Now

> *Beloved, we are [even here and] now God's children; it is not yet disclosed (made clear) what we shall be [hereafter], but we know that when He comes and is manifested, we shall [as God's children] resemble and be like Him, for we shall see Him just as He [really] is.*

> 1 John 3:2

In reality, it is the choices we make today that determine whether we will enjoy the moment or waste it by worrying. Sometimes we end up missing the moment of today because we are too concerned about tomorrow.

Another definition of *anxiety* is "uneasiness and distress about future uncertainties."[6] The definition that God gave me follows along the same lines: "Anxiety is caused by trying to mentally or emotionally get into things that are not here yet (the future) or things that have already been (the past)."

One of the things we need to understand is that God wants us to learn how to be *now* people. For example, 2 Corinthians 6:2 (KJV) says: "Behold, now is the day of salvation" and Hebrews 4:7 says, "Today, if you would hear His voice and when you hear it, do not harden your hearts."

We need to learn to live now. Too many times we spend our mental time in the past or the future. This may sound a little comical to you, but I have had so many problems with this tendency in my life that God once revealed to me that I was in anxiety even when I was brushing my teeth!

While I was brushing my teeth, I was already thinking about the next thing I wanted to do. I was in a hurry, and my stomach was already tied in knots.

When you and I don't really give ourselves to what we are doing at the moment, we become prone to anxiety. Brushing our teeth may seem a simplistic matter, but I believe that is exactly the kind of everyday situation that often gives us the most problems.

I can remember when I was first baptized in the Holy Spirit. My mind was such an awful mess that I had trouble with the most ordinary things of life. I would get up in the morning, get my three little kids off to school and my husband off to work, and then start in on what I needed to get done that day. But I couldn't keep my mind on anything.

I would be in the bedroom making my bed when all of a sudden I would realize I hadn't loaded the dishwasher. So I would rush into the kitchen to do that, leaving the bed only partially made.

As I was loading the dishwasher I might think, "You know, I really need to go downstairs and get the meat out of the freezer so it will thaw in time for dinner."

So I would rush downstairs to get the meat out of the freezer. As I did so I might see the dirty laundry piled up and decide I really needed to stop and get it into the washer.

Just then I might think of a phone call I needed to make and would run back upstairs to attend to that chore. In the midst of all that rush and confusion I might suddenly remember I needed to go to the post office and get some bills in the mail. So off I would hurry to do that errand.

By the time the day was over, I had a worse mess than I had when I started out. Now everything was half done, and I was frustrated and worn out. Why? Simply because I never gave myself totally to one thing.

One Thing at a Time

Keep your foot [give your mind to what you are doing].

Ecclesiastes 5:1

Do you know why we don't give ourselves to one thing? Because we are too concerned with getting on to the next thing. We need to do what the writer of Ecclesiastes has told us to do—keep our mind on what we are doing at the moment. If we don't do that, we will lose our footing or balance in life, and nothing will make any sense!

We must make a decision to live in the now, not in the past or the future, because getting into yesterday or tomorrow when we should be living in today causes us to lose our anointing for today. We have to take one day at a time because that is the only way we are going to get where we are going.

We live in such an instant society that we want somebody just to wave a magic wand over us and make everything all better. But things just don't happen that way. Change comes one day at a time.

One Day at a Time

Do not worry or be anxious about tomorrow, for tomorrow will have worries and anxieties of its own. Sufficient for each day is its own trouble.

Matthew 6:34

In John 8:58 Jesus referred to Himself as "I AM." If you and I, as His disciples, try to live in the past or the future, we are going to find life hard because Jesus is always in the present. That's why He told us not to be concerned about yesterday or tomorrow.

If we try to live in the future or the past, life is going to be hard. But if we will live in the now, we will find the Lord there with us. Regardless of what situations life brings our way, He has promised never to leave us or forsake us but to always be with us and help us (see Hebrews 13:5; Matthew 28:20).

Giving ourselves to one thing at a time in the now is not just a physical matter, it is a mental and emotional matter as well. For example, we can be standing in one place physically, but be having a conversation with someone in our mind someplace else.

When we go on to the next thing mentally, it creates unnecessary pressure upon us. When we do come back to the present, we may not be clear as to what went on while we were mentally absent.

That is why the devil constantly tries to snatch our minds away and take us off somewhere else. He wants us to miss out on what is happening in the now.

I remember one time when I was angry about something my husband had done. In those days, I would get mad and stay mad for days. Finally Dave said something that really got my attention: "Wouldn't it be pitiful if Jesus came tonight, and you had spent your last day on earth like this?" That gave me something to think about.

You and I don't need to be anxious about tomorrow when we have all we can handle today. Even if we manage to solve all our problems today, tomorrow we will just have more to deal with, and even more the next day.

Why waste time being anxious when it is not going to solve anything? Why be anxious about yesterday which is gone or tomorrow which has not yet arrived? Live in faith now. Fear not and don't be anxious.

4

GOD'S THOUGHTS ARE HIGHER THAN OUR THOUGHTS

Are you always trying to figure everything out? Many of us have fallen into that ditch. Instead of casting our cares upon the Lord, we go through life carrying every bit of it.

When we are trying to figure everything out, we are exalting our reasoning above God's thoughts and plans for our life. We are placing our ways higher than His ways.

Second Corinthians 10:5 tells us that we should "lead every thought and purpose away captive into the obedience of Christ." The third signpost is "Cast All Your Care and Avoid Reasoning." When we do that, we will stop trying to figure everything out and learn to cast our care upon the Lord and enter into His rest.

Enter God's Rest

For we who have believed (adhered to and trusted in and relied on God) do enter that rest.

Hebrews 4:3

This passage refers to the children of Israel entering the land of Canaan rather than wandering in the desert. But we can apply it to our lives: if we are not resting, then we are not really believing and trusting, because the fruit of belief and trust is rest.

Sometimes I am tempted to try to figure out every detail of what's happening or the reason things are happening. But I know that when I do that I am not really trusting God.

In Proverbs 3:5 we are told, "Lean on, trust in, and be confident in the Lord with all your heart and mind and do not rely on your own insight or understanding." In other words, we are told, "Trust God and don't try to figure things out on the basis of what you see," not, "Trust God while you are trying to figure everything out"!

I realized that with my mouth I had been telling God I trusted Him while in my mind I was still trying to figure out everything for myself. What Proverbs 3:5 tells us to do is to trust in the Lord with all of our heart and all of our mind!

That means we must give up excessive reasoning.

Reasoning Contrary to the Truth

But be doers of the Word [obey the message], and not merely listeners to it, betraying yourselves [into deception by reasoning contrary to the Truth].

James 1:22

When God revealed to me that I had to give up excessive reasoning, it was a real challenge to me because I was addicted to it. I couldn't stand it if I did not have everything figured out.

For example, God told us to do some things in our ministry several years ago that I didn't have the slightest idea how to go about doing. One of those things was going on television on a daily basis. Of course, that multiplied the workload and financial responsibility of the ministry by five. It required more employees and more space.

But God never called me to figure out exactly how to accomplish everything He asked me to do. He called me to seek *Him*, not the answer to my problems, then obey what He tells me to do.

I didn't know where to get the money to do all the things God told us to do, or the space or the people. But I have had enough experience with God to know that if I will just stay in the shade, under the shadow of His wing, worshipping and praising Him, taking my part of the responsibility but casting my care on Him, He will bring everything to pass in accordance with His will and plan.

My part of the responsibility is to do whatever He shows me to do. All He asks of me is to say, "I'm going to start taking steps, Lord, and I believe You are going to provide." But I can assure you that God is never going to ask me to worry or to try to figure out how He is going to do everything He is leading me to do.

When we worry, we lose our peace, and when we try to figure everything out, we fall into confusion. Staying in peace is abiding under the shadow of the Almighty!

One time I asked the Lord, "Why are we all so confused?" He answered by saying, "If you will stop trying to figure things out, then you won't be confused."

The beginning of confusion is a signpost warning that we are about to take a wrong turn and get into trouble.

Confusion is the result of reasoning with our own understanding when we should be trusting in the Lord with all our heart to make the way for us according to His plan. When we trust that His thoughts are higher than our thoughts, we can stop confusion before it starts.

Endless Conversations

> *Do not be anxious [beforehand] how you shall reply in defense or what you are to say. For the Holy Spirit will teach you in that very hour and moment what [you] ought to say.*
>
> Luke 12:11–12

Sometimes we not only try to figure out ahead of time what we ought to *do*, we also try to figure out what we ought to *say*.

At home you may be needing to confront your spouse about some issue between the two of you. At work you may be needing to ask your boss for a raise or reprimand an employee about his inappropriate behavior. Whatever the situation may be that is facing you right now, you may be full of anxiety.

Why not make a decision to trust God instead of planning and rehearsing a conversation over and over in your head? Why not simply believe God wants you to deal with what is placed in front of you without figuring out ahead of time what you are going to say?

You may want to have a general idea of what you need to present, but there is a balance to be maintained. If you become obsessive and keep going over the situation in your head, that is a sign you are not depending upon the anointing of the Lord. You are depending on yourself, and you are going to fail.

Do you know that you and I can say a few words under God's anointing and bring peace and harmony, or we can say two hundred words in our own flesh and cause total havoc and confusion?

Sometimes we rack our brains trying to come up with a plan to handle a difficult situation. Once we think we have finally decided just what we are going to do, the troubling thought pops into our head, "Yes, but what if . . . ?" And we end up more confused than ever.

I remember one night lying in bed mentally dealing with a situation that was causing me to be restless. Eventually I found myself in one of those endless imaginary conversations: "If I say this, they will say that. If that happens, I'm going to get upset! Then what am I going to do?"

I knew I had to discuss some unpleasant things with some people I didn't want to offend, and I knew it wouldn't be easy. Even though I didn't want those involved to be angry with me, I also didn't want to shirk my responsibility by being a "men-pleaser" (see Ephesians 6:6 KJV and Colossians 3:22 KJV). I needed a sense of peace and confidence about the matter.

God's peace is always available—but we must choose it. We must choose to stand either in the hot sun of worry—and be sweaty, miserable, thirsty, and dry—or in the cool, comforting shade of God's peace.

God's Plans for Us Are Good!

For I know the thoughts and plans that I have for you, says the Lord, thoughts and plans for welfare and peace and not for evil, to give you hope in your final outcome.

Jeremiah 29:11

Because of my abusive home environment as a child I learned to make sure that everything I said was just right before I opened my mouth to speak. I was afraid if I said the wrong thing, I would be made to suffer for it.

I spent many years of my life outlining conversations in my head in order to make sure that everything was going to sound just right. Eventually, of course, my mind developed the habit of thinking negatively and defensively.

Because of my insecurities and my fear of being rejected, I would spend days trying to figure out the meaning of some casual remark made to me by someone who had meant nothing by it.

God doesn't want us using our minds that way. It is a useless waste of time. Our heavenly Father has a plan for our life. His thoughts are above our thoughts, and His ways are above our ways (see Isaiah 55:8–9). Neither you nor I will ever figure Him out.

After struggling for years, I finally said to the Lord, "What is my problem?" The Lord spoke something to me then that changed my life. He said, "Joyce, because of the way you were raised, fear is embedded in your thinking processes."

Of course, the Lord had been working with me from the time I was filled with the Holy Spirit to root that fear out of me. Even though I had come a long way, I realized I still had a long way to go.

Despite all that, He said to me, "Joyce, everything is going to be all right!" When He said that, it was like a breakthrough. It reminded me of what I used to say to my kids when they would come to me upset and crying: "It's okay! Mama will fix it. Everything is going to be all right." Even though the message was simple, I have reminded myself of it on countless occasions.

I remember one time in particular when my ministry team and I were scheduled to hold a seminar. Although we had reordered the tape labels we needed for the seminar, we had worked our way down to the last one. When we called the company, it appeared the order had been lost. Even though we had sent the initial order in well ahead of time, now we had run out of time, and we had to put in a special rush order.

The day after the new shipment date, the labels still had not arrived! Instead of allowing that situation to get to me, I simply said, "Everything is going to be all right." Sure enough, by the time I got home, the people at the office had called to tell me the labels had arrived right after I left the office.

Developing Trust

We glory in tribulations also: knowing that tribulation worketh patience; And patience, experience; and experience, hope.

Romans 5:3–4 (KJV)

How many times have you frustrated yourself and gotten all upset needlessly over these kinds of situations? How many years of your life have you spent saying, "Oh, I'm believing God. I'm trusting God," when, in reality, all you were doing was worrying, talking negatively and trying to figure out everything on your own? You may have thought you were trusting God because you were saying, "I trust God," but inside you were anxious and panicky. You were trying to learn to trust God, but you were not quite there yet.

Do I mean that developing trust and confidence is simply a matter of saying, "Don't worry; everything will be all right"? No, I don't. Trust and confidence are built up over a period of time. It usually takes some time to overcome an ingrained habit of worry, anxiety, and fear.

That is why it is so important to "hang in there" with God. Don't quit and give up, because you gain experience and spiritual strength every round you go through. Each time you become a little stronger than you were the last time. Sooner or later, if you don't give up, you will be more than the devil can handle.

Only God Can Really Help

You are He Who took me out of the womb; You made me hope and trust when I was on my mother's breasts. I was cast upon You from my very birth; from my mother's womb You have been my God. Be not far from me, for trouble is near and there is none to help.

Psalm 22:9–11

I have been walking with God now for a long time, so I have some experience behind me and have been through some hard times. But I have never forgotten the many years the devil controlled and manipulated me. I remember the nights I used to spend walking the floor crying, feeling like I just couldn't make it.

I remember running to my friends and others I thought might be able to help me. Eventually I got smart enough to stop running to people—not because I didn't like them or trust them, but because I knew they really could not help me—only God could.

I heard one speaker say, "If people can help you, you don't really have a problem."

I used to get so aggravated at my husband because when he would be having problems or going through rough times, he wouldn't tell me about it. Then two or three weeks after he had won the victory, he would say, "I was really going through a rough time a few weeks ago."

Before he would finish, I would ask, "Why didn't you tell me?"

Do you know what he would say?

"I knew you couldn't help me, so I didn't even ask!"

I am not saying it is wrong to share with someone you love and trust what is going on in your life, but Dave understood a truth that I needed to put into practice in my own life. There are times that only God can help. Although I would have liked to be able to help my husband, I really couldn't. Only God could, and he needed to go to Him.

The Lord once told me that we need to learn how to suffer privately. One of the verses He gave me along this line is Isaiah 53:7, "He was oppressed and He was afflicted, Yet He opened not His mouth" (NKJV). Once you reach a certain point in your walk with God, this is one of the golden rules for gaining even more strength in Him.

Cast All Your Care upon the Lord

Casting all your care upon Him, for He cares for you.

1 Peter 5:7 (NKJV)

In my walk with the Lord, I wanted to get to the point where I had stability, did not worry, was not full of unnecessary reasoning, and could cast all my care upon Him.

My husband has a special gift in this area. He has been through a lot with God, and over the years the Lord has given him a real sense of peace and security. (It is a good thing because I was such a worrier that if we had both been like me, we never would have made it.)

I was the household bookkeeper and took care of paying the bills. Every month I would get out the calculator and begin adding up all the bills. I would work myself into a frantic mess worrying about how we were going to pay them all.

Dave, on the other hand, would be in the family room playing with the kids. They would be putting rollers in his hair and crawling all over his back while they all watched television. I would hear them giggling and laughing and having a great time.

Pretty soon I would get mad at Dave because he was enjoying life while I was so miserable.

But that is the way it goes. When we are miserable, we get angry at anybody who won't be miserable with us.

I would be out in the kitchen wringing my hands and saying, "Oh, dear God, I trust You. I believe You are going to come through for us again this month." I was saying the right words, but I was worried and miserable.

The end of the month would come, and, sure enough, God would do a miracle in our finances. Then, of course, I would have the next month to worry about. Even though I knew we were right in the middle of the will of God, I would still worry.

Trusting God is one of those areas in which we have to get experience for ourselves. It doesn't come by going through a prayer line or having hands laid on us. It isn't something someone else can give us. We have to get it for ourselves over a period of time.

Cry Out to God

Be merciful and gracious to me, O Lord, for to You do I cry all the day.

Psalm 86:3

But finances are not the only area in which I have had to learn to trust God. There have been times in my life when I have hurt so badly that I have lain on my office floor and held onto the legs of the furniture to keep from running away from God. I have had to stretch out on my face and cry out to Him, "Lord, You have *got* to help me. If You don't do something, I can't hang on any longer."

It is in desperate times like that we get to know God really well. To be honest, crying out to the Lord like a little child and depending totally on Him is healthy. When we cry out, we don't have to worry about how we sound or how pretty we look.

I am sure there have been times in my life when I looked like an absolute idiot as I cried out to the Lord, but I did it anyway.

In Which Direction Are You Headed?

I have learned how to be content (satisfied to the point where I am not disturbed or disquieted) in whatever state I am.

Philippians 4:11

Don't get discouraged with yourself if you are not quite where you would like to be. It takes time and experience to learn how to cast all your care upon the Lord and stay under His shadow in the secret place.

The question is not, "Where are you right now?" Instead, the question is, "In which direction are you headed?"

Are you learning? Are you willing to change? Are you open to grow? The very fact that you are reading this book right now indicates that you are serious about overcoming fear, anxiety, and insecurity. Now all you need to do is get some experience in casting all your care upon the Lord so that you can avoid vain reasoning.

Fulfill Your Responsibility but Cast Your Care

Roll your works upon the Lord [commit and trust them wholly to Him; He will cause your thoughts to become agreeable to His will, and] so shall your plans be established and succeed.

Proverbs 16:3

I think the reason I have always tried to figure everything out is because of my lifelong fear of failure. I have always been a responsible person, and I have always wanted things to turn out right. But in addition to the responsibility that I took, I also took the care.

God wants us to *fulfill our responsibility,* but *cast our care.* Why does He want us to cast our care? Because He cares for us.

I don't know about you, but I spent too many years of my life tormenting myself with worry and anxiety, trying to handle things that I could not handle or trying to handle things that were not mine to handle. As a result, years of my life were wasted.

If you want to be really frustrated, just go around all the time trying to do something about something you can't do anything about. If you do, it is going to frustrate you unbearably.

"Oh, Well"

Cease from anger and forsake wrath; fret not yourself—it tends only to evildoing.

Psalm 37:8

Whenever I find myself in a situation I can't do anything about, I have found that a good way to cast my care upon the Lord is simply to say, "Oh, well."

Take, for example, the morning that Dave spilled his orange juice in the car and got a little of it on my sweater. Immediately he said, "Devil, I'm not impressed." And I said, "Oh, well." So that problem was solved, and we pressed forward with the rest of our day.

Some things just aren't worth getting upset about, yet many people do. Unfortunately a large majority of Christians are upset, fretful, and full of anxiety *most* of the time. It is not the big things that get to them; it is the little things that don't fit into their plans. Instead of casting their care and just saying, "Oh well," they are always trying to do something about something they can't do anything about.

On more than one occasion that simple phrase "Oh, well" has really helped me to make it through.

One time our son Danny made a mistake at the very end of a paper he was writing for homework. So he crumpled up his paper and proceeded to start all over again. Eventually he ended up getting mad and upset and wanted to give up altogether.

So his father and I began to work with him on just saying, "Oh, well." It worked. After that when he was tempted to give up, we said, "Danny," and he would say, "Oh, well." Then he would go back to whatever he was doing and complete it.

Be Well Balanced

Be well balanced.

1 Peter 5:8

Sometimes in trying situations our anxiety gets in the way of our doing what we should. All we can do is our best, then trust God with the rest.

We function best when we have a calm, well-balanced mind. When our mind is calm, it is without fear, worry, or torment. When our mind is well-balanced, we are able to look the situation over and decide what to do or not to do about it.

Where most of us get in trouble is getting out of balance. Either we move into a state of total passivity in which we do nothing, expecting God to do everything for us, or we become hyperactive, operating most of the time in the flesh. God wants us to be well-balanced so that we are able to face any situation of life and say, "Well, I believe I can do certain things about this situation, but no more."

This happens to many of us at income tax time. We think we have paid in enough throughout the year to meet our tax obligation. Then we find out that we still owe money. The time is usually short, and we don't know how to get the money the government demands.

Instead of getting distraught and full of fear and worry, we need to go before God and say, "Well, Lord, I'm believing You to help me in this situation, but is there something You want me to do?"

God may show us to take a part-time job for a while to earn what we need to pay off our taxes. He may show us a way to borrow the money, along with a plan to pay it back quickly. Whatever it is God shows us to do about our problem, we need to be diligent enough to do it. Then we need to trust Him with the outcome.

Sometimes we think we should be doing more than we are to solve our problems or meet our needs. But if we rush ahead without getting God's direction, we will be acting in the flesh, and all our efforts will be in vain. Sometimes we just have to make a determination to rest even though our mind is yelling, "What are you going to do?"

We must be confident that the God we serve does not require us to do more than we know how. Once we have done all we know to do, we can trust God with the rest. That is what I call faith and balance.

A Man of Faith and Balance

[Urged on] by faith Abraham, when he was called, obeyed and went forth to a place which he was destined to receive as an inheritance; and he went, although he did not know or trouble his mind about where he was to go.

Hebrews 11:8

Abraham was a man of faith and balance. Think for a moment about his situation.

In obedience to the Lord, Abraham left behind his family, his friends, and his home to set out on a journey to some unknown place.

I am sure that every step of the way the devil was screaming in his ear, "You fool! Where do you think you're going? What are you going to do when night comes? Where are you going to sleep? What are you going to eat? Come on, Abraham, what are you doing out here? What makes you think this was God's idea anyway? Do you know of anybody else God has told to do this?"

Don't Trouble Your Mind

And He said to them, Why are you disturbed and troubled?

Luke 24:38

Despite what the devil was screaming at him, Abraham went on. The Bible says that although he did not know where he was going, he did not *"trouble his mind"* about it (Hebrews 11:8).

Sometimes we trouble our own mind! Some of us love to worry so much that if the devil did not give us something to worry about, we would go dig something up!

Let's think about our mind for a moment. What is our mind supposed to be full of? It is supposed to be full of praise, full of the Word of God, full of exhortation and edification, full of hope, and full of faith.

Now let's take a brief inventory of the thoughts we think throughout the day. It is sad to say, but most of us would have to admit that our mind is full of worry, fretfulness, fear, figuring, plotting, planning, theorizing, doubt, anxiety, and uneasiness.

As a result, some of the gears of faith in our mind have cobwebs in them. We need to blow away those cobwebs and lubricate the gears of faith with the oil of the Holy Spirit—even though it may be hard when those gears of faith begin to roll again after so many years of disuse!

Like Abraham, we need to move out in faith and do what we can, then trust God with the rest and not trouble our mind about it. We need to get our faith in gear, but leave our mind at rest.

Don't waste your life. Determine what is your responsibility and what is not. Don't try to take on God's responsibility. Do what you can do, what He expects you to do, then leave the rest to Him. Fulfill your responsibility, but cast your care.

Conclusion

Verse two of Psalm 91 carries a similar message to that of verse one which we examined earlier.

He who dwells in the secret place of the Most High shall remain stable and fixed under the shadow of the Almighty [Whose power no foe can withstand]. I will say of the Lord, He is my Refuge and my Fortress, my God; on Him I lean and rely, and in Him I [confidently] trust! (Psalm 91:1–2)

Our Refuge and Fortress

Both of these verses show us that we do not need to be worried, anxious, or fretful because we can put our trust in God and place our confidence in Him.

But verse two not only says that God is our refuge, it also says that He is our fortress.

A refuge is different from a fortress. A refuge is a secret place of concealment in which the enemy cannot find us. If we are hidden in God, then Satan cannot locate us. We can see what is going on, but the devil cannot see us. He doesn't know where we are because we are hidden from his sight under the shadow of the Almighty.

A fortress, on the other hand, is a visible place of defense. The enemy knows we are there, but he cannot get to us, because we are inaccessible to him—as in the old Western movies in which the soldiers built a strong wooden fort as protection against their enemies.

We can either be in the hiding place where we see the enemy, but he doesn't see us, or we can be in a visible fort where the enemy plainly sees us but cannot get to us because we are surrounded by God's protection.

Verse two is just as important as verse one because the rich promises of this whole chapter are dependent upon the conditions of these two verses being met. "He will give His angels [especial] charge over you to accompany and defend and preserve you in all your ways [of obedience and service]" (v. 11) if the conditions of verses one and two are met—if we are obedient to them.

Leaning on Him

For we have heard of your faith in Christ Jesus [the leaning of your entire human personality on Him in absolute trust and confidence in His power, wisdom, and goodness].

Colossians 1:4

In verse two of Psalm 91 when the psalmist says, "I will say of the Lord," He is not just referring to lip service. "Saying of the Lord" does not mean just memorizing Scriptures and repeating them out loud. To "say of the Lord" requires that we truly trust in Him, that we place our confidence totally in Him, that we lean on Him completely.

According to Colossians 1:4 that is really what faith is—the leaning of the entire human personality on God in absolute trust and confidence in His power, wisdom, and goodness.

Some time ago the Lord showed me how we often lean on Him. Because of our fears, we lean somewhat on Him. But we keep enough weight on our own feet so that if God moves away, we will keep standing on our own.

We can tell when we are not really leaning on God because our thoughts will go something like this: "Yes, Lord, I trust You, but just in case You don't come through I have an alternative plan to fall back on."

That isn't trusting God totally and completely! God wants us to trust Him without reserve, with no thoughts or plans for failure.

Is the Lord really your refuge? Is He really your fortress? Do you really lean and rely on Him and trust in Him? Or are you just giving Him lip service?

If you have proven verses one and two for yourself, the rest of Psalm 91 is full of wonderful, marvelous promises for you.

He Will Deliver and Cover You

For [then] He will deliver you from the snare of the fowler and from the deadly pestilence. [Then] He will cover you with His pinions, and under His wings shall you trust and find refuge; His truth and His faithfulness are a shield and a buckler.

Psalm 91:3–4

The first of these wonderful, marvelous promises are found in verses three and four which speak of the Lord's deliverance and protection.

Both the shield and the buckler are forms of protection used during combat. Oftentimes the shield was large enough to cover the whole body of a person, protecting him from the arrows of the enemy. Some shields were rounded rather than flat and offered more protection from arrows that might fly from the right or the left.[1]

The buckler, on the other hand, was a small shield worn on the arm or held by the hand. It was used more in hand-to-hand fighting and would provide all-around protection as the warrior turned to fight the enemy.[2] This is similar to the imagery found in Psalm 125:2 which says, "As the mountains are round about Jerusalem, so the Lord is round about His people."

Regardless of the situation in which you and I may find ourselves, God is for us. It may seem hopeless to us, but if the Lord is for us, who can be against us (see Romans 8:31)?

The Lord is with us because He has promised, "I will never leave you nor forsake you" (Hebrews 13:5 NKJV). He is under us because the Bible says that He upholds us with His promise (see Psalm 119:116). He is over us because we are told in Psalm 91:4, "He will cover you with His pinions, and under His wings shall you trust and find refuge."

Now get this picture firmly embedded in your mind. God is around you. He is for you. He is with you. He is under you, and He is over you. The devil is the only one who is really against you—and as long as you are dwelling in the secret place of the Most High, stable and fixed under the shadow of the Almighty, the enemy cannot find you or get to you!

If all this is true, why should you be afraid?

You Shall Not Be Afraid

You shall not be afraid of the terror of the night, nor of the arrow (the evil plots and slanders of the wicked) that flies by day, Nor of the pestilence that stalks in darkness, nor of the destruction and sudden death that surprise and lay waste at noonday. A thousand may fall at your side, and ten thousand at your right hand, but it shall not come near you. Only a spectator shall you be [yourself inaccessible in the secret place of the Most High] as you witness the reward of the wicked. Because you have made the Lord your refuge, and the Most High your dwelling place.

Psalm 91:5–9

You and I need to learn how to hide ourselves in God. If we can learn how to dwell in that secret place, we can give the devil a nervous breakdown. We will be able to sit still and watch him try to get at us, but he won't be able to because we will be inaccessible to him.

Some years ago, God made a great transition in my life. At the time, I was already saved and baptized in the Holy Spirit, but I was still struggling and having a lot of problems. Then the Lord began to teach me that in His presence is fullness of joy and that the only way I would ever have any stability in my life was to dwell in His presence.

At that point in my life, I was so tired of the ups and downs that I yearned for stability. I didn't want to be an emotional mess. I didn't want to be controlled by my circumstances. I didn't want to spend the rest of my days screaming at the devil. I wanted to get on with my life and be able to receive and enjoy all the blessings the Bible said were mine as a child of God.

When I got to that point, the Lord started teaching me about dwelling in His presence. For years I studied all about it and more and more began to apply it in my life.

Now, years later, I can hardly begin to tell you what a transition there has been in my life. I have become so happy and so stable. That doesn't mean I never have problems. That doesn't mean I never struggle. But it does mean that in the midst of the problems and struggles of life, I am able to stay in His presence and remain stable.

Psalm 91 is not just a nice piece of inspiring literature. It is true, and I can verify its truth with my own life.

If you will only learn to dwell in that secret place, then the devil will no longer have the upper hand over you. He will no longer have control over you.

When you have made the Lord your refuge and the Most High your dwelling place, you will be able to sit and watch the reward of the wicked, but no evil will befall you.

No Evil Shall Befall You

There shall no evil befall you, nor any plague or calamity come near your tent. For He will give His angels [especial] charge over you to accompany and defend and preserve you in all your ways [of obedience and service]. They shall bear you up on their hands, lest you dash your foot against a stone.

Psalm 91:10–12

The Amplified Bible translation lays out so clearly that this angel of protection is present if we are walking in obedience and serving God.

One of the women who works for me was sitting in a boat one day. She had just been reading and confessing verse ten about no calamity coming near her tent because of God's angelic charge over her. All of a sudden, the boat hit a wave, she fell over, and her head hit the side of the boat.

Then she was perplexed. She didn't understand how she could be claiming and confessing a verse of protection, then get hurt. When she asked the Lord about it, He said to her, "You aren't dead, are you?" Even though she may not have thought of it that way, His angels did protect her.

How many times do you think you might have been killed if God's angels had not protected you? Probably more times than you would like to even think about!

We don't need to be complaining about what we don't see God doing. We need to be thanking Him for what He is doing.

You Shall Tread on the Enemy

You shall tread upon the lion and adder; the young lion and the serpent shall you trample underfoot.

Psalm 91:13

Luke 10:19 (NKJV) is a cross reference to this verse and further explains what the lion, adder, scorpion, and serpent represent: "Behold, I give you the authority to trample on serpents and scorpions, and over all the power of the enemy, and *nothing* shall by any means hurt you."

The lion, adder, serpent, and scorpion all represent the enemy. God has given us the authority to trample or tread on them. The authority, *exousia*, that He has given to us is a "delegated authority" from Jesus to us.[3] If we choose to use it, we can tread on our enemy. That is our place in God when we assume our rightful position.

Because We Love Him

Because he has set his love upon Me, therefore will I deliver him; I will set him on high, because he knows and understands My name [has a personal knowledge of My mercy, love, and kindness—trusts and relies on Me, knowing I will never forsake him, no, never]. He shall call upon Me, and I will answer him; I will be with him in trouble, I will deliver him and honor him.

Psalm 91:14–15

Notice that in order to qualify for God's blessings and protection we must have a personal knowledge of His name. We cannot depend upon a relationship with God through our mother or father or friend. We must have a relationship with the Lord for ourselves. We must go to the hiding place, the secret place, and spend time there with God.

A lot of times all we think about is the "deliver me" part of this passage, and we say, "Deliver me, deliver me, deliver me." But deliverance is a process. When we have trouble, first of all, God will be *with* us in that trouble. He will strengthen us and take us through it victoriously. *Then* He will deliver us and honor us.

For many years, God was *with* me in the trials and troubles I was going through while I was trying to overcome my past. But when He began to *deliver* me He also began to honor me.

When you have trouble, do you run to the phone, or to the throne? At first it may seem hard, but you need to come to the point in your life where you run to God and not to people when you are in trouble or a decision needs to be made. There is no reason to call up a bunch of people who barely know what they are doing in order to ask them what you should be doing.

Most of us have more than enough to do just trying to run our own lives without attempting to give advice to others.

Instead, learn to run to God. Learn to run to that secret place, that dwelling place, that hiding place. Learn to say, "Lord, nobody can help me but You. I am totally dependent upon You."

Many times, God will anoint somebody else to help us, but if we turn to others first, He is insulted. We need to learn *to go to God first* and say, "Lord, if You are going to use somebody to help me, You are going to have to choose and anoint that person because I don't want just anybody trying to tell me what to do. I want a word from You, or I don't want anything."

With Long Life

With long life will I satisfy him and show him My salvation.

Psalm 91:16

Sometimes it is easy to see that certain sins of the flesh such as alcoholism, drugs, and sexual promiscuity, can lead to death. But we tend to soft-pedal sins like worry, anxiety, and reasoning. We rationalize them away saying that surely these are not sins. And yet they are. They too wear on our body and lead us to an early death through heart attack, ulcers, or high blood pressure.

But God's plan for us is to be satisfied with long life and to experience the wonderful, marvelous promises of this psalm.

As you travel down the road of life, the next time you are attacked by the devil, put into practice the commands of Psalm 91:1–2—dwell in the secret place of the Most High under the shadow of the Almighty, leaning on Him and making Him your refuge and your fortress.

Follow the Signposts

But after I am raised [to life], I will go before you.

Mark 14:28

So the signposts along the way are: (1) trust God and don't worry; (2) fear not and don't be anxious; (3) cast all your care and avoid reasoning.

In order not to veer off to the right or to the left, pay attention to these signposts. If you do find yourself veering to one side or the other, correct yourself to keep from getting into a collision or going off into a ditch.

On the Christian journey, one of the main reasons for veering off the road is worry. In John 15:5, Jesus said, "Apart from Me [cut off from vital union with Me] you can do nothing." Meditate on that verse and let the word *nothing* grip you. Worry can do nothing to change your situation. Instead the attitude of faith does not worry, fret, and have anxiety concerning tomorrow; because faith understands that wherever it needs to go, Jesus has already been there.

It is not necessary to know and understand the reason behind everything that is going on in your life; trust that whatever you need to know, the Lord will reveal to you. Choose to be satisfied to know the One Who knows and does all things well.

Part Two

———— ✑ ————

Scriptures to Overcome Worry

Read and confess the following Scriptures to help you live a worry-free life.

> Anxiety in a man's heart weighs it down, but an encouraging word makes it glad. (Proverbs 12:25)

> All the days of the desponding and afflicted are made evil [by anxious thoughts and forebodings], but he who has a glad heart has a continual feast [regardless of circumstances]. (Proverbs 15:15)

> You will guard him and keep him in perfect and constant peace whose mind [both its inclination and its character] is stayed on You, because he commits himself to You, leans on You, and hopes confidently in You. (Isaiah 26:3)

> Therefore I tell you, stop being perpetually uneasy (anxious and worried) about your life, what you shall eat or what you shall drink; or about your body, what you shall put on. Is not life greater [in quality] than food, and the body [far above and more excellent] than clothing? Look at the birds of the air; they neither sow nor reap nor gather into barns, and yet your heavenly Father keeps feeding them. Are you not worth much more than they? (Matthew 6:25–26)

Therefore do not worry and be anxious, saying, What are we going to have to eat? or, What are we going to have to drink? or, What are we going to have to wear? (Matthew 6:31)

So do not worry or be anxious about tomorrow, for tomorrow will have worries and anxieties of its own. Sufficient for each day is its own trouble. (Matthew 6:34)

The cares and anxieties of the world and distractions of the age, and the pleasure and delight and false glamour and deceitfulness of riches, and the craving and passionate desire for other things creep in and choke and suffocate the Word, and it becomes fruitless. (Mark 4:19)

Peace I leave with you; My [own] peace I now give and bequeath to you. Not as the world gives do I give to you. Do not let your hearts be troubled, neither let them be afraid. [Stop allowing yourselves to be agitated and disturbed; and do not permit yourselves to be fearful and intimidated and cowardly and unsettled.](John 14:27)

My desire is to have you free from all anxiety and distressing care. (1 Corinthians 7:32)

Do not fret or have any anxiety about anything, but in every circumstance and in everything, by prayer and petition (definite requests), with thanksgiving, continue to make your wants known to God. And God's peace [shall be yours . . . that peace] which transcends all understanding shall garrison and mount guard over your hearts and minds in Christ Jesus. (Philippians 4:6–7)

Whatever is true, whatever is worthy of reverence and is honorable and seemly, whatever is just, whatever is pure, whatever is lovely and lovable, whatever is kind and winsome and gracious, if there is any virtue and excellence, if there is anything worthy of praise, think on and weigh and take account of these things [fix your minds on them]. (Philippians 4:8)

Casting the whole of your care [all your anxieties, all your worries, all your concerns, once and for all] on Him, for He cares for you affectionately and cares about you watchfully. (1 Peter 5:7)

Prayer to Overcome Worry

Father,

Help me not to worry. I realize worry does me no good, but in fact only makes my situation worse. Help me keep my mind on good things that will benefit me and Your kingdom.

Lord, I am thankful You are taking care of me. You have a good plan for my life. I am going to start taking the steps You have shown me to take to fulfill that plan. I place my trust in You and in Your Word. I cast all my cares on You because I know You care for me. In Jesus' name, amen.

PRAYER FOR A PERSONAL RELATIONSHIP WITH THE LORD

———— ❧ ————

If you have never invited Jesus, the Prince of Peace, to be your Lord and Savior, I invite you to do so now. Pray the following prayer, and if you are really sincere about it, you will experience a new life in Christ.*

———————————

Father,

You loved the world so much, You gave Your only begotten Son to die for our sins so that whoever believes in Him will not perish, but have eternal life.

Your Word says we are saved by grace through faith as a gift from You. There is nothing we can do to earn salvation.

I believe and confess with my mouth that Jesus Christ is Your Son, the Savior of the world. I believe He died on the cross for me and bore all of my sins, paying the price for them. I believe in my heart that You raised Jesus from the dead.

I ask You to forgive my sins. I confess Jesus as my Lord. According to Your Word, I am saved and will spend eternity with you! Thank You, Father. I am so grateful! In Jesus' name, amen.

* See John 3:16; Ephesians 2:8–9; Romans 10:9–10; 1 Corinthians 15:3–4; 1 John 1:9; 4:14–16; 5:1, 12–13.

ENDNOTES

———— ❧ ————

Straight Talk on Stress

Chapter 1

1. *Webster's II New College Dictionary* (Boston/New York: Houghton Mifflin Company, 1995), s.v. "prudence."
2. Compiled from the following sources:
   H. R. Beech, L. E. Burns and B. F. Sheffield. *A Behavioural Approach to the Management of Stress*. Ed. Cary L. Cooper and S. V. Kasl. Chichester: John Wiley & Sons, 1982, pp. 8, 9 and 11.
   Randall R. Cottrell, "The Human Stress Response," in *Grolier Wellness Encyclopedia: Stress Management*, 1st ed. (Guilford: The Dushkin Publishing Group, 1992), V. 13, pp. 34, 35.
   Webster's II, s.v. "adrenal gland," "endocrine gland," "pituitary gland."

Straight Talk on Loneliness

Chapter 2

1. *Webster's II New Riverside University Dictionary*, s.v. "lone."
2. *Webster's II*, s.v. "lonely."
3. *Webster's II*, s.v. "lonesome."
4. *Webster's II*, s.v. "alone."
5. *Webster's II*, s.v. "grief."
6. *Webster's II*, s.v. "grieve."
7. Based on *Webster's II*, s.v. "depression."

Straight Talk on Depression

Chapter 1

1. *Noah Webster's First Edition of an American Dictionary of the English Lan-*

guage (San Francisco: The Foundation for American Christian Education, 1967 and 1995 by Rosalie J. Slater. Permission to reprint the 1828 edition granted by G. & C. Merriam Company), s.v. "depression."

2. *Webster's, 1828 Edition,* s. v. "discouraged," "discouragement."
3. *Webster's II New College Dictionary* (Boston/New York: Houghton Mifflin Company, 1995), s.v. "discourage."
4. W. E. Vine, *An Expository Dictionary of New Testament Words* (Old Tappan: NJ, Fleming H. Revell, 1940), Vol. I, p. 300.

Chapter 2

1. James E. Strong, "Greek Dictionary of the New Testament," in *Strong's Exhaustive Concordance of the Bible* (Nashville: Abingdon, 1890), p. 77, entry #5479, s.v. "joy," Acts 20:24.
2. Strong, "Hebrew and Chaldee Dictionary," p. 37, entry #2304 from entry #2302, s.v. "joy," Nehemiah 8:10.
3. Strong, "Hebrew," p. 27, entry #1523, s.v. "joy," Habakkuk 3:18; Zephaniah 3:17.

Straight Talk on Discouragement

Chapter 1

1. *Webster's II New College Dictionary* (Boston/New York: Houghton Mifflin Company, 1995), s.v. "oppress."
2. *Webster's II,* s.v. "aggressive," "enterprising."

Chapter 2

1. Watchman Nee, *The Spiritual Man*, Vol. 1 (New York: Christian Fellowship Publishers, Inc., 1968), p. 145.

Chapter 4

1. *Webster's II,* s.v. "disappoint."

Straight Talk on Insecurity

Chapter 4

1. Helen Hayes with Katherine Hatch, *My Life in Three Acts* (New York: Harcourt Brace Jovananovich, 1990), pp. 39, 66.
2. Mary Kittredge, *Helen Hayes* (New York: Chelsea House Publishers, 1990), p. 64.

Chapter 6

1. *Webster's II New College Dictionary* (Boston/New York: Houghton Mifflin Company, 1995), s.v. "conform."

Straight Talk on Worry

Introduction

1. *Webster's New World College Dictionary*, 3rd ed., s. v. "dwell."

Chapter 3

1. *Webster's New World College Dictionary*, 3rd ed., s. v. "anxiety."
2. *Webster's*, 3rd ed., s. v. "apprehension."
3. *Webster's II New College Dictionary*, s. v. "foreboding."
4. *Webster's II*, s.v. "anxious."
5. *Webster's II*, s.v. "anxiety."
6. *Webster's II*, s.v. "anxiety."

Conclusion

1. Merrill F. Unger, *Unger's Bible Dictionary* (Chicago: Moody Press, 1966), p. 89.
2. Unger, p. 90.
   James Strong, *The Exhaustive Concordance of the Bible* (Nashville: Abington 1890, "Greek Dictionary of the New Testament," p. 30, entry #1849, "delegated influence:—authority. . . ."

ABOUT THE AUTHOR

Joyce Meyer has been teaching the Word of God since 1976 and in full-time ministry since 1980. She is the bestselling author of more than sixty inspirational books, including *How to Hear from God*, *Knowing God Intimately*, and *Battlefield of the Mind*. She has also released thousands of teaching cassettes and a complete video library. Joyce's *Enjoying Everyday Life* radio and television programs are broadcast around the world, and she travels extensively conducting conferences. Joyce and her husband Dave are the parents of four grown children and make their home in St. Louis, Missouri.

TO CONTACT THE AUTHOR WRITE:

Joyce Meyer Ministries
P. O. Box 655
Fenton, Missouri 63026
or call: (636) 349-0303
Internet Address: www.joycemeyer.org

Please include your testimony or help received from this book
when you write. Your prayer requests are welcome.

To contact the author in Canada, please write:
Joyce Meyer Ministries Canada, Inc.
Lambeth Box 1300
London, ON N6P 1T5
or call: (636) 349-0303

In Australia, please write:
Joyce Meyer Ministries—Australia
Locked Bag 77
Mansfield Delivery Centre
Queensland 4122
or call: 07 3349 1200

In England, please write:
Joyce Meyer Ministries
P. O. Box 1549
Windsor
SL4 1GT
or call: (0) 1753-831102

BOOKS BY JOYCE MEYER

Battlefield of the Mind

Battlefield of the Mind Study Guide

Approval Addiction

Ending Your Day Right

In Pursuit of Peace

The Secret Power of Speaking God's Word

Seven Things That Steal Your Joy

Starting Your Day Right

Beauty for Ashes Revised Edition

How to Hear from God

How to Hear from God Study Guide

Knowing God Intimately

The Power of Forgiveness

The Power of Determination

The Power of Being Positive

The Secrets of Spiritual Power

The Battle Belongs to the Lord

Secrets to Exceptional Living

Eight Ways to Keep the Devil Under Your Feet

Teenagers Are People Too!

Filled with the Spirit

Celebration of Simplicity

The Joy of Believing Prayer

Never Lose Heart

Being the Person God Made You to Be

A Leader in the Making

"Good Morning, This Is God!" Gift Book

Jesus—Name Above All Names

When, God, When?

Why, God, Why?

The Word, the Name, the Blood

Tell Them I Love Them

Peace

The Root of Rejection

If Not for the Grace of God

If Not for the Grace of God Study Guide

JOYCE MEYER SPANISH TITLES

Las Siete Cosas Que Te Roban el Gozo (Seven Things That Steal Your Joy)

Empezando Tu Día Bien (Starting Your Day Right)

BY DAVE MEYER

Life Lines